THE RURAL LAWYER

The Rural Lawyer takes a close look at the challenges facing small-town America, where populations are dwindling and aging lawyers are not being replaced by new graduates. With interviews and personal accounts, the book shows how incentive programs can address this access-to-justice crisis. It specifically examines the South Dakota Rural Attorney Recruitment Program, which is the first program of its kind in the US and has seen great success in helping to attract new lawyers to small towns. Chapters also explore the larger context of rural economic development and its relationship to the law. With insightful analysis and real-life examples, *The Rural Lawyer* provides readers with a deep understanding of the challenges facing rural communities and the role that lawyers can play in helping these areas thrive.

Hannah Haksgaard is a professor at the University of South Dakota Knudson School of Law. Hannah has written extensively about the rural lawyer shortage, with two prior book chapters and five law review articles on the topic.

The Rural Lawyer

HOW TO INCENTIVIZE RURAL LAW PRACTICE AND HELP SMALL COMMUNITIES THRIVE

HANNAH HAKSGAARD

University of South Dakota

Shaftesbury Road, Cambridge CB2 8EA, United Kingdom

One Liberty Plaza, 20th Floor, New York, NY 10006, USA

477 Williamstown Road, Port Melbourne, VIC 3207, Australia

314–321, 3rd Floor, Plot 3, Splendor Forum, Jasola District Centre, New Delhi – 110025, India

103 Penang Road, #05-06/07, Visioncrest Commercial, Singapore 238467

Cambridge University Press is part of Cambridge University Press & Assessment, a department of the University of Cambridge.

We share the University's mission to contribute to society through the pursuit of education, learning and research at the highest international levels of excellence.

www.cambridge.org
Information on this title: www.cambridge.org/9781009542845

DOI: 10.1017/9781009542821

© Cambridge University Press & Assessment 2025

This publication is in copyright. Subject to statutory exception and to the provisions of relevant collective licensing agreements, no reproduction of any part may take place without the written permission of Cambridge University Press & Assessment.

When citing this work, please include a reference to the DOI 10.1017/9781009542821

First published 2025

A catalogue record for this publication is available from the British Library

Library of Congress Cataloging-in-Publication Data
NAMES: Haksgaard, Hannah, author.
TITLE: The rural lawyer : how to incentivize rural law practice and help small communities thrive / Hannah Haksgaard, University of South Dakota.
DESCRIPTION: Cambridge, United Kingdom ; New York, NY : Cambridge University Press, 2025. | Includes index.
IDENTIFIERS: LCCN 2024044535 | ISBN 9781009542845 (hardback) | ISBN 9781009542821 (ebook)
SUBJECTS: LCSH: Country lawyers. | Practice of law.
CLASSIFICATION: LCC K115 .H35 2025 | DDC 340.023/73091734–dc23/eng/20240920
LC record available at https://lccn.loc.gov/2024044535

ISBN 978-1-009-54284-5 Hardback
ISBN 978-1-009-54283-8 Paperback

Cambridge University Press & Assessment has no responsibility for the persistence or accuracy of URLs for external or third-party internet websites referred to in this publication and does not guarantee that any content on such websites is, or will remain, accurate or appropriate.

Contents

List of Figures		*page* vii
List of Maps		ix
List of Tables		xi
Acknowledgments		xiii
1	Introduction	1
2	The Rural Lawyer	12
3	Policy Responses	28
4	Choosing Rural Practice	42
5	Entering a Rural Community	63
6	Acceptance	77
7	Legal Work	90
8	Mentorship	109
9	The Finances of Practice	125
10	Community Impact	142
11	Staying or Leaving	154
12	Conclusion	166
	Postscript	174
Appendix: Participating Attorneys		175
Index		183

Figures

2.1	John B. Miniard	*page* 12
3.1	Dylan Kirchmeier	28
3.2	Legislative timeline	33
4.1	Kirby Krogman	42
4.2	Agricultural background of participants	44
4.3	Reasons for choosing rural	54
4.4	Persisting placement based on distance from home county	60
5.1	Cole Romey, William Hustead, and Austin Schaefer	63
5.2	Lawyer placements by community population	65
5.3	County seat placements and their persistence	66
6.1	Jennifer English	77
7.1	Cassie Wendt	90
7.2	Criminal work	98
8.1	Zach Pahlke	109
8.2	First hiring situation and persistence	111
9.1	Rachel Mairose	125
9.2	Lawyer hourly rates	135
10.1	Rachelle Norberg	142
11.1	Amy Jo Janssen and family	154
11.2	Year of participant departure	156
12.1	Dusty Ginsbach	166

Maps

3.1 Qualifying counties *page* 33
8.1 Location of satellite offices 114

Tables

9.1 Prosecutor minimum salaries — *page* 132
12.1 Suggestions for improvement — 170

Acknowledgments

I must start by thanking the rural lawyers who shared their ideas, stories, and hopes with me. Without a group of rural lawyers who were willing to give their time and experience, this book would not have happened. As I neared completion of this manuscript, I sent it to those lawyers and administrators who granted me interviews for fact-checking. Feedback and comments related to fact-checking were integrated, though no one demanded any change in my analysis.

A number of entities and people at the University of South Dakota provided support. Funding for this research was provided by the University of South Dakota Knudson School of Law and a Chiesman Research Award from the Political Science Department. Seven students helped with managing citations, transcripts, editing, and figures: Andrew Falcone, Tessa Dalberg, Kaylee ("Joey") O'Daniel, Madyson Fleckenstein, Bryce Drapeaux, Cameron Morgan, and Isabella Erickson. Three law librarians gave their time and expertise: Susan Benton, Sarah Kammer, and Justin Huston. Administrative assistance came from Heather McDonald, Teresa Carlisle, Tracy Hummel, and Saumbra Hall. My faculty colleagues provided feedback at a 2023 faculty workshop and then more informally throughout the process.

Next comes a group of people who willingly gave me feedback on written versions of this book. My mom's book club provided a first and critical batch of non-lawyer readers, and I particularly thank Mary Pat Bierle and Julieanne Bauer for their extensive comments. Matthew Sparks, Michael McKey, Lisa Pruitt, Margaret Raymond, Neil Fulton, Steve Macias, Quinn Yeargain, Shirley Mays, Kathy Abrams, Beth Colgan, Elizabeth Chambliss, and Emily Prifogle read portions of my manuscript and provided feedback; I thank them for their assistance. Workshop readers at the 2022 and 2023 Law & Rurality Workshop similarly provided useful feedback.

This is my first book, and I had a lot to learn during the process. Michele Statz provided advice that got my research off the ground. Nancy Levit served as a mentor during the submission and contracting process. Patrick Garry, Lisa Pruitt, and Frank Pommersheim all provided professional and personal advice as I navigated the book-writing process for the first time. I thank everyone for their support and assistance. Matt Gallaway and the entire editing team at Cambridge University Press were very kind in helping me with the publication process.

My parents deserve thanks for watching the kids while we trekked across South Dakota doing interviews. My husband, Jesse Haksgaard, was crucial to this book at every step. He drove me all across South Dakota to meet with lawyers, bringing his camera and taking the photos included in this book. Having met the lawyers and visited their rural communities, he served as my primary sounding board throughout the writing and editing process, and for that I am sincerely thankful.

1

Introduction

In the summer of 2022, I was in the middle of South Dakota in the small town of Fort Pierre (population 2,115) attending a conference about strengthening rural communities.[1] During the first day of the conference, rural community members – none of them lawyers – talked about different programs and strategies they had used to strengthen their rural communities. I spent that first day listening to these rural stories and reflecting on the many concerns raised that could easily be addressed by a local lawyer: the small businesses needing to incorporate. The organizations that would be better off as nonprofits. The communities trying to plan housing developments that needed legal advice on deeds. The cities weighing opportunities but needing compliance advice.

At supper, after I confessed to being a lawyer, I sorely disappointed my tablemates by acknowledging my absolute lack of knowledge on business formation law. Plus, I could not provide advice to the librarian seated next to me about handling liability risks for renting out the local library space to private parties. But that relatively simple legal question might be a critically important one for a rural community where the library has the only rentable space for events – the space sorely needed for baby showers, graduation celebrations, and ninetieth birthday parties. What became obvious throughout that first day is that a local lawyer, invested in improving a rural community, could make so many of the ideas and projects more viable. Yet the conference on strengthening rural communities had not once mentioned access to lawyers, or – perhaps more accurately – the lack of access to lawyers.

On the second day of the conference, my morning began as I stepped into the hotel elevator and came face-to-face with a retired Chief Justice of the Supreme Court of South Dakota – David Gilbertson. As South Dakota's longest-serving Chief Justice, Gilbertson spent his last decade on the bench as a champion for South Dakota's Rural Attorney Recruitment Program – the inspiration for this book and a

---

[1] Unless otherwise noted, the population sizes throughout this book are drawn from the most recent Census data available. *Explore Census Data*, U.S. CENSUS BUREAU, https://perma.cc/3L9P-SHW3 (last visited Feb. 16, 2024).

program aimed at replenishing South Dakota's rural lawyers. In that short elevator ride, we talked about South Dakota's shortage of rural lawyers and the incentive program South Dakota developed to replenish the supply of rural lawyers. An incentive program was not always needed. According to Gilbertson, "at one time, access to legal services in rural South Dakota existed."[2] The problem is, now retiring rural lawyers are not being replaced.

Rural areas nationwide are suffering a shortage of lawyers. The American Bar Association ("ABA") releases an annual profile on the legal profession. The most recent findings, released in 2023, report more than 1.3 million lawyers in the United States, but show disproportionate placement in urban areas.[3] In the 2020 report, the ABA tracked county-level data on where lawyers practice. Calling the rural areas with few lawyers "Legal Deserts," the ABA report captures in comprehensive data what rural-focused advocates have been saying for years: There is a widespread and growing rural lawyer shortage across the nation.[4]

When this shortage came to light in South Dakota, the state invested in a rural lawyer incentive program because the state invests in rural communities. This investment came despite South Dakota being a fiscally conservative state, and one of the country's most conservative states overall.[5] When Chief Justice Gilbertson and leaders of the state bar began advocating for a program to draw more lawyers to rural South Dakota, they focused on both community needs and the economic viability of rural law practice. Investing in recruiting a new rural lawyer is not only about providing a stable job to one person. That new lawyer helps make a community more vibrant and functional.

Rural county and municipal governments need lawyers – for prosecutorial and defense work, for abuse and neglect cases, to serve as judges – and having local lawyers in rural areas means the government need not pay for travel, keeping costs low. Rural governments also need lawyers to serve in advisory roles and provide legal representation to the government when litigation arises. When there are no local lawyers, small local governments – often running on shoestring budgets – end up paying lawyers to travel from bigger towns. In some cases, small towns just do not hire legal counsel, even for important matters.[6]

Lawyers also serve private clients in rural communities, providing critical legal services to residents who would otherwise need to travel, use online services, or entirely forgo meeting their legal needs. Attorneys not only know the law, but

---

[2] Hon. David Gilbertson, *Reflections on the Rural Practice of Law in South Dakota: Past, Present, and Future*, 59 S.D. L. REV. 433, 433 (2014).
[3] A.B.A. *Profile of the Legal Profession* (2023), A.B.A., https://perma.cc/8SBW-MG4F.
[4] A.B.A. *Profile of the Legal Profession* (2020), A.B.A., https://perma.cc/42ZK-SLD4.
[5] Brad Dress, *Here Are the 50 Legislatures Ranked from Most to Least Conservative*, THE HILL (Dec. 6, 2022), https://perma.cc/ZVM4-U3HJ.
[6] Town of Wood v. Good Shield, 188 N.W.2d 757, 757 (S.D. 1971) (noting that "the Town of Wood (pop. 132) has not responded or appeared because of lack of funds to employ counsel").

they also guide clients through stressful times with legal and nonlegal problems. Studying rural lawyers over thirty years ago, Donald Landon explained that lawyers are "frequently expected to act outside their specialty to provide business and economic advice, or provide clients with a sympathetic ear or organizational know-how."[7] Michele Statz, an anthropologist of law, describes lawyers as "bear[ing] the burden of the problem – the crisis – so it may be solved in a dignified and just way."[8] This guiding role may be particularly important in rural communities where there are few other services available.

Lawyers tend to be involved citizens, often serving on boards or running for office. Lawyers are problem solvers, both for their clients and their larger communities. While urban areas have plenty of law-educated individuals to fill these roles, a rural community may have no one with a law degree. Similarly, larger communities probably have government employees who write grants; rural areas probably do not.[9] A few lawyers in any rural community can shift the level of expertise for local entities, making nonprofits and other organizations more viable. When rural lawyers help community members form nonprofits or businesses, shopping stays local, providing jobs and keeping sales tax local. Strong local businesses and nonprofits can then keep rural communities vibrant despite countervailing economic forces. There are some lawyers in rural South Dakota that have made clear and identifiable impacts on the growth of their rural communities even outside of their legal jobs. For example, Kelsea Kenzy Sutton in Burke, population 579, graduated from law school in 2014 and now serves as counsel to the local bank in her hometown. Since returning home, Sutton has proven herself as a capable grant-writer, obtaining funds to create a splash pad in her small town.[10]

These contributions can help rural places sustain their communities. To sustain a population that prevents school consolidation. To sustain local businesses that create a stable tax base. To sustain churches, community halls, and local cafés. To avoid becoming the kind of community that Michelle Wilde Anderson labels as "border-to-border low-income" when she writes about city and county governments where economic distress has taken hold across an entire community, not just in small pockets.[11] As Anderson demonstrates, border-to-border low-income communities struggle to survive, let alone thrive, because the tax base simply cannot provide services. Rural areas are often poor, but they are not all destined to this downward spiral.

---

[7] DONALD D. LANDON, COUNTRY LAWYERS: THE IMPACT OF CONTEXT ON PROFESSIONAL PRACTICE 5 (1990).
[8] Michele Statz et al., *"They Had Access, but They Didn't Get Justice": Why Prevailing Access to Justice Initiatives Fail Rural Americans*, 28 GEO. J. ON POVERTY L. & POL'Y 321, 375 (2021).
[9] MICHELLE WILDE ANDERSON, THE FIGHT TO SAVE THE TOWN: REIMAGINING DISCARDED AMERICA 108 (2022).
[10] Renee Ortiz, *"I Think This Project is About Love": New Splash Pad Opens in Burke*, KELOLAND (Aug. 7, 2022), https://perma.cc/PY9J-TD2G.
[11] ANDERSON, *supra* note 9, at 5.

Some reading this book may wonder why we should care about these rural communities. Why, in the face of decades of population loss and economic stagnation, should investments be made to sustain and improve rural America? Why not, as one commentator suggested, "pack rural America up" and have rural residents "move elsewhere" if they want better jobs and more satisfying lives?[12] As a product of rural America, I find this perspective misguided. Of course we should care about the people and places of rural America. Just like we should care about so many other people and places that make America the beautiful, diverse, pluralistic society she is. Because this entire book is premised on the idea that rural America matters, it is worth explaining why it does, both to me and to the other people who reside there.

All four of my grandparents were born in rural America in the 1910s and 1920s. Two in southeastern Kentucky, deep in the rural foothills of the Appalachian Mountains where the ancient mountains are so close together the sun disappears hours before dark and roads are hard to build. Two in southeastern South Dakota, out on the prairies where the wind is constant and the droughts of the 1930s pushed many families – including those of my grandparents – from their farms into small towns. My mother grew up in rural Kentucky in her parents' home county. My father grew up in several South Dakota towns. My parents settled outside of Yankton, South Dakota, on an acre of land on the Missouri River bluffs that sometimes requires four-wheel drive for winter access. But the steep gravel road to their home is worth the sweeping views of the Missouri. The neighboring cow pasture of my childhood has now been replaced with beautiful houses for commuters and vacationers, but the trees and sweeping views remain.

Rural areas and rural history have always been a part of my life. My great-great-uncle penned a moving poem about homesteading and breaking the virgin sod of rural South Dakota.[13] That poem now prominently hangs in my office. My South Dakota grandmother taught high school English in some tiny towns and published a historical essay about rural South Dakota.[14] An aunt in Kentucky keeps relics and documents from the family's rural past; a cousin who is already writing about the history and culture of Appalachia hopes to write a book chronicling the family history my aunt has preserved.[15] We often visited family in rural areas of South Dakota and Kentucky. We frequented small towns for their festivals, bakeries, and stores. I drove thirty minutes through rural South Dakota to buy my prom and wedding dresses in a town of 1,000. We hiked in state and National Parks. My children are

---

[12] Allan Golombek, *Sorry New York Times, Rural America Cannot be Saved*, REALCLEARMARKETS (Dec. 18, 2018), https://perma.cc/ZKL3-HEZM.

[13] Rudolf G. Ruste, *Last of the Virgin Sod* (1912) (full text available in Hilmer H. Laudre, *The Fruitful Plains*, 61 TRANSACTIONS KAN. ACAD. SCI. 16, 16–17 (1958)).

[14] Doris Alsgaard, *Start with One Cabin*, in DAKOTA PANORAMA 79 (J. Leonard Jennewein & Jane Boorman, eds. 1961).

[15] MATTHEW R. SPARKS & OLIVIA SIZEMORE, HAINT COUNTRY: DARK FOLKTALES FROM THE HILLS AND HOLLERS (2024).

growing up in a similar world. We live in a town of 10,000 in South Dakota, but frequently interact with more rural communities.

Being in rural spaces is normal for me, and I never questioned whether rural people and places deserved to survive and be nourished. In law school in Berkeley, I once did a class presentation about law in rural areas, and a classmate commented how they had "never thought" about rural people or places and why they matter. For a student body attuned to the diversity and inequities of America, I learned that rural America was a blind spot for many of my classmates. For many urban Americans, feelings of apathy toward rural America turned to anger following the 2016 election of President Donald Trump.[16] Angry accusations were thrown at rural America – too white, too conservative, too self-interested, too powerful. But those labels do not accurately capture the reality of rural America.

Defining and categorizing what counts as rural is difficult. The Census Bureau's definition is a good place to start, that "rural" is any area not designated as urban. Under the 2020 Census, urban areas require only 2,000 housing units or a population of 5,000.[17] Using this definition, 20 percent of Americans live in rural areas, with 80 percent in urban areas.[18] Yet the rural-designated areas make up about 97 percent of the country's landmass, playing a critical role in the economic structure of the United States.

Much of that rural land is used for agriculture. Farms alone, without considering any related industries, contributed 164.7 billion dollars to the United States gross domestic product in 2021.[19] American farmers grow most of the domestically consumed food. American agricultural exports were 192 billion dollars in 2022. Of course, food does not just grow – it requires labor. In 2022, 1.3 percent of United States employment was on farms, accounting for 2.6 million jobs.[20] Other rural industries, including food processing and tourism, employ even more workers.

Imagine for a moment we indulged the angry commentators telling rural Americans to pack up and move to cities if they want services like libraries, pools, healthcare, and legal representation. Rural communities would dwindle, decreasing the labor pool available for agricultural work. Those agricultural workers could relocate to cities, and farms could bus in 2.6 million workers to farm our food. All of America might start to resemble the exploitative farm labor system in parts of California where farm laborers live hours from worksites, requiring them to take

---

[16] Lisa R. Pruitt, *The Women Feminism Forgot: Rural and Working-Class White Women in the Era of Trump*, 49 U. TOL. L. REV. 537, 553 (2018).
[17] Michael Ratcliff, *Redefining Urban Areas Following the 2020 Census*, U.S. CENSUS BUREAU (Dec. 22, 2022), https://perma.cc/5NGJ-96QG.
[18] *Nation's Urban and Rural Populations Shift Following 2020 Census*, U.S. CENSUS BUREAU (Dec. 29, 2022), https://perma.cc/26R3-EN8E.
[19] *Ag and Food Sectors and the Economy*, ECON. RSCH SERV., U.S. DEP'T OF AG. (Jan. 26, 2023), https://perma.cc/Z879-RV53.
[20] *Id.*

buses and carpools to far-flung fields where they are underpaid for long hours of work and often face unnecessary safety risks. While those farm workers (who are hypothetically enjoying the services available in larger communities) take long bus-rides into rural areas to work long hours, not only do the workers lose the benefits of the services available where they live, their children are left without parent supervision in those urban areas. This system does not benefit anyone. Keeping rural communities strong means keeping schools, hospitals, and other services strong, which in turn keeps workers local.

Investing in rural communities is not just about investing in white communities. Rural America is already diverse and becoming more racially and ethnically diverse. In 2020, 24 percent of rural Americans were people of color.[21] Significant populations of Native American, Black Americans, Latinx Americans, and Asian Americans live in rural America, though largely concentrated in different regions. In South Dakota, where I conducted my research, Native Americans are the largest minority population. Nationwide, a higher percentage of Native Americans are rural than any other group. Calculations vary depending on how rural is defined, but the best calculation is that over half of Native Americans live in rural communities.[22] Reservations are mostly rural, and often remote, making strong local communities even more important.

To argue that rural America does not deserve investment, or that its population should give up and move to cities, is dismissive of the economic and cultural value of rural America. Native American communities cherish land that has long been inhabited by their ancestors. Black Americans and Latinx Americans live in rural communities connected to generations of their ancestors. New immigrants of color are establishing strong communities in rural parts of the country. Descendants of much earlier European immigrants continue to keep ancestral traditions alive in rural areas. In my corner of South Dakota, you will find the Yankton Sioux Tribe maintaining its culture and small towns holding festivals that celebrate the roots of European settlers, including Danish Days, Czech Days, Schmeckfest, and more. The traditions alive in Native American and other rural communities make rural America vibrant. Neglecting the rural parts of our country and asking these rural populations to abandon their connection to the land and traditions is both deeply offensive and ill advised.

Rural America also offers a different type of lifestyle. Most Americans prefer to live in urban areas, with each Census showing growth in urban areas and decline in rural. While more of the United States population prefers to live in big cities, there are many people who *want* a rural or small-town lifestyle. Those people who want

---

[21] D. W. Rowlands & Hanna Love, *Mapping Rural America's Diversity and Demographic Change*, BROOKINGS (Sept. 28, 2021), https://perma.cc/WW7Q-G6GM.

[22] Sarah Dewees & Benjamin Marks, *Research Note – Twice Invisible: Understanding Rural Native America*, FIRST NATIONS DEV. INST. (Apr. 2017), https://perma.cc/7K2V-LLE9.

to leave rural communities largely have the capacity to do so, as has been demonstrated through population shifts over time. Those who stay in rural communities often want to stay. The difference in lifestyle cannot be discounted. If we invest in rural opportunities that create more jobs and better stability, there will be more opportunities for rural residents to stay where they have kinship and community ties.

Rural investment could also open the opportunity for increased diversity. More Native Americans might return to their home reservations if those communities were strengthened. More new immigrants might settle in small towns where housing and land are affordable. European immigrants, like my ancestors, often settled on free land provided by the Homestead Act. Modern immigrants might be attracted to rural areas with affordable housing so long as there is a need for workers. Huron, South Dakota, while not technically rural with a population over 14,000, does provide an example of increasing diversity in a relatively isolated and small town. In 2000, Huron was 96 percent white and had a falling population. Since taking purposeful recruitment and investment in education and affordable housing programs, Huron has grown and diversified its population. By 2022, Huron's population was only 69 percent white, with 16 percent of the population born outside the country. Even more telling for the future of Huron, 46 percent of the K-12 students in Huron are of Asian or Latinx descent.[23] That community growth did not just happen; it required available jobs and an invested community.

Rural areas matter and deserve investment to remain viable and even thrive. Yet lawyers, just one of the tools available to help rural areas, are in steep decline. Retirements and deaths have left too many small towns without a local lawyer, and too many rural residents without access to legal services. Without accessible legal services, businesses may not form, estate plans may not be written, and communities may wither.

Though the rural lawyer shortage impacts nearly every jurisdiction, policy responses have been lacking. Only North Dakota, South Dakota, and Illinois have programs that pay rural lawyers directly. Several other states have legal incubators to train rural lawyers before they begin practice. Various states have also experimented with funding rural summer internships or other methods of connecting aging attorneys with potential successors. There have also been attempts to leverage technology – especially during the COVID-19 pandemic – to have urban lawyers serve the legal needs of rural residents remotely. Urban lawyers and law students also serve rural legal needs in many states through traveling clinics that temporarily provide services in rural areas. Then there are the programs aimed at creating education pathways. A number of law schools offer rural courses or clinics, with a few more offering loan forgiveness for rural practice.

Law professor Lisa Pruitt has been at the forefront of documenting the rural lawyer shortage in the United States and describing the responses to that shortage,

---

[23] PBS NewsHour, *South Dakota Town Embraces New Immigrants Vital to Meat Industry*, S.D. PUB. BROAD (July 2, 2016), https://perma.cc/UL7D-TK6A.

including conducting the only existing study about lawyer and law student opinions on rural practice.[24] In surveying the policy responses attempted by different states, Pruitt concludes that the "current institutional responses ... provide little hope for reversing" the rural lawyer shortage.[25] As she says, "[o]nly a handful of States have been willing to spend money" on these programs, with South Dakota standing out among the states for "put[ing] its money where its mouth is."[26]

Indeed, in 2013 South Dakota became the nation's leader in trying to alleviate the rural lawyer crisis by creating what would become known as the Rural Attorney Recruitment Program. This program, as a partnership between the State of South Dakota, the State Bar of South Dakota, and the local rural communities, provides stipends for rural lawyers. For a decade, South Dakota has been touted as the nation's leader in solving the rural lawyer crisis, but in the beginning, no one knew whether the lawyers entering South Dakota's program would stick around. In fact, some have been dismissive of the program, arguing "there is no demonstrated evidence" that lawyers will stay rural.[27]

Now, a decade after the program was launched, I have the first opportunity to analyze the long-term success of the program. In short, it has gone well. Not every lawyer who participated in the program has stayed, and not every participant has enjoyed rural legal practice, but the vast majority of them have. This book is a study of new rural lawyers that includes analysis of how a stipend influences the first few years of rural law practice. In this way, the book provides a comprehensive study of the Rural Attorney Recruitment Program participants in the first ten years of the program, from 2013 until 2023. The analysis of how a *program* can help new rural lawyers should offer lessons for recruitment and retention in rural areas across the country.

South Dakota, with a population of just over 900,000 in 2024, remains a very rural state despite major growth in some of the state's largest cities. South Dakota *has* lawyers – 2,026 by latest count.[28] Those lawyers are just disproportionately located in the state's three biggest towns and its capital city. In 2013, when the program began, 65 percent of South Dakota's lawyers lived in Sioux Falls, Rapid City, Aberdeen, and Pierre.[29] In 2023, those same four cities contained 72 percent of South Dakota's

---

[24] Lisa R. Pruitt et al., *Justice in the Hinterlands: Arkansas as a Case Study of the Rural Lawyer Shortage and Evidence-Based Solutions to Alleviate It*, 37 U. ARK. LITTLE ROCK L. REV. 573 (2015).
[25] Kelly V. Beskin & Lisa R. Pruitt, *A Survey of Policy Responses to the Rural Attorney Shortage in the United States*, in ACCESS TO JUSTICE IN RURAL COMMUNITIES: GLOBAL PERSPECTIVES 7, 7 (Daniel Newman & Faith Gordon, eds. 2023).
[26] *Id.* at 25.
[27] Brian L. Lynch, *Access to Legal Services in Rural Areas of the Northern Rockies: A Recommendation for Town Legal Centers*, 90 IND. L.J. 1683, 1693 (2015).
[28] A.B.A. *Profile of the Legal Profession* (2022), A.B.A., https://perma.cc/Y9YX-CLEX.
[29] Ethan Bronner, *No Lawyer for Miles, So One Rural State Offers Pay*, N.Y. TIMES (Apr. 8, 2013), http://perma.cc/4M6L-UADA (for articles behind paywalls, like with the *New York Times*, click "view the live page" to view the original).

lawyers.[30] This is not to say that there are too many lawyers in South Dakota's largest communities. In fact, South Dakota ranks near the bottom of lawyers per capita, and there are excess legal jobs available in the state, including in these larger communities.

While more lawyers are entering practice in South Dakota's larger communities, the same is not happening in rural places. The state's rural communities are losing baby boomer lawyers to retirement at a steady clip, and simultaneously have declining numbers of high school graduates, thus shrinking the pool of potential replacement lawyers. Even when a rural student manages to overcome educational disadvantages to make it through college and law school, it is not always easy for those new lawyers to see a viable path into rural practice.[31] The path of least resistance is often to take a salaried job in the biggest cities or the state capital; after all, the firms are always hiring.

After decades of rural lawyer loss, South Dakota actually did something about it. In 2005, Chief Justice Gilbertson started using his annual speech to the legislature to address the growing rural lawyer shortage. In 2011, two prominent South Dakota attorneys with deep rural connections – Bob Morris and Pat Goetzinger – formed a working group through the state bar called Project Rural Practice. After years of work and advocacy by Chief Justice Gilbertson and Project Rural Practice, in 2013 the South Dakota Legislature passed a law authorizing a pilot program to fund sixteen lawyers who would practice in rural areas. A participating lawyer signs a contract agreeing to stay in their rural community for five years and practice law at least thirty-five hours a week. At the end of each year, the participating attorney receives a stipend from the Rural Attorney Recruitment Program for 12,513.60 dollars. After five years the stipend ends and the program hopes that participants will stay permanently in their rural practices.

The law was signed on March 25, 2013, and went into effect on July 1, 2013. Immediately the search began for new lawyers willing to commit to rural practice with the support of this stipend. On May 7, 2014, the first participant began the program. As of July 1, 2023, a total of thirty-two attorneys have taken part in the Rural Attorney Recruitment Program. At the ten-year anniversary, twenty-four of those attorneys were currently practicing law in their rural communities, with one more teaching middle school in her rural community. Only seven participants left their rural communities.

The conclusions of this book are largely based on qualitative interviews I conducted with lawyers who have participated in the Rural Attorney Recruitment

---

[30] John Hult, *Rural Lawyer Recruitment Efforts Show Local Results, but Fail to Alter Urban-Rural Divide*, S.D. SEARCHLIGHT (Jan. 15, 2023), https://perma.cc/LFA3-LX52.

[31] Bart Pfankuch, *Rural Schools in S.D. Face Unique Challenges That Can Affect Learning*, S.D. NEWS WATCH (Nov. 7, 2019), https://perma.cc/VXQ5-N9YG; ROBERT WUTHNOW, THE LEFT BEHIND: DECLINE AND RAGE IN SMALL-TOWN AMERICA 61 (2018).

Program. The interviews were semistructured, where I asked the same open-ended questions, allowing interviewees to share their own stories. All thirty-two lawyers who have ever participated in the program met with me to discuss their time in rural practice and their views on the program. Every attorney who remains in their rural community invited me into their law office for an in-person interview, letting me learn about their small towns and their workspaces. To get a better sense of their rural practices, I watched several participants in court, attended a city council meeting where a participant served as counsel, watched a different participant present at a continuing legal education event, read appellate briefs filed by participants, and – among other activities – toured an oil field where one participant works when he's not practicing law. For participants who left their rural communities, interviews were either in person or on Zoom.

In addition to my core interviews with participating lawyers, I interviewed a dozen mentoring attorneys and a number of key players who brought this program into existence. I also interviewed four lawyers who had strong interest in participating in the Rural Attorney Recruitment Program but did not do so. Then there were some less formal conversations I had with people who knew the lawyers. A talkative woman in an airport had hired a lawyer I interviewed. One of my mom's friends knew a lawyer from when he was a kid on swim team; another of her friends had taught a couple of the lawyers in college courses. Hotel clerks were happy to share their views on the local lawyers I was visiting. A few of my current students grew up in some of these towns and shared their perspectives. A friend-of-a-friend is the son of one of the mentoring attorneys. These conversations with nonlawyers helped add context to my main interviews, providing a different perspective on rural lawyers. Also providing a different perspective were interviews with rural lawyers and policymakers from other states.

Relying on those interviews, *The Rural Lawyer* provides a modern account of how new rural lawyers settle into their careers. Though it also captures the story of the first ten years of South Dakota's Rural Attorney Recruitment Program, the story is broader than just thirty-two lawyers in one state. Instead, it draws lessons from these lawyers' experiences to help other rural lawyers improve their practices and other states craft similar programs. Chapter 2 looks at rural lawyers across America, starting with a historical perspective, considering changes in the profession, and ending with a description of rural lawyers today. Chapter 3 turns to various policy responses to the rural lawyer shortage, looking at what jurisdictions have tried in attempts to combat the growing shortage, including South Dakota's Rural Attorney Recruitment Program.

Then the book pivots to the issues facing new rural lawyers. Throughout the remaining chapters, data from the interviewed South Dakota lawyers is used to provide evidence of how one program has succeeded (or not) in addressing issues faced by new rural lawyers. Chapter 4 looks at the backgrounds of those lawyers, discussing how they ended up in rural legal practice, including why they attended law school and why they had an interest in practicing in rural communities. This can help law schools and rural communities understand how to recruit new rural lawyers.

The South Dakota program requires buy-in from local communities, so Chapter 5 focuses on the process of participants getting programmatic approval. Chapter 5 also covers some more practical steps of starting a practice, such as finding office space and housing. Chapter 6 looks at whether the lawyers were accepted or not in their new rural practices. This includes whether the lawyers have felt welcomed in their communities, whether the lawyers were accepted by local lawyers, and whether community members brought business to the lawyers. Chapter 7 turns to the actual practice of law, surveying practice areas.

While the feedback on the Rural Attorney Recruitment Program is overwhelmingly positive, two common themes arose when participants expressed concerns about rural practice: mentorship and finances. Chapters 8 and 9 address those two concerns. The concerns, though, do not amount to insurmountable barriers to success. Indeed, the program has been very successful. Chapters 10 and 11 summarize that success and look to the future. Chapter 10 looks at the communities and what services those lawyers provided, including a robust discussion of whether rural communities benefit from having lawyers. Chapter 11 returns to a focus on the lawyers themselves with a look at their longevity in rural practice as well as their thoughts on the long-term viability of rural practice.

South Dakota's program can serve as proof that rural attorney financial incentives work. Throughout the book I reflect on ways that the South Dakota program has worked and on ways that it could do better. Yet, there may be challenges for other states that do not have the same rural-friendly coalitions existing in South Dakota leadership. South Dakota is large in square miles, but small in population. It is, after all, the kind of state where a young professor can strike up a conversation with a retired Chief Justice in the elevator of a Holiday Inn Express. In larger states, it might be harder to build the connections and coalitions that made it possible for South Dakota to create the nation's first program. The success in South Dakota, though, should inspire other states to invest in doing the same.

2

The Rural Lawyer

FIGURE 2.1 John B. Miniard

Born in southeastern Kentucky in May 1865, John B. Miniard entered life in a poor, rural region of Appalachia. The Civil War had just ended. Though no fighting took place in Miniard's home of Leslie County, Kentucky, deserting soldiers raided rural communities and small towns in the area.[32] Like in much of Appalachia, the people

---

[32] SADIE WELLS STIDHAM, LESLIE COUNTY, KENTUCKY 1878–1978: A FOLK HISTORY OF FACTS AND FICTION 72 (1978).

in Leslie County were subsistence farmers at the time.[33] There were no roads to speak of. The people were isolated, traveling on horse or mule and using creek beds for passage.

When Miniard reached adulthood, he decided to become a lawyer. Legal education was sparse, especially in the rural reaches of the country. Early American education had largely been through apprenticeships or the independent reading of law books.[34] Though some universities had begun appointing professors of law in the late 1700s, they were mostly in New England, and plenty of lawyers were still trained through apprenticeships rather than higher education institutions.[35] This makes sense. The American population was spread wide; travel was difficult. Even apprenticeships were not available everywhere. Instead, some aspiring lawyers simply read legal texts. With no law school to attend in rural eastern Kentucky, Miniard crossed the border to "read the law" in Turkey Cove, Virginia. Likely, Miniard journeyed to Turkey Cove because he was able to borrow one or more law books, much like Abraham Lincoln travelled around Illinois to borrow the law books that provided his legal education.[36] Even in 1900 most American lawyers had not attended law school.[37]

After finishing what legal education he was able to obtain, Miniard returned to rural Kentucky and began his legal career. Miniard served as a prosecutor for Leslie County starting in 1905, running in two elections. After serving as prosecutor, Miniard transitioned to private practice, where he had a long career in his rural community. Rural lawyers at this time saw various degrees of financial success. Some only "eked out a bare living at the law," but others "became rich country lawyers."[38] It was a career that offered, but did not guarantee, a decent livelihood.

With no roads and no railroads, Miniard truly "rode" circuit in a saddle, working in his home county as well as nearby counties. In 1926, at this point in his sixties, he travelled through the mountains to Harlan County to try a case. A snowstorm hit during trial. After the trial ended, Miniard decided to brave the weather and set off for home. His legs froze to his stirrups, leading to frostbite, gangrene, then death. In January of 1926, Miniard's life and rural law career ended.

A CHANGING NORM

Though we do not know much about Miniard's legal practice, we know that he tried cases and served as a local prosecutor, living and working in the rural community

---

[33] STEVEN STOLL, RAMP HOLLOW: THE ORDEAL OF APPALACHIA (2017).
[34] Brian J. Moline, *Early American Legal Education*, 42 WASHBURN L.J. 775, 779 (2004).
[35] ALBERT J. HARNO, LEGAL EDUCATION IN THE UNITED STATES 24 (1953).
[36] ALBERT A. WOLDMAN, LAWYER LINCOLN 20 (1936).
[37] Moline, *supra* note 34, at 801; LAWRENCE W. FRIEDMAN, A HISTORY OF AMERICAN LAW 464, 542 (3d ed. 2001).
[38] FRIEDMAN, *supra* note 37, at 491.

where he was born. In these ways, Miniard's career looks a lot like the prototypical rural lawyer of American yesteryear, often portrayed in our imaginations by Abraham Lincoln and the fictional Atticus Finch.[39] Of course, the legal profession has always offered different paths. Even early on, there were elite lawyers who made policy for the new country.[40] But Miniard and most rural lawyers were not that. Instead, rural lawyers were running active practices, representing local parties in mostly local disputes.

These rural or "country" lawyers are almost mythical. In fact, Judy Cornett and Heather Bosau write about "the myth of the country lawyer."[41] In this framing, country lawyers are do-gooders embedded in their hometown communities. They are admired by their neighbors, value community members, do not hold themselves aloof, possess knowledge (both legal and practical), are generalists in their practices, are unconcerned with pecuniary gain, and defend the underdog. Cornett and Bosau call this view of rural lawyers a myth because it leads society to judge all lawyers by a standard of high community involvement. In our modern society, there is a disconnect between the prototypical country lawyer and how most lawyers practice law.

Instead of America's lawyers being generalist lawyers practicing in their rural hometowns, the lawyers of today are mostly specialists in cities. Most new lawyers continue to go into private practice, choosing to work for law firms rather than the government or legal aid. While small law firms (one to ten attorneys) used to be a dominant hiring block, recent shifts have moved hiring away from the smallest firms. Nationwide, for the class of 2022, 58 percent went into private practice, but under 30 percent of those law firm jobs were in small firms. Only 184, or half of 1 percent of new graduates in the class of 2022, started their own solo practices. Nationwide, students are heading to big firms instead of small.[42] Those big firms are in cities, which continue to attract the vast majority of new law school graduates. For South Dakota's only law school, a third of all graduates joined law firms with one to ten attorneys.[43] Yet even though South Dakota graduates are heading to small firms, those firms are almost always in the state's biggest towns. Unfortunately, available nationwide data does not collect size of community for recent graduates, but we know that not enough students are heading to rural practice to replace retiring lawyers.

---

[39] WOLDMAN, *supra* note 36; Cynthia L. Fountaine, *In the Shadow of Atticus Finch: Constructing a Heroic Lawyer*, 13 WIDENER L.J. 123 (2003).

[40] STEVEN J. MACIAS, LEGAL SCIENCE IN THE EARLY REPUBLIC: THE ORIGINS OF AMERICAN LEGAL THOUGHT AND EDUCATION (2016).

[41] Judy M. Cornett & Heather H. Bosau, *The Myth of the Country Lawyer*, 83 ALB. L. REV. 125, 125, 131, 138, 147, 156 (2020).

[42] *Jobs & JDs: Employment for the Class of 2022*, N.A.L.P. (2023), https://perma.cc/K225-SD2J; *Employment Outcomes as of March 15, 2023 (Class of 2022 Graduates)*, A.B.A. (2023), https://perma.cc/HJL7-U5ER.

[43] *Employment Summary for 2022 Graduates*, A.B.A. (2023), https://perma.cc/Y8NW-ALFT.

Of course, there is nothing nefarious about this change. America becomes more urban and less rural at every census. The law becomes more complicated every year. Consider how lawyers need to deal with the shifting terrain of the administrative state; new fields of law; technological development; and the strengthening of the corporate firm. Put it all together and it makes sense that more lawyers work in cities in specialized roles. As lawyers become siloed in specialties, fewer Americans interact with local lawyers in positive ways. At least since Shakespeare wrote *Henry VI*, lawyers have been disliked – or at least the punchline of jokes.[44] Most Americans do not think lawyers are ethical, and Gallup polls show that sentiment has only increased in recent years.[45]

Urbanization and specialization in the legal field has been a slow but steady transition. Yet every step down that path removes more lawyers from small-town generalist practices. For almost a century, starting only a handful of years after Miniard's death, authors have been decrying the loss of rural lawyers. In 1939: "The country lawyer … is no more."[46] In 1950: "The county-seat lawyer and the small-town advocate are pretty much gone."[47] Then there was at least a bit of resurgence. The GI Bill brought more students to law school, including from more precarious economic backgrounds, like rural communities.[48] Some of those new lawyers returned to their rural hometowns.[49] That massive governmental subsidy provided a path to education that kept the rural practice of law alive, at least for a few decades. Yet even during these decades with more rural lawyers, the legal needs of poor rural residents were still not being met.[50]

By the 1970s, the rural out-migration of young adults coupled with the retirement of the GI Bill-funded lawyers finally caught up with rural communities. Small-town lawyers really were disappearing this time. A 1967 article described how "many rural areas" were facing the "absence of any lawyers or the advanced age of those available. In many counties there are no lawyers, in others there are only a few who may be employed as judges or county attorneys."[51]

The slow march over time of specialization and urbanization took lawyers from small towns. Even though the number of lawyers per capita has proliferated nationwide as the law became more complicated and omnipresent, rural communities saw the relative decline of lawyers. Lisa Pruitt has observed this in Arkansas.[52] Other

---

[44] WILLIAM SHAKESPEARE, 2 HENRY VI act 4, sc. 2 ("The first thing we do, let's kill all the lawyers.").
[45] Megan Brenan & Jeffrey M. Jones, *Ethics Ratings of Nearly All Professions Down in U.S.*, GALLUP (Jan. 22, 2024), https://perma.cc/2ZZU-FWKB.
[46] BELLAMY PARTRIDGE, COUNTRY LAWYER 317 (1939).
[47] Robert H. Jackson, *The County-Seat Lawyer*, 36 ABA J. 497 (1950).
[48] FRIEDMAN, *supra* note 37, at 543.
[49] Gilbertson, *supra* note 2, at 434.
[50] Mark Kessler, *Expanding Legal Services Programs to Rural America: A Cast Study of Program Creation and Operations*, 73 JUDICATURE 273, 274 (1990).
[51] William M. Barvick, *Legal Services and the Rural Poor*, 15 U. KAN. L. REV. 537, 550 (1967).
[52] Pruitt et al., *supra* note 24.

studies back up these observations – rural lawyer numbers are continuing to drop, leaving more rural communities without lawyers, and leaving more individuals without legal representation.[53]

There are a variety of explanations for this. The legal profession now requires seven years of higher education, which almost always is done away from rural hometowns. Students travel to larger communities to get educated and might not return. This is a far cry from the education received by rural lawyers like Miniard and Lincoln. "Reading the law" required only law books. Perhaps the books needed to be obtained from a different community, but the education could happen at home. In 1855, Abraham Lincoln responded to a young man who had sought a legal apprenticeship in his firm. Lincoln rejected the aspiring lawyer, but wrote an encouraging letter telling him that it was fine to read the law alone and that it "is of no consequence to be in a large town while you are reading. I read at New Salem, which never had three hundred people living in it. The books, and your capacity for understanding them, are just the same in all places."[54] That is no longer true.

A few law schools offer online law degrees. As of 2024, the ABA had approved five fully online programs.[55] A dozen more schools have approved hybrid programs that provide legal education partially in-person and partially online. Of the full-time programs, only one is public. The rest are private, and their average tuition per year is over $46,000. This is unaffordable for students heading to rural practice and looking at a future without high salaries or the benefits of loan forgiveness programs available for public interest lawyers or graduates of elite schools. Notably, not a single online program appears on the list of most affordable law schools, a list dominated by public institutions in rural states, including South Dakota, Nebraska, North Dakota, and Montana.[56]

For most rural students, it still makes sense to attend a residential law school that provides lower cost, local networking, and in-person learning. Some rural students will choose to attend online law schools despite the higher cost, but the fully online law schools are all in cities, and their events and networks will not be focused on rural America. The local connections built by attending regional law schools will not materialize with online institutions. But the bigger problem is

---

[53] Cliff Collins, *Attracting Rural Lawyers*, OR. ST. BAR BULL. 17, 18 (Feb./Mar. 2024); Ashli R. Tomisich, New Lawyers' Perceptions of Learning the Rural Practice of Law (2023) (Ph.D. dissertation, University of Wyoming); Alan Romero, *Assessing and Addressing the Need for Rural Lawyers in Wyoming*, WYO. LAW. 26 (Oct. 2021).

[54] Letter from Abraham Lincoln to Isham Reavis (Nov. 5, 1855), in UNCOLLECTED LETTERS OF ABRAHAM LINCOLN 61–62 (Gilbert A. Tracy, ed., 1917).

[55] *ABA-Approved Law Schools with Approved Distance Education J.D. Programs*, A.B.A. https://perma.cc/ZDK8-PLLW (last visited Feb. 26, 2024).

[56] *20 Most Affordable Law Schools 2024*, BEST VALUE SCHS. (Jan. 26, 2024), https://perma.cc/8C8S-RRM8.

likely student loans. Student loan debt is a major issue for all law school graduates, and I have written before about how rural practitioners fall between the cracks of traditional loan forgiveness programs.[57] While rural lawyers have incomes closer to public interest lawyers than big city firm lawyers, none of the public interest loan forgiveness programs cover rural lawyers in private practice. Because fewer loan forgiveness programs are available for these rural practitioners, student debt is an even larger burden.

There are other factors as well. Two-career households can have a harder time finding work for both parties in smaller communities. Earnings in rural and urban communities have separated, with rural workers earning substantially less than their urban peers. Student loans loom large, pushing new lawyers to pursue lucrative job options. Competition for spots in law schools has also increased. Students from rural school systems face educational deficiencies.[58] Not enough rural students are entering law schools. Even for those who do enter, not enough are returning home. Outsiders rarely take law jobs in rural communities, perhaps because of their own preferences for urban amenities and perhaps because of the reputation that rural America is skeptical of outsiders. Whatever it is that has kept Americans from choosing to practice law in rural communities, the impact is that rural communities are now facing a shortage of rural lawyers.

Donald Landon conducted the last deep study of rural lawyers, publishing his findings in 1990. His research was done in Missouri from 1982 to 1983 and though Landon spoke with attorneys from small towns, he included towns up to 20,000 in his study. Following Landon, there was a long time with no significant study of rural lawyers. A few law review articles here and there profiled rural lawyers, and there have been occasional memoirs.[59] Advice books by rural lawyers came out in 2013 and 2016.[60] In 2017, an edited volume about rural practice in Australia arrived.[61] In 2020, the Wyoming State Bar surveyed its membership about rural lawyers and then in 2023 Ashli R. Tomisich finished a dissertation about new rural lawyers in Wyoming.[62] Law professor Elizabeth Chambliss has a forthcoming article studying the practice of rural attorneys in South Carolina.[63] All of this work is helpful in understanding my study because it provides context to the way that the new lawyers

---

[57] Hannah Haksgaard, *Rural Practice as Public Interest Work*, 71 ME. L. REV. 209, 218 (2019).
[58] Kai A. Schafft & Catharine Biddle, *Education and Schooling in Rural America*, in RURAL AMERICA IN A GLOBALIZING WORLD: PROBLEMS AND PROSPECTS FOR THE 2010S 561–62 (Connor Bailey, Leif Jensen & Elizabeth Ransom, eds., 2014).
[59] Among these are DALE BUMPERS, THE BEST LAWYER IN A ONE-LAWYER TOWN (2004), and CHRIS CALLAHAN, BAR TALES: STORIES FROM A SOUTHERN RURAL LAW PRACTICE (2012).
[60] BRUCE M. CAMERON, BECOMING A RURAL LAWYER (2013); ALVIN LEAPHART, HOW TO PRACTICE LAW IN A SMALL TOWN & MAKE MONEY DOING IT (2016).
[61] THE PLACE OF PRACTICE: LAWYERING IN RURAL AND REGIONAL AUSTRALIA (Trish Mundy, Amanda Kennedy & Jennifer Nielson, eds., 2017).
[62] Romero, *supra* note 53; Tomisich, *supra* note 53.
[63] Elizabeth Chambliss, *Rural Legal Markets*, 12 TEX. A&M L. REV. (forthcoming 2025).

in South Dakota are experiencing rural practice. One common theme emerging from this work is that while there are difficulties in rural practice, the field is not dead. As Landon concluded, "rural law practice is alive and, for the most part, well."[64]

I'm not convinced there was ever a heyday for rural lawyers, though aspects of the past look appealing. Take Miniard, for example. His education was cheap. His practice was local. We think his income was stable for the time and place, though it did not build generational wealth or even generational access to high-quality education. Miniard's son was a moonshiner by profession, his granddaughter a coal miner's wife with a sixth-grade education who subsistence farmed to feed her family, his great-granddaughter an astute businesswoman, and his great-great-granddaughter a rural lawyer in the same Appalachian community. That modern-day rural lawyer is my cousin; Miniard my great-great-grandfather.

Between Miniard's life and mine, his rural community and family went through poverty, law-breaking during prohibition, a starvation-level drought in the 1930s, educational deficiencies caused by a poor and isolated school system, and the growth and demise of coal reliance. But there was also modernization that brought the family out of poverty and into the contemporary broader world. There was some out-migration, including by my own mother. My cousin received her law degree from the University of Kentucky, leaving her rural community for higher education and the first few years of her career. She graduated first in her class and could have stayed at her large urban firm for a successful career. Instead, she came home to practice in rural Appalachia. Yet her rural practice is nothing like Miniard's. She neither rides a mule nor risks her life for her law practice. Highways now connect what was once an area so isolated that when Mary Breckinridge set out to test the functionality of a rural nursing program, she chose Leslie County to prove that the program could function in even the most rural and remote region of America.[65]

The rural lawyers of today are not the rural lawyers of the 1800s (like Abraham Lincoln) or the 1900s (like Miniard or Atticus Finch). Education, technology, and other societal changes have, in many ways, changed the daily life of a rural lawyer. The famous country song "Mammas Don't Let Your Babies Grow Up to Be Cowboys" offers a caution against the hard life faced by rural cowboys.[66] It offers a better option: "Let 'em be doctors and lawyers and such." Lawyering – even rural lawyering – is supposed to offer an easier rural life for those who pursue it. This was true for Lincoln, Miniard, and Atticus Finch. It is true today. Yet despite a career that offers so much, not enough young people are choosing the profession.

---

[64] LANDON, *supra* note 7, at 2, 121.
[65] MARY BRECKINRIDGE, WIDE NEIGHBORHOODS: A STORY OF THE FRONTIER NURSING SERVICE (1952).
[66] ED BRUCE, MAMMAS DON'T LET YOUR BABIES GROW UP TO BE COWBOYS (United Artists, 1975).

RURAL LIFE WITHOUT LAWYERS

In the myth of the country lawyer that Cornett and Bosau describe, these local rural lawyers are present in rural communities to ensure fairness and access to justice to everyone. If this is what rural lawyers do, then perhaps rural lawyers should be viewed "as the great equalizers in American democracy."[67] They at least have that potential. And at some junctures, rural lawyers have represented the most vulnerable members of their communities. In his fictional closing argument, Atticus Finch told his rural jury that "in this country our courts are the great levelers."[68] But in the real world, lawyers are not accomplishing this.

In Loka Ashwood's book *For-Profit Democracy* about rural places, government, and democracy, lawyers play a limited – and mostly negative – role.[69] One key argument in Ashwood's book is that rural Americans are losing land ownership to corporate control, with the corporations using the law and lawyers to take rural land. That is true, but nowhere does Ashwood mention access to lawyers as a way to combat these types of losses. Instead, Ashwood almost exclusively discusses lawyers as outsiders working for corporations against rural interests. The rural lawyers that appear in the book are mainly hired by companies, thus representing outside interests rather than the downtrodden rural residents with whom Ashwood is concerned. The same narrative appears in Jennifer Sherman's work about rural communities, with lawyers appearing only briefly and portrayed as working with outside forces against local interests.[70]

At least Ashwood and Sherman take note of what lawyers are doing in rural communities. Other rural writers seem to simply forget about lawyers. In preparing to write this book, I read a lot of books about rural America, and most of them did not acknowledge lawyers. Some books acknowledge the frustration that rural people feel about the law and its application, but never turn to discussing the role lawyers can play.[71] At other times, lawyers appear only in passing. In one book about rural America, a brief mention is made that rural lawyers exist, but only urban lawyers are interviewed.[72] In another book, a part-time lawyer busy raising five kids makes an appearance, as does a colonial house renovated to a law office.[73] And while that book covers the high social esteem that lawyers hold and their potential unaffordability for small farmers, it never describes the work those lawyers are doing.

---

[67] Cornett & Bosau, *supra* note 41, at 156.
[68] HARPER LEE, TO KILL A MOCKINGBIRD 205 (1960).
[69] LOKA ASHWOOD, FOR-PROFIT DEMOCRACY: WHY THE GOVERNMENT IS LOSING THE TRUST OF RURAL AMERICA 67, 73, 102, 105, 148 (2018).
[70] JENNIFER SHERMAN, DIVIDING PARADISE: RURAL INEQUALITY AND THE DIMINISHING AMERICAN DREAM 183 (2021).
[71] *See, e.g.*, CYNTHIA M. DUNCAN, WORLDS APART: WHY POVERTY PERSISTS IN RURAL AMERICA 37 (1999).
[72] ELIZABETH CURRID-HALKETT, THE OVERLOOKED AMERICANS 2, 25, 107, 224 (2023).
[73] WUTHNOW, *supra* note 31, at 22, 34, 82, 104.

Those writing about rural communities from an academic or policy standpoint seem to simply forget that lawyers may play a unique role in rural communities. There are quite a few lawyers (and one anthropologist) who focus their academic work on the study of rural lawyers, but those studying rural communities have yet to incorporate lawyers into their main focus of study. Part of the problem may be that modern rural communities often lack lawyers. Perhaps the rural lawyer shortage is now so bad that rural sociologists just do not run into lawyers or their clients when they study rural communities, though one suspects the role of law and lawyers could play a more prominent role in the study of rural communities.

Lawyers appear more often in local histories of rural South Dakota. In preparation for this book, I also undertook reading memoirs and histories written by residents of the counties I study. In these books, lawyers are often mentioned in passing as part of the fabric of society. A self-described cowman runs into a prosecutor and judge.[74] A sheep herder explains that his rural community had "mechanics, farm laborers, kitchen mechanics, clerks, schoolma'ams, lawyers, nurses, preachers, ex-soldiers, merchants, and musicians – every class and occupation you could think of."[75] A retired historian reminisces about her youth, mentioning that there were two lawyers in Presho in 1922, a town that had zero lawyers a century later.[76]

These older texts about rural South Dakota take for granted that lawyers will be part of a rural community, yet lawyers are now missing from many such communities. When lawyers are in a rural community, they do a lot of things. They appear in court in criminal and civil cases. They advise businesses and governments. They draft documents and provide advice. When lawyers are absent, some of these things simply do not happen. In criminal cases, where the government pays a prosecutor and a defendant is entitled to representation, lawyers will still be present. Those lawyers, though, will often travel from larger communities to provide legal services, going home at the end of the day, taking with them their pay, their community investment, and their legal knowledge. Or those criminal lawyers will do only part-time work.

Judges are likely, but not guaranteed, to be licensed lawyers. There have been nonlawyer judges for a long time, though progressively more and more judges are law-trained. Today, most states require that judges have law degrees and licenses, but nonlawyer judges remain, especially in tribal and rural courts. As the Supreme Court announced in 1879, "[a]s respects the administration of justice, [each state] may establish one system of courts for cities and another for rural districts."[77] That rule is still good law. Nothing says that rural and urban residents receive the same judicial system.

---

[74] W. H. HAMILTON, DAKOTA: AN AUTOBIOGRAPHY OF A COWMAN 12 (1941).
[75] ANDREW B. GILFILLAN, SHEEP 284 (1929).
[76] DOROTHY HUBBARD SCHWIEDER, GROWING UP WITH THE TOWN: FAMILY & COMMUNITY ON THE GREAT PLAINS 65 (2002).
[77] State of Missouri v. Lewis, 101 U.S. 22, 30 (1879).

In 1976, the Supreme Court considered a challenge to nonlawyer judges in Kentucky, where large communities were required to have law-trained judges and small communities were not. The Supreme Court endorsed this urban–rural difference, in part because "it is a convenience to those charged to be tried in or near their own community, rather than travel to a distant court where a law-trained judge is provided."[78] While generous of the Supreme Court to take into account the travel burdens on rural people, the Court only took into account these travel burdens to justify the state allowing less-qualified judges in rural places. Even today, rural areas are more likely to have judges without any legal training.[79]

When rural areas do have law-trained judges, those judges often travel or serve as only part-time judges. Traveling judges have less connection to rural communities. Part-time judges develop conflicts of interest. A full-time, local, law-trained judge sounds wonderful, but many rural economies cannot support the expense.

Even when a law-trained judge sits at the front of a courtroom, there may be no lawyers at counsel table. Litigants in rural areas often have no access to lawyers, instead representing themselves. In 2023, the *Wall Street Journal* ran a story about rural Kansas courtrooms where judges were taking a more active role in helping self-represented clients successfully navigate the legal system.[80] The same has been observed in northern Minnesota and Wisconsin.[81] Fewer lawyers, low funding of legal aid services, and poor rural economies all contribute to a court system where judges find themselves helping litigants in ways traditionally done by lawyers.[82] While some litigants appearing without attorneys would have hired a local attorney if available, there are many other rural residents who simply could not afford an attorney no matter what. And thus, the economic realities of rural life come to bear on the question of whether rural lawyers are still a viable part of contemporary America.

LAWYERS AND THEIR CLIENTS

There are a variety of ways to be a rural lawyer. The classic conception is an office on Main Street with one or more lawyers serving private clients in the local community. The rural lawyer is thought of as an independent entity, making money from clients rather than being employed by any agency or organization. They may do criminal or civil litigation; they may draft estate plans; they may form businesses

---

[78] North v. Russell, 427 U.S. 328, 336 (1976).
[79] Sara Sternberg Greene & Kristen M. Renberg, *Judging Without a J.D.*, 122 COLUM. L. REV. 1287, 1301 (2022).
[80] Shannon Najmabadi, *Courts Come to Order with Judges, Litigants – but No Lawyers; Some Judges Are Helping Divorcées Fill Out Paperwork, But Have to Avoid Getting Too Involved*, WALL ST. J. (Oct. 7, 2023).
[81] Michele Statz, *On Shared Suffering: Judicial Intimacy in the Rural Northland*, 55 L. & SOC'Y REV. 5, 24–25 (2021).
[82] Najmabadi, *supra* note 80.

or mediate divorces. But whatever they do, they do legal work for fee-paying clients who walk into their offices from the local communities. For many rural lawyers, this is the case.

There are other ways to be a rural lawyer. Some rural lawyers work directly for businesses, like a local bank. Very few rural lawyers do impact litigation, also called strategic litigation, where they bring lawsuits meant to effect wider policy changes.[83] Instead, even impact litigation that affects rural America is often brought by specialists in cities. Some rural lawyers work for the government, though government agencies at both the federal and state level tend to be in more populated areas.

Another type of rural lawyer starts in a small town, then ascends to political power. Rural lawyers have served in all levels of government, including as president, as Lincoln made famous.[84] More often, of course, their political careers start and end in local elections, often with election as the local prosecutor. They serve on school boards and city councils. Many become judges; some become justices. There are fewer but still substantial numbers who join state or federal legislative bodies. Some continue to identify as rural lawyers even after they ascend to the highest levels of government. Dale Bumpers, a senator from Arkansas, titled his autobiography, *The Best Lawyer in a One-Lawyer Town*, laying claim to an identity as a rural lawyer despite his many years in Washington.[85] When rural law practices produce political leaders, those lawyers may have a positive impact on the larger world, but the small towns lose their practicing lawyers.

A final way to be a rural lawyer is to work for a legal aid office. American legal aid organizations originated in American cities, privately financed by donors or bar organizations.[86] The first big push for legal aid in rural America came in the 1960s when the federal government funded legal aid offices through the Office of Economic Opportunity as part of President Lyndon Johnson's War on Poverty.[87] Even then, most of the funding for legal aid went to urban areas.[88] Rural areas saw some, though. As a few examples: A single lawyer funded to provide legal services to migratory workers in Ulysses, Kansas.[89] Legal aid offices on rural reservations.[90] A New Jersey lawyer who was so insistent in providing services to his farmworker

---

[83] Sarah Vogel, The Farmer's Lawyer: The North Dakota Nine and the Fight to Save the Family Farm (2021).
[84] Friedman, *supra* note 37, at 494–95.
[85] Bumpers, *supra* note 59.
[86] Felice Batlan, *Archival Confrontations and Rewriting the History of Legal Aid in the U.S.*, in Histories of Legal Aid: A Comparative and International Perspective 287–88 (Felice Batlan & Marianne Vasara-Aaltonenpage, eds. 2021).
[87] E. Clinton Bamberger Jr., *Legal Services Program of the Office of Economic Opportunity*, 41 Notre Dame Law. 847 (1966).
[88] *Id.* at 849; Barvick, *supra* note 51, at 544; Kessler, *supra* note 50, at 273.
[89] Bamberger, *supra* note 87, at 849.
[90] Monroe E. Price, *Lawyers on the Reservation: Some Implications for the Legal Profession*, 1969 L. & Soc. Ord. 161 (1969).

clients that he faced criminal trespass charges for visiting clients on the farm that employed them.[91]

Writing in 1966, the director of the Legal Services Program at the Office of Economic Opportunity pushed for full-time legal aid attorneys, arguing against using private attorneys who would then receive compensation for their work. His skepticism focused on financial cost, the depth of services provided, and the need to still have clients vetted for indigency. Yet, he was open to paying private attorneys "in sparsely populated areas where there is no other feasible method to provide free legal assistance."[92] The Office of Economic Opportunity's legal aid funding did not last long enough to test this.

In 1974, federal legal aid funding was moved to the Legal Services Corporation ("LSC"), where it remains today.[93] During the early years of LSC, there was momentum to provide legal aid in rural areas.[94] Now, LSC funds 131 legal aid providers across the country.[95] The primary way lawyers work for legal aid organizations is as full-time employees, though it is also possible for legal aid organizations to hire part-time lawyers or to pay hourly rates to lawyers for taking cases. Paying local lawyers to take cases is known as "judicare," modeled off of Medicare where government funds go to private providers for taking on low-income clients. The judicare model has largely been rejected by LSC and a preference remains for full-time attorneys.[96]

Legal aid offices provide substantial representation to people in or near poverty but are constrained in the types of clients and cases they can take. In a 2017 report, LSC found that 75 percent of low-income rural residents faced a civil legal issue, compared against only 71 percent of all low-income Americans.[97] Despite the higher need in rural areas, legal aid funding disproportionately flows to urban areas.[98] Add in that law firms volunteering to help legal aid providers are concentrated in urban areas, and the services provided through legal aid are disproportionately urban. Even when LSC-funded organizations are supposed to equally cover urban and rural areas, their offices are likely located in urban centers, requiring travel for rural residents. Without a doubt, rural America needs more legal aid funding, offices, and attorneys.

The need for more rural legal aid lawyers brings me to one of the debates about rural lawyers. On one side are those spending time and resources to advocate for more private practice rural lawyers. On the other are those who think resources should be directed at creating more legal aid positions in rural areas.

---

[91] State of New Jersey v. Shack, 58 N.J. 297, 277 A.2d 369 (1971).
[92] Bamberger, *supra* note 87, at 851.
[93] Warren E. George, *Development of the Legal Services Corporation*, 61 CORNELL L. REV. 681 (1976).
[94] Kessler, *supra* note 50, at 280.
[95] *Our Grantees*, LEGAL SERVS. CORP., https://perma.cc/3AWC-MJ9X (last visited Feb. 23, 2024).
[96] George, *supra* note 93, at 722.
[97] *The Justice Gap: Measuring the Unmet Civil Legal Needs of Low-income Americans*, LEGAL SERVS. CORP. (2017), https://perma.cc/4GZQ-A27N.
[98] Matt Reynolds, *Help Wanted*, 110(2) A.B.A. J. 38, 41 (Apr./May 2024).

The entire Rural Attorney Recruitment Program in South Dakota is premised on the first idea – that it is worth investing societal resources to bring more private practice attorneys to rural areas. But not all agree. Take Jennifer English, a rural South Dakota lawyer who completed her five years in the Rural Attorney Recruitment Program and remains in her rural community. English thinks the lack of paying clients is the "true barrier" to rural practice. English does not see the need for more private practice attorneys in rural areas; instead, "what is needed is low-income services." Instead of incentivizing private practice in communities with insufficient paying clients, English thinks the investment should be to set up legal aid offices in every county and provide funding for lawyer salaries. English speaks of her own experience based on five years in rural practice where she found plenty of clients with legal problems, yet few clients that could pay.

So far, I have introduced data about the presence (or, more specifically, lack) of rural lawyers. But another way to think about this issue is from an "access to justice" angle. Broadly speaking, this means people having access to legal services or legal outcomes that serve their needs. Declining access to justice is related to declining numbers of rural lawyers, though the two are not the same. Law professors Daria Fisher Page and Brian Farrell argue persuasively that these are two distinct, but related, phenomena.[99] This is, of course, true. My argument is that putting more lawyers in rural America is necessary, though not sufficient, to provide access to justice.[100]

Simply because there are lawyers in a given community does not mean those lawyers can solve the legal problems for all community members. Private practice lawyers have to pay their overhead costs and thus require fee-paying clients. Public defenders work on the government's dime, but only when clients meet certain requirements. Prosecutors work *with* victims, but not *for* them. Local legal aid attorneys are the closest to truly focused on providing access to justice. There are also nonlawyer ways to achieve access to justice, but rural areas are short on services as well. The lack of services in rural America, coupled with the difficulties of providing legal assistance in rural areas, means that low-income residents struggle even more to access the legal system in a meaningful way.[101] In short, rural Americans are most often not accessing resources in ways that achieve true access to justice.

Certainly, there should be more legal aid attorneys. Most low-income individuals are unable to get legal assistance, either through a legal aid organization or from

---

[99] Daria Fisher Page & Brian R. Farrell, *One Crisis or Two Problems? Disentangling Rural Access to Justice and the Rural Attorney Shortage*, 98 WASH. L. REV. 849 (2023).

[100] Larry R. Spain, *The Opportunities and Challenges of Providing Equal Access to Justice in Rural Communities*, 28 WM. MITCHELL L. REV. 367, 367 (2001); Eric W. Schultheis, *The Social, Geographic, and Organizational Determinants of Access to Civil Legal Aid Services: An Argument for an Integrated Access to Justice Model*, 11 J. EMPIRICAL LEGAL STUD. 541, 542 (2014).

[101] Spain, *supra* note 100, at 369.

a private lawyer.[102] The federal government, the states, and private donors should fund more offices and salaries. Despite all of the good reasons to increase funding for legal aid, there are also good reasons to financially support new private practice lawyers in rural areas. LSC-funded legal organizations are restricted by Congress in the types of clients and cases they can take. Local private attorneys can pick up the prohibited cases. Plus, one reason that rural areas desperately need more legal aid is that there are insufficient local lawyers to take on pro bono cases for indigent community members.[103] More private practice attorneys cannot possibly serve all legal needs, but each attorney can do something. Chapter 10 provides data on how the South Dakota rural lawyers engaged in pro bono work, supporting the idea that even private practice attorneys help to meet the needs of low-income rural residents.

Focusing on creating opportunities for private practice lawyers to move to rural areas and encouraging them to take pro bono cases will serve fewer poor clients than hiring those same attorneys as legal aid attorneys, but it is better than the remaining alternatives. In 2000, the ABA created the Rural Pro Bono Delivery Initiative, which focused on "the redistribution of human and financial resources from urban areas to rural areas."[104] The ABA recognized the same concerns I have raised here – that there are not enough rural lawyers; the rural lawyers that do exist have conflicts, limited access to support staff, and travel demands; and that full-time staff attorneys at legal aid offices cannot keep up with demand. The ABA's idea was to leverage technology to have urban attorneys provide pro bono services in rural areas. But these technology-based plans to provide remote services are never sufficiently successful. Rural America lags behind in broadband access. High rates of poverty limit access to technology, and it turns out that rural clients like face-to-face interactions. As anthropologist of law Michele Statz says: "There's this sort of 30,000-foot view that we'll put in the technology and people can just attend court differently," but "it's so much more than that. It's so much more than just a hearing."[105] Resources are better spent putting lawyers on the ground in rural communities. The ABA program sunset in 2003.[106]

The keen interest in funding more legal aid attorneys is largely born out of the widespread poverty and poor economic conditions in rural communities. Rural economies are an important part of the story of rural lawyers and the clients they can serve. In later chapters about the finances of rural practice and pro bono work, I address specifically how the rural lawyers I interviewed are managing to serve both paying and nonpaying clients. In Chapter 10 I make the argument that lawyers help

---

[102] Schultheis, *supra* note 100, at 544.
[103] Spain, *supra* note 100, at 377.
[104] Greg McConnell, *The Center for Pro Bono Creates New Project: The Rural Pro Bono Delivery Initiative*, 4(1) DIALOGUE: A.B.A. DIV. FOR LEGAL SERVS. 25 (Winter 2000).
[105] Jack Karp, *A Mountain to Climb: The Inaccessibility of Rural Courts*, LAW360 (Dec. 1, 2023), https://perma.cc/N25F-63SQ.
[106] *Rural Pro Bono Project*, A.B.A., https://perma.cc/NA6A-S32M (last visited Feb. 28, 2024).

the economies of their small towns. Most of these lawyers have found themselves busy with fee-paying clients, though a few have struggled to develop enough fee-paying clients to make the practice of law financially successful. Most of the rural lawyers in my study have enough work. While they pick up pro bono work on the margins, they *can* fill their days with fee-paying clients.

The argument that financial investment in legal aid services would be a more worthy alternative is one critique leveled against the South Dakota program. Another is that the program has not been very successful in bringing rural attorneys into Indian Country.[107] Two of the attorneys joined the program in Indian Country and more in border communities with substantial Native American populations, but not enough. I have heard this criticism leveled against the program and its advocates several times. The response is complicated, and probably unsatisfying.

Lawyers knowledgeable about practice in South Dakota have concerns that attorneys will struggle financially in Indian Country. Under this theory, a rural lawyer's bread and butter fee-earning cases are in probate and estate planning. In Indian Country, with much of the land held in trust, there is less wealth to pass generation to generation. While estate planning is more complicated in Indian Country, fewer clients can pay for sophisticated estate planning. Thus, lawyers cannot rely on estate planning to sustain their practices. South Dakota's Native American communities are poor. It is not a lack of legal need in those communities, it is a lack of funds to pay. Of course, much of rural America is poor, but in Indian Country the land ownership structure removes a form of wealth that often translates to using lawyers.

The 2020 Census shows that the five United States counties with the highest percentage of residents living below the poverty rate are in South Dakota.[108] All of those counties are rural, remote, and include Federal Indian Land. The numbers of attorneys in those counties are telling. Todd County, encompassing the reservation of the Rosebud Sioux Tribe, has a poverty rate of 55.5 percent, the single highest poverty rate in the entire country. Todd County has only five resident lawyers: a retired and two active tribal judges as well as two in-house tribal lawyers. While providing critical legal services in the county, these lawyers are not representing individual clients directly.

Mellette County, which ranks second nationwide for highest poverty rate and has substantial amounts of trust land belonging to the Rosebud Sioux Tribe, has one resident lawyer. That lawyer is a participant in the Rural Attorney Recruitment Program. He supplements a slow private practice with government work as the county's part-time prosecutor. The top ten highest poverty counties rounds out with four more reservation counties in South Dakota: Oglala Lakota, Jackson, Corson,

---

[107] The term "Indian Country" is both a legal and a conversational term. Its legal definition appears in 18 U.S.C. § 1151.
[108] Andrew DePietro, *Counties with the Highest and Lowest Poverty Rates in the U.S.*, FORBES (Feb. 28, 2022), https://perma.cc/66NC-V39H.

and Ziebach, which have a *combined* total of seven licensed resident lawyers, several of whom work in-house for tribes and do not provide direct client services. In the data I tracked in South Dakota, the poorer a county, the more difficult it is to keep private practice lawyers. This is unsurprising. Lawyers need to make a living and at some point there are too few paying clients to sustain a business. The economic circumstances of a rural area matter.

There are also other factors that go into low placement in Indian Country. Dakota Plains Legal Services, an LSC-funded legal aid provider, serves rural Native American populations. Like many rural legal aid providers, Dakota Plains is rarely fully staffed and often hiring.[109] In March of 2024, it was advertising for three open lawyer positions.[110] If a lawyer wants to move to rural Indian Country in South Dakota, it is very likely they can get a job through Dakota Plains, a job that comes with a guaranteed salary, benefits, and built-in mentor attorneys. Tribal governments also need attorneys, again offering full-time salaries. It is easy to understand why attorneys choosing to work in Indian Country would prefer to take jobs offering full-time employment, rather than self-employment in a solo law office. In other words, the attorney shortage is so bad on South Dakota reservations that funded salaried positions are open. Someone would have to affirmatively want to move to a reservation *and* be in private practice to use the Rural Attorney Recruitment Program in Indian Country. It turns out those people are rare.

Indian Country is not the only type of rural community that can struggle to support a local lawyer. Bedroom communities, where many residents commute to a larger community for work, have similar issues. In bedroom communities, like Salem where Jennifer English works, it becomes too easy for potential clients to take their legal business to larger firms in the city. Thus, one potentially counterintuitive observation: In my study, the further a lawyer is from a city, the easier it is to build a book of paying clients. Though that held true only so long as a lawyer did not practice in a county so remote and rural that it suffers from persistent poverty.

I have laid out in this section some of the ways that rural lawyers can (or cannot) serve rural clients. There are lots of potential clients with unfulfilled legal needs across rural America. There are insufficient lawyers to serve those clients. There are too few government lawyers, there are too few legal aid lawyers, and there are too few private practice lawyers. Data, narratives, and scholarship firmly support the position that there are too few lawyers. Yet there must be another step – a real attempt to remedy the disproportionate lack of access to lawyers in rural America.

---

[109] Reynolds, *supra* note 98, at 41–43.
[110] *Career Center*, ST. BAR S.D. NEWSL. 59–60 (March 2024).

3

Policy Responses

FIGURE 3.1 Dylan Kirchmeier

Today, Dylan Kirchmeier is a rural lawyer in South Dakota. Kirchmeier is the prosecutor for Roberts County, which has just over 10,000 people. The Sisseton Wahpeton Oyate reservation covers most of the county, including the county seat of Sisseton where Kirchmeier practices.

In 2013, though, Kirchmeier was a high school student serving as a page in the South Dakota legislature. One day, while attending a committee hearing, Kirchmeier heard debate about a proposed bill to provide incentive payments for rural South Dakota lawyers. That bill became law. Kirchmeier decided to become a lawyer with the intention of using the program to start a career in rural South Dakota. In 2020, Kirchmeier graduated law school and entered the program.

The legislative process that Kirchmeier saw led to South Dakota's Rural Attorney Recruitment Program, the nation's first – but certainly not last – attempt at solving the rural lawyer shortage. This chapter introduces various policy responses to the rural lawyer shortage, including South Dakota's legislation and strategies tried in other states. After surveying what is happening across the country, this chapter introduces the rest of the lawyers who have taken part in the South Dakota program.

TURNAROUND OPPORTUNITIES

Rural lawyers are declining in number, and the real question is whether the trend can be reversed. There are skeptics – a Kansas judge says there is no "realistic solution" to the lack of rural lawyers.[111] A North Dakota justice told me his own state's Rural Attorney Recruitment Program is not going to solve access to justice problems. But there are also those who see rural communities, and rural law practice, as having a level of resiliency that will allow growth.

In writing more broadly about rural communities, David Brown and Kai Schafft track the reversals of migration to and from rural areas since the 1970s.[112] The turnarounds in rural population growth have been brief, and overall rural areas have lost population, especially in comparison to urban and suburban communities. But there have been moments when rural areas have become popular, most recently during the COVID-19 pandemic as more space became appealing and remote work became possible. With greater internet connectivity, living in rural America is less isolating than it once was and rural people now have access to much of the information available to those in urban areas. Brown and Schafft argue that movement to rural areas will only occur when rural economic conditions are good. Certainly, for lawyers a rural legal practice will be more tempting when the economy is good enough that clients can pay. On the other hand, rural practice may be more enticing when urban lawyers are struggling in a down economy.

Sarah Thorne was a law student at the University of South Dakota during the 2008 financial crisis when lawyer jobs were in short supply. Thorne was part of a law school cohort where many new graduates were, in her words, "going to have to just go out on our own and attempt to wing it" in law practice. The firms in cities were not hiring; many government agencies had hiring freezes. At Thorne's law school orientation, Chief Justice Gilbertson of the South Dakota Supreme Court spoke about pursuing practice in small towns. Later, when Thorne had to draft legislation for a class assignment, she drafted legislation authorizing loan forgiveness for rural lawyers. Amazingly, when Thorne surveyed her fellow law students for her research, over 80

---

[111] Najmabadi, *supra* note 80 (sharing view of The Honorable Glenn Braun, Chief Judge of Kansas's 23rd Judicial District).

[112] DAVID L. BROWN & KAI A. SCHAFFT, RURAL PEOPLE AND COMMUNITIES IN THE 21ST CENTURY: RESILIENCE AND TRANSFORMATION 33–37 (2d ed. 2019).

percent said they would consider rural practice in exchange for partial student loan forgiveness. This is not exactly what Brown and Schafft predict about rural migration because the rural economy was not good at the time, but it (at least hypothetically) offered some comparative advantages, including loan forgiveness as an offset to poor economic conditions. Of course, there was no loan forgiveness program for rural lawyers, and 80 percent of Thorne's classmates did not head out to practice in rural South Dakota. Yet, that law student paper planted seeds for policy changes to come.

Thorne's paper was passed onto Chief Justice Gilbertson, who was already advocating for some sort of program to incentivize rural practice. Gilbertson started his career as a rural attorney in 1975 in his hometown of Sisseton, population 2,428. After he became a member of the Supreme Court, Gilbertson regularly drove across rural South Dakota for decades. After noticing rural firm after rural firm disappear as attorneys retired or died, Gilbertson began to think about how to recruit new rural attorneys. Early on, Gilbertson realized the financial limitations faced by new graduates with high student loans. In consultation with the executive director of the state bar association, he decided that "the best way to encourage small town attorneys" would be "some kind of a financial incentive to take the fear" out of going to a small town.

As the state's Chief Justice, Gilbertson addressed the legislature every year in his State of the Judiciary Address. Gilbertson started talking about the rural lawyer shortage in these addresses in 2005. For several years the legislature did not respond to Gilbertson's call to action. But then in 2013 State Senator Mike Vehle came to visit Gilbertson a few days after the speech. Vehle sponsored legislation, but in an environment where other work was already happening behind the scenes.

Pat Goetzinger, a lawyer practicing in South Dakota's second-largest city, was elected as the state bar president for the 2011–2012 term. Goetzinger came from rural South Dakota, having grown up in Martin, population 941. Goetzinger saw the lawyers in his hometown disappearing during the same time that Chief Justice Gilbertson was starting to talk about the hollowing out of the rural bar. Goetzinger read Thorne's law school paper, and, at the urging of Gilbertson, Goetzinger spoke with Thorne about her idea for incentivizing rural practice. Tom Barnett, the executive director of the state bar, was crucial in forging these connections for Goetzinger and in ultimately supporting his vision. Goetzinger adopted rural recruitment as his project for his year as state bar president.

Once Goetzinger decided to focus on rural lawyers during his term as state bar president, he still needed to *do* something. With the help of Tom Barnett, Goetzinger launched a task force, bringing Bob Morris – a small-town attorney and past president of the state bar – to chair the task force, which became known as "Project Rural Practice." The task force began by bringing together stakeholders, including county commissioner representatives and municipal representatives, then brought together what Goetzinger called the "big three" – the state bar, the Unified Judicial System (basically, the judiciary and the administrative wing of the judiciary), and the state's only law school at the University of South Dakota. With the law school under the deanship of Tom Geu, originally from rural western Nebraska, the "big three" were all led by men who grew up in rural America.

Goetzinger heard skepticism from many people, but he had Chief Justice Gilbertson, Barnett, Geu, and Morris on his side, meaning the judicial system, the law school, and the state bar had a strong coalition to make *something* happen to resolve the rural lawyer shortage. These men worked hard and built a coalition. They also encountered what Goetzinger called "serendipitous things." Bob Morris simply called it "dumb luck." For example, meeting the ABA leadership at a conference and getting national attention through an ABA resolution regarding rural lawyers, which in turn made the national and local news. Goetzinger credits the ABA resolution and media coverage "as a catalyst to crafting legislation" the following year. It helped that Goetzinger's law partner David Lust was the house majority leader in South Dakota and was an "advocate" and "natural" ally in the legislative effort once Senator Vehle decided to take action.

THE LEGISLATION

A year after Goetzinger's state bar presidency and the ABA resolution on rural lawyers, and after years of hearing Chief Justice Gilbertson talk about rural lawyers in his State of the Judiciary address, Senator Mike Vehle "took the initiative to walk into Chief Justice Gilbertson's office and say 'are you gonna do something about this, or just talk about it?'" Vehle mentioned stipends for medical professionals and asked about pursuing a similar program for lawyers. Suddenly, there was a partner in the legislature willing to make this happen. The Project Rural Practice Task Force, by then co-chaired by Goetzinger and Morris, stepped back into an advisory role while the program moved through the legislative process. Vehle was not a lawyer, though the prior summer a rural lawyer named Shane Penfield had told Vehle that "small towns really need attorneys" to fix client and community problems, including to spur economic development.[113]

In 2013, Vehle introduced legislation. Vehle's first legislation had funding going to law students rather than practicing lawyers; those law students had to have connections to South Dakota; and counties under 12,000 in population could participate.[114] The legislation failed in the Senate, but Vehle was undeterred. He listened to critiques, amended the language of the bill, and took advantage of a procedural workaround by "hoghousing" (or taking over) a bill about transfer on death deeds.[115] By doing this, Vehle was able to substitute in his rural lawyer bill, this time getting

---

[113] *See generally* Justin Simard, *The Birth of a Legal Economy: Lawyers and the Development of American Commerce*, 64 BUFF. L. REV. 1059 (2016).
[114] S.B. 218, 2013 Leg., 88th Sess. (SD 2013).
[115] H.B. 1096, 2013 Leg., 88th Sess. (SD 2013).

enough votes. Chief Justice Gilbertson found extra money in his judiciary budget to fund the 50 percent match from the state. Lust helped obtain funding approval in the House of Representatives. It passed both chambers and was signed into law on March 21, 2013, by Governor Dennis Daugaard.

What South Dakota passed into law in 2013 was truly unique. Nothing similar had ever happened in a state legislative body in the United States. States had long used financial incentives to attract medical professionals to rural or underserved areas. But incentivizing lawyers to go rural was new. While there was thoughtful planning behind the bill, a lot of fast decisions had to be made. There was no model legislation to follow; no sister state with a law to copy. Instead, the South Dakota team did their best to write something entirely new.

This initial legislation called the program the Recruitment Assistance Pilot Program, limited to a maximum of sixteen attorneys and only available until 2017. Counties under 10,000 in population could participate in the program. Under the legislation, participating attorneys had to stay for five years. If they left before serving five years, they would have to repay the stipends they had received. The stipend amount was calculated based on 2013 tuition at the University of South Dakota School of Law. Unfortunately, "everyone was so giddy" that the bill might actually pass that future inflationary increases were not built into the bill. To be fair, very little could have been done in 2013 to create an effective escalator clause in the legislation. Because a portion of the funding comes directly from the state, any future inflationary increases would need approval from the legislature, secured on an annual basis. Now, program administrators are thinking about how to get legislative approval for an escalator clause, though even with such a clause the budgeting process would need legislative approval. If the stipend were growing with inflation, it would be over 16,000 dollars per year in 2024, rather than stuck at 12,513.60 dollars per year as it was calculated in 2013.

One key piece of the legislation is defining which counties are eligible to participate. The 2013 legislation allowed counties under 10,000, which is admittedly arbitrary. The population line could have been drawn anywhere. Chief Justice Gilbertson originally picked 12,000 as the cutoff, which the first proposed legislation used. The final legislation decreased that population cutoff to 10,000. That population line includes most of South Dakota's counties as indicated by the darker counties in Map 3.1.

Senator Vehle insisted that counties have "skin in the game," so a cost-sharing provision was included to make sure that local counties paid a portion. Counties had to pay 35 percent of the stipend; the state bar 15 percent; and the state – through the Unified Judicial System – 50 percent. That basic structure has remained, though the legislation has been amended three times, as shown in Figure 3.2. This continued legislative intervention has always been to expand, rather than restrict, the program. In other words, whatever happened to get the conversative South Dakota legislature on board with funding rural lawyers was not a fluke. The people working behind the scenes feel like luck was involved with the legislative approval, yet the

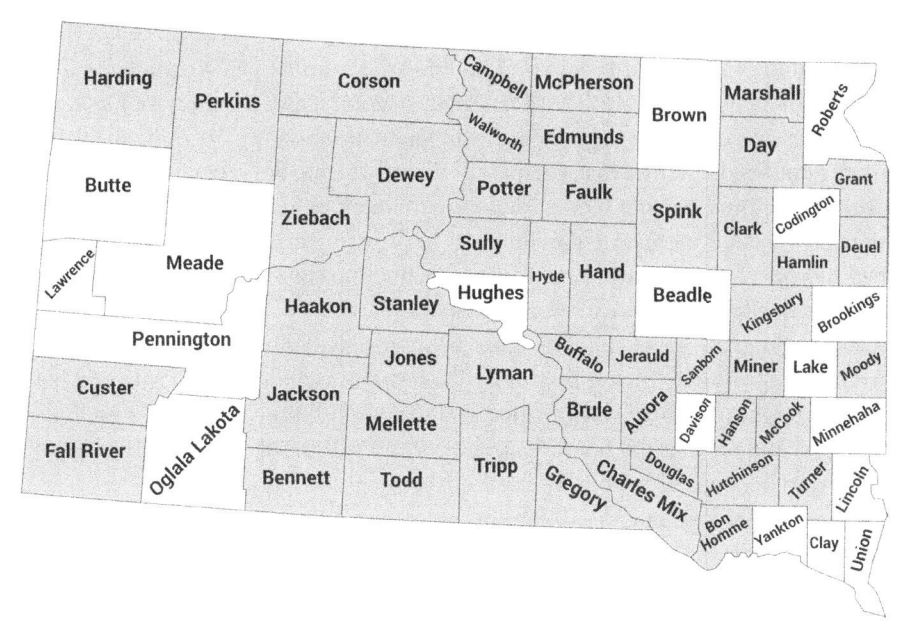

MAP 3.1 Qualifying counties[116]

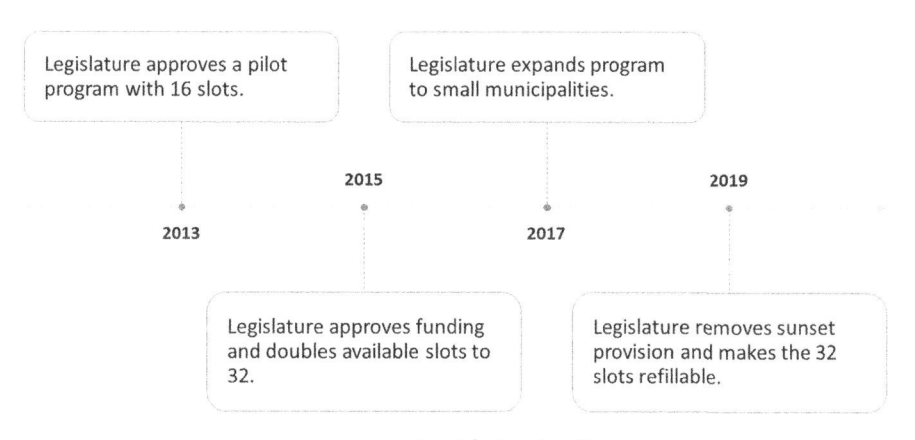

FIGURE 3.2 Legislative timeline

- 2013: Legislature approves a pilot program with 16 slots.
- 2015: Legislature approves funding and doubles available slots to 32.
- 2017: Legislature expands program to small municipalities.
- 2019: Legislature removes sunset provision and makes the 32 slots refillable.

constant reapproval and expansion from the South Dakota legislature demonstrates that the political branches feel things are going well enough to continue investing in the program.

As the timeline in Figure 3.2 encapsulates, the three additional legislative actions occurred in 2015, 2017, and 2019. In 2015, the legislature approved 500,000 dollars

[116] Created under A Creative Commons Attribution-ShareAlike 4.0 International License at mapchart.net on Jan. 26, 2024.

in expenditure authority to fund the incentive payments.[117] That same legislation extended the time frame to 2022 and doubled the number of slots, allowing thirty-two attorneys to participate. Two years later, in 2017, legislation removed the "pilot program" language and expanded the program to allow small municipalities in more populated counties to participate.[118] Then, in 2019, the program was extended again – this time making the legislation permanent by removing the sunset provision entirely and increasing the ability of lawyers to participate by allowing thirty-two attorneys to participate at any given time, but imposing no limits on the ultimate number of attorneys who can ever participate.[119]

More programmatic changes have been decided at an administrative level without requiring legislative approval. These have included changes to pro bono requirements, mandatory mentorship, and making full-time prosecutors ineligible. The trial and error of the South Dakota program was inevitable, but also not problematic. The team of people invested in the program's success have been able to navigate necessary changes to keep the program working for South Dakota. Chief Justice Gilbertson retired in 2021, and current South Dakota Supreme Court Chief Justice Steven Jensen now talks about the program as one that is flexible except where constrained by legislation. Jensen's view is a useful one – one of the takeaways from the interviews I conducted is that flexibility is important. Because the program was a first-of-its-kind approach, the people running the program have been open to change over time. The Project Rural Practice task force continues to innovate, including, in October 2024, setting up several new working groups to strategize future improvements. Because the authorizing statute is broadly written to allow various locations and types of practice, the program has been more successful for more rural attorneys than a narrowly drawn program would have been.

OTHER POLICY RESPONSES

At the same time that South Dakota was working its way through the first ten years of the Rural Attorney Recruitment Program, other states were considering whether to attempt something similar. In 2021, North Dakota, through administrative rule rather than legislation, created a program almost exactly like South Dakota's. The usage in North Dakota has been different, with only four participating attorneys and all four being practitioners who were already in their rural areas when they applied for and received the stipend. One more state – Illinois – offers a stipend to rural lawyers. Illinois is substantially less at only 10,000 dollars maximum, though requiring only a one-year commitment. Illinois has seen higher numbers of participants, but substantially lower rates of retention in rural communities.

---

[117] S.B. 178, 2015 Leg., 19th Sess. (SD 2015).
[118] H.B. 1053, 2017 Leg., 92nd Sess. (SD 2017).
[119] H.B. 1046, 2019 Leg., 94th Sess. (SD 2019).

There has been interest in developing similar funded programs in other states, but nothing else has come to fruition. Most of the failed bills were much more constrained anyway. For example, sometimes only for rural public defenders or only for tuition reimbursement.[120] Work continues across the country. As just a few examples: Kansas is currently studying solutions to its rural lawyer shortage.[121] The Oregon State Bar recently extended its Loan Repayment Assistance Program to cover rural settings.[122] The Colorado Access to Justice Commission received a 627,000-dollar grant to work on solutions to the rural lawyer shortage.[123] The Dakotas have certainly made the biggest dollar investment for paying practicing lawyers, though other states have invested in different types of programs, which are worth analyzing.

In 2023, law professor Lisa Pruitt collected and categorized different state policy responses to the rural lawyer shortage.[124] Though the programs are constantly in flux and programs have already changed, her categorizations remain useful to understanding policy responses. Beyond stipends to practicing lawyers, like South Dakota, North Dakota, and Illinois have done, there are incubators, succession planning programs, channeling urban resources to rural areas, and expanding pathways to rural practice. There is an even newer strategy being tested in several states, expanding licensing opportunities for lawyers in rural areas.

Incubator programs are designed for new graduates to learn how to launch a law practice. They are often, but not always, associated with law schools. The ABA tracks incubators, reporting over seventy-five programs in existence since 2007, a few of which are rural focused.[125] The incubator system is largely directed at solo practitioners serving low- and middle-income clients. They offer a modest stipend, but provide substantial structured mentorship.

Montana and Arkansas have created rural-focused incubators. Montana Legal Services Association has a rural-focused incubator program with a 24-month commitment from new practicing lawyers. The lawyers go to underserved rural areas, but are given substantial mentorship and training along with loan forgiveness.[126] In Arkansas, the current incubator program is administered by a faculty member at the William H. Bowen School of Law and targeted specifically to its alumni.[127] Lawyers

---

[120] *See, e.g.*, S.B. 461, 2019 Leg., 104th Reg. Sess. (Wis. 2019).
[121] Rachel Mipro, *Kansas Supreme Court Justice Tackles State's Severe Shortage of Rural Attorneys*, KAN REFLECTOR (Dec. 2, 2022), https://perma.cc/C5CY-H5JM.
[122] Collins, *supra* note 53, at 17, 20–21.
[123] Elaine Tassy, *Nearly Half of Colorado Counties Have 10 or Fewer Attorneys*, CPR NEWS (Dec. 19, 2023), https://perma.cc/L5AC-FP8C.
[124] Beskin & Pruitt, *supra* note 25, at 7–26.
[125] *Results of the Legal Incubator Lawyers' Survey April 2021: ABA Standing Committee on the Delivery of Legal Services*, A.B.A. (2021), https://perma.cc/55EK-XMU3.
[126] *Rural Incubator Project for Lawyers*, MONT. LEGAL SERVS. ASS'N, https://perma.cc/ZLX8-4GXP (last visited Feb. 28, 2024).
[127] *Rural Practice Incubator Project*, U.A. LITTLE ROCK, https://perma.cc/MM79-AZ43 (last visited Feb. 28, 2024).

work in underserved rural areas, receiving up to 10,000 dollars in start-up costs for an eighteen-month commitment. Both programs require participants to engage in pro bono work; both programs aim to provide the necessary support to make the lawyers launch successfully. The incubator mentorship in Arkansas has relied on volunteer attorneys. After a solid start, the Arkansas incubator was without a director for several years, stalling placements in rural areas. It turns out that sustaining rural-focused incubators has been difficult. California had one briefly, but it shuttered before really getting off the ground.[128] Arkansas, though, is discussing significant improvements to its program.

Other states have developed programming aimed at facilitating succession planning in rural areas. These programs, though, are less developed. Much has been done to connect law students with retiring lawyers, but less to facilitate the actual transition of the firm. In my own interviews with new and retiring attorneys, I heard varied perspectives about what retiring lawyers expect. Some retiring lawyers view succession planning as a way to sell a firm and book of business for a profit. Aspiring rural lawyers in South Dakota told me that they walked away from retiring lawyers trying to charge too much. On the other hand, some retiring rural lawyers see succession planning as an investment to ensure a new attorney comes to town to take care of their clients. A lawyer like this, instead of charging the new attorney for "buying" the practice, might sell a building or its contents, but then spend time and lose money helping the new attorney take over. No program has successfully targeted resources at older attorneys as an incentive for them to train and hand off offices.

Then there are the programs that bring urban lawyers and resources to rural areas. A Minnesota project called "Justice Buses" encapsulates one strategy – taking lawyers from more urban areas, putting them on buses, and having them bring legal services to more rural communities.[129] These types of programs are most often conducted through legal aid offices and law school clinics. Short-term legal assistance is not as good as permanent local counsel. However, these programs are usually providing free services to clients that likely could not afford to hire a local lawyer, even if one were present.

Another way to leverage urban resources to serve rural communities is through the use of technology. For decades, there have been proponents of using technology to provide legal services in rural areas. However, rural areas still have technological deficiencies that prevent this from being a real, long-term solution. Urban lawyers providing representation in rural areas may successfully fill gaps in legal assistance, but it cannot be a primary path forward. Urban attorneys are unfamiliar with local norms, both in and outside of the courtroom. Local issues often need

---

[128] Pruitt et al., *Hinterlands, supra* note 24, at 664 n. 227.
[129] *Justice Buses: Putting Wheels on Justice*, REACH JUST., https://perma.cc/7HVN-CNT2 (last visited Feb. 28, 2024).

local solutions, though specialized attorneys in urban areas certainly provide critical assistance in more complicated matters when rural lawyers want to make referrals.

The largest grouping of state programing can be lumped together and generally described as pathway programs, though those come in a variety of packages. Nebraska has the most robust system, with the Rural Law Opportunities Program.[130] Nebraska recruits rural high school students as they enter college, providing an undergraduate scholarship and exposure to law school and rural law practice. This program sees students through four years of undergraduate education and three years of law school. That long-term investment means that Nebraska is only now seeing graduating lawyers come out the other side, with several initial graduates choosing not to practice in rural areas. Other programs are less time- and resource-intensive, but also attempt to encourage prelaw students to consider rural practice.

Law schools themselves take part in encouraging rural practice by offering rural courses and clinics to law students. Law school students take part in job fairs and mentorship programs with rural attorneys. Summer stipends for law students, whether through the school or state bar, can bring those students to rural areas when no local attorney can afford to pay a summer intern. Those funded stipends can help with building connections between aspiring rural lawyers and rural practitioners.

There is also an opportunity for each school to support rural lawyers after graduation through Loan Repayment Assistance Programs ("LRAPs"). In looking through LRAP terms for the top 140 law schools, my best guess is that about seven law schools would cover rural practice, with only Michigan and Berkeley explicitly mentioning rural practice in their policies.[131] LRAPs are generally only available at larger, more expensive schools, but they can provide loan forgiveness for rural practitioners not covered by federal loan forgiveness.

Finally comes the nascent policies focused on easing licensure requirements with the goal of expanding the pool of attorneys willing to go to rural areas. In 2023, the Nevada Supreme Court issued a rule allowing twelve months of limited practice for law school graduates working full time for legal aid, rural prosecutor, or rural public defender offices.[132] Several more states have policies that allow alternative pathways to full licensure, though the programs are not aimed specifically at rural lawyers. In South Dakota, a committee has recommended a pathway program to licensure for traditional public service jobs or for private practitioners working in communities that qualify for the Rural Attorney Recruitment Program.[133] The South Dakota Supreme Court, in 2024, continues to move forward with the proposal, which would

---

[130] *Rural Law Opportunities Program*, NEB. COLL. OF L., https://perma.cc/S2LE-HRLJ (last visited Feb. 28, 2024).
[131] Haksgaard, *supra* note 57.
[132] *Nevada Supreme Court Adopts Changes to SCR 49.5 re: Limited Practice of Law*, ST. BAR NEV. (Oct. 19, 2023), https://perma.cc/SQ9M-MVPK.
[133] *South Dakota Bar Licensure Assessment*, NAT'L CTR. ST. CTS. (Dec. 2023), https://perma.cc/G8JJ-S72C.

create a pilot program allowing students heading to rural areas or public interest jobs an option to submit a portfolio rather than take the traditional bar exam.

All of these programs – from funding for lawyers, to recruitment, to loan forgiveness, to eased licensing requirements – can play a role in recruiting and retaining rural lawyers. For a relatively young policy issue, a lot has been tried. Without a doubt, some rural lawyers have been incentivized by these various programs. This book's focus is on the South Dakota program because it was the first and remains the most expansive. Now with a ten-year history to study, there is enough information to start understanding how a rural lawyer incentive program works in practice.

THE SOUTH DAKOTA LAWYERS

After Governor Dennis Daugaard signed the initial legislation in 2013, the recruitment process began in South Dakota for the rural attorneys and rural communities who wanted those lawyers. Jake Fischer was the first participant to enter the program, Clay Anderson the second. Then, in the first ten years of the program, thirty more lawyers followed with signed contracts and boots on the ground in their rural communities. Those thirty-two attorneys – and their successes and failures – are the focus of this book. A bit more about those attorneys is needed by way of introduction.

At the ten-year mark of the program, in 2023, there were twenty-four participating attorneys practicing law in their rural communities. Twenty-four of thirty-two attorneys, then, are still in their rural communities. The other eight left rural practice. Three participants – Jake Fischer, Casey Jo Deibert, and Amanda Work – completed their five years then left their rural communities. Fischer returned to Minnesota, his wife's home and where he attended law school. Deibert and Work both moved to Pierre, South Dakota, where they work as government lawyers.

Five participants left during their five-year obligations. Evan Hoel had – by far – the shortest stint. He was in rural practice for only three weeks before moving to Rapid City to work as a full-time public defender. During those three weeks, Hoel had done some work as an assistant prosecutor but had not yet taken on any of his own clients. I include Hoel in the study because I think his experience is useful to understanding the initial stress and concerns that most of these participants had about rural practice. Hoel, though, never acquired clients and never practiced law, so his experience is not reflected in discussions of the practice of law.

Elizabeth Steptoe was in practice less than a year before deciding to step away from the practice of law. Steptoe, though, has deep connections to her rural community, and did not move after leaving rural practice. Instead, she still lives on the same farm but teaches in the local school. Also lasting less than a year was Ryan McKnight, who similarly left for a teaching job. But for McKnight, his job offer was to teach at a college on the other side of the state. McKnight is unique because his wife Brittany Kjerstad McKnight graduated from law school in the same year, and they entered rural practice together. However, the county commissioners were not going to approve and fund two participants. Accordingly, only McKnight had a contract even though Kjerstad McKnight could have been a participant. Kjerstad McKnight is not included in the thirty-two lawyers that form this study, though I interviewed her in the same fashion as those thirty-two lawyers. I bring in her story as appropriate throughout the book because her experiences are very similar to other new rural attorneys.

Two attorneys made it into their second year before departing. Amanda LaCroix was in rural practice for over a year, but health insurance and other factors pushed her to leave. She took a salaried job with the state government in Pierre, which she still holds today. Kasen Lambeth was in rural practice exactly two years before receiving a job offer in the larger community of Vermillion, South Dakota, where he moved. The book explores these departures in more detail, including an analysis of whether the departures can be viewed as policy failures, or whether they are inevitable transitions that happened as part of changing lives.

Of the twenty-four participants still in their rural communities, twelve had finished their five-year commitments by the ten-year anniversary in 2023. Of those twelve with completed contracts, most are full-time rural lawyers, while four attorneys are doing something less than full-time rural practice, though all four continue to be at least a part-time rural attorney. Those four part-time rural attorneys are Dusty Ginsbach who works in the oil fields of northwestern South Dakota; Clay Anderson who is more of a businessman than a lawyer; Jennifer English who contracts with a nearby larger county to do involuntary commitments; and Ashley Anson who is connected with a firm in a larger community, splitting her time between her rural office and its larger office, with plans to transition to a career in counseling.

The other eight attorneys who have finished their five-year contracts are full-time rural practitioners. Kristian Ellendorf, Austin Hoffman, Amy Jo Janssen, Kristen Kochekian, Zach Pahlke, Victor Rapkoch, Jackson Schwandt, and Stephanie Trask are all rural lawyers with no intention of leaving the full-time practice of law.

Then there are the twelve attorneys who were in their five-year contract window in 2023 at the ten-year anniversary. Dylan Kirchmeier and Kathy Zenner are both full-time prosecutors in rural communities with intentions to stay. Kirby Krogman, Rachel Mairose, Abigail Monger, and Mason Juracek have part-time prosecutor positions and part-time private practices – again, they all plan to stay in their rural communities. Then, finally, Rachelle Norberg, Derrick Johnson, Cody Miller, Cole Romey, Austin Schaefer, and Cassie Wendt are rural lawyers who either practice solo or with small law firms – and, again, they all intend to stay.

This group of thirty-two lawyers makes up the Rural Attorney Recruitment Program participants from the first ten years of the program. Their experiences are valuable in telling us about the realities of rural practice in today's world. This includes where the pressure points are that require assistance, and, therefore, how a rural lawyer incentive program can help.

While there is no racial diversity among the participants, there is diversity of gender, background, and political affiliation. Overall, the participants tend to be from rural backgrounds and tend to be conservative, yet there are participants from larger cities and participants who are politically liberal. There have been seventeen men and fifteen women participate in the program. Equal numbers of women and men (four each) have left the rural practice of law either during or after the five-year commitment.

THE WIDER PERSPECTIVE

New lawyers begin rural legal careers every year, and the story this book tells is a small-scale version of what happens every year in jurisdictions across the United States when new lawyers start practicing in rural areas. But it also tells a story unique to South Dakota, because South Dakota provides a stipend to support its new rural lawyers.

In 2024, NPR ran a story with the headline "One of the World's Greatest Instrument Collections Is in South Dakota, of All Places."[134] Can you imagine South Dakota, *of all places*, having a museum? Apparently that is hard to imagine, at least for NPR. Can you imagine South Dakota, *of all places*, being the nation's leader in incentivizing rural practice? I hope so, because it is. Though when the *New York Times* first introduced this program to the national media in 2013, the *Times* did not even mention South Dakota in the headline. Instead, it simply announced that "one rural state" had created a rural lawyer incentive program.[135]

South Dakota does not often make headlines for being the best at anything. We have the nation's best musical instrument museum. We have the nation's best trust laws (or worst, depending on your perspective). The museum came about by happenstance. The part-time legislature has been able to craft those trust laws with major industry help and as part of a larger economic strategy. Just like relaxed credit card laws boosted the state's economy, so does the trust industry. South Dakota's innovations in legislation have nearly always been about earning money, not spending money. It's not so obvious why South Dakota innovated a program for rural lawyers, even though this government spending is partially for the benefit of helping local economies.

Sometimes it feels like lightning struck in South Dakota – a fiscally conservative state became the nation's leader in funding rural attorney recruitment. But the real story leading up to the funded incentive program is a story of hard work by invested leaders who were willing to put in years of advocacy to solve a crisis. There were multiple modes of advocacy occurring simultaneously, with multiple people

---

[134] Elizabeth Rembert, *One of the World's Greatest Instrument Collections Is in South Dakota, of All Places*, N.P.R. (Jan. 2, 2024 5:23 PM ET), https://perma.cc/T8FG-KXGM.
[135] Bronner, *supra* note 29.

making a difference. There were also, quite frankly, a lot of people with power who care deeply about rural America. This is a state where rural continues to matter, and rural investment is part of the state identity. Combine all of this, and South Dakota has a funded program to help ease the rural lawyer shortage in the state.

The first-in-the-nation aspect led me to do this deep study of how the program and its participants are faring. But let me be clear. Just because my interviews are with South Dakota lawyers does not mean that only South Dakota lawyers can learn from their experiences. In fact, myself and others have heard similar feedback from rural lawyers in other states. I conducted interviews with rural lawyers and policymakers in Arkansas, Colorado, Illinois, Iowa, North Dakota, and Wisconsin. Those lawyers face similar constraints and challenges. Elizabeth Chambliss interviewed private practice lawyers at various career stages in South Carolina's poorest rural counties.[136] Ashli Tomisich interviewed new lawyers in Wyoming.[137] Even accounting for jurisdictional difference and the different rural lawyers targeted in these studies, the reality of rural practice appears more similar than not across the country.

---

[136] Chambliss, *supra* note 63.
[137] Tomisich, *supra* note 53.

4

Choosing Rural Practice

FIGURE 4.1 Kirby Krogman

In the lower forty-eight, it is hard to find a place more rural than where Kirby Krogman grew up, a ranch twenty-two miles from the nearest town.[138] "Town" here refers to White River, South Dakota, a remote county seat with a population of 533 – not exactly a population center, even for South Dakota. Krogman attended a one-room country schoolhouse and now practices law in White River. Kasen Lambeth, in contrast, started his life in a 13,000 person Utah town, then moved to Las Vegas, Nevada, at thirteen, spending his formative years in one of America's biggest cities. Lambeth ended up practicing law in Elk Point, South Dakota, with a population of

---

[138] KROGMAN QUARTER HORSES, https://perma.cc/ZVP7-637R (last visited July 4, 2023).

2,124. The paths that brought Krogman and Lambeth to rural practice are vastly different, but both entered careers as rural lawyers in small-town South Dakota.

We all have instincts on what a rural lawyer looks like and why they might choose rural practice, but we have little data on what actually incentivizes lawyers to choose rural practice. Studies from Arkansas (surveying law students) and Missouri (surveying lawyers) provide some answers.[139] Using those studies for comparison and relying on data collected about law school students and graduates, I analyze how the thirty-two Rural Attorney Recruitment Program participants entered rural practice. This chapter focuses on *why* those attorneys chose to practice law in rural South Dakota. It considers where and how they grew up, whether they knew lawyers as children, why they chose to go to law school, and why they ultimately decided to work in rural areas. The lessons learned from these interviews can help guide policymakers in determining where to place resources and at what point to recruit lawyers for rural areas.

GROWING UP

The perceived wisdom is that rural lawyers are generally from rural areas and recruiting lawyers is easier if the recruitment is for lawyers who are returning home. Overall, rural residents tend to be from rural areas – 80 percent of rural Americans grew up in a rural area or a small town.[140] In Missouri in the 1980s, 87 percent of the surveyed rural lawyers were from rural communities.[141] Lisa Pruitt's Arkansas study in the 2010s focused on law students, finding that law students from rural counties were "especially open" to rural law practice.[142] Depending exactly on how rural is defined, 80 to 85 percent of the Rural Attorney Recruitment Program participants are from rural areas or small towns. There are a few, however, from metropolitan areas.

Twenty-one of the thirty-two participants are originally from South Dakota, with one more who started her life in Idaho before moving to the family ranch in rural South Dakota as a child. The other ten participants hail from around the country: Indiana, Iowa, Minnesota, Montana, Nebraska, New Jersey, North Carolina, Utah/Nevada, West Virginia, and a military kid who grew up in various places, but always thought of his grandparents' ranch in South Dakota as "home." Half of the participants ended up practicing very close to, or even in, their hometowns, while the other half are not in the place where they grew up. Almost all of the lawyers who relocated are in a smaller town than where they grew up. Only five participants grew up in towns over 25,000, and four of those five participants left rural

---

[139] Pruitt et al., *Hinterlands*, *supra* note 24; LANDON, *supra* note 7.
[140] WUTHNOW, *supra* note 31, at 28.
[141] LANDON, *supra* note 7, at 20.
[142] Pruitt et al., *Hinterlands*, *supra* note 24, at 630–33.

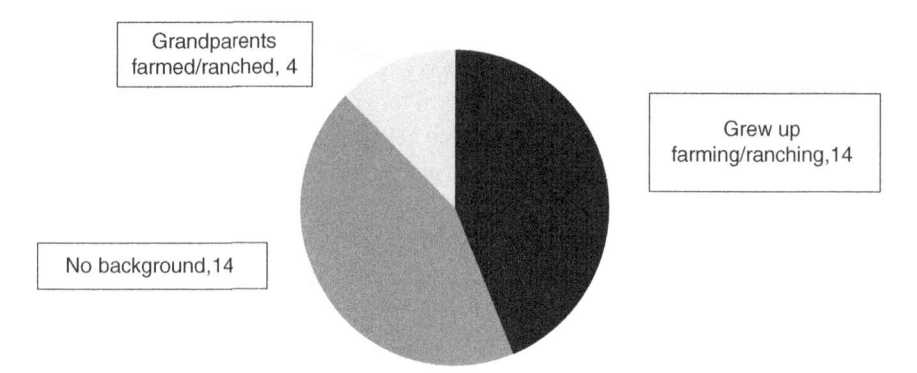

FIGURE 4.2 Agricultural background of participants

practice. Participants from St. Paul, Minnesota; Las Vegas, Nevada; and South Dakota's two biggest cities – Rapid City and Sioux Falls – all departed the program. Participants who grew up in smaller communities were more likely to stay in their rural communities.

The agricultural industry is important to rural areas, and a potential driver for educated young adults to return home. Figure 4.2 shows the agricultural background of the participating lawyers. Nearly half grew up in farming or ranching families, a few grew up in town but spent time on their grandparents' farms and ranches, then almost half did not grow up tied closely to agriculture. Most lawyers who grew up on farms or ranches have nothing to do with actual agricultural work, though it is common for these lawyers to do legal work for the family farm or ranch. A couple of participants actively farm or ranch with their families, and several chose to live on the family farm or ranch and commute to town for work.

A last important childhood factor is whether these lawyers were exposed to lawyers in their childhoods. Very few participants came from lawyer families. Over half of the participants said they did not know lawyers as children and were not exposed to what lawyers did. One participant "was taught to fear lawyers as a kid." When he was a child, "distrust" of lawyers "was very high" in his small, rural community.

A few more participants, all from small towns, said they knew about the lawyer (singular) in their small town, and a few had a closer relationship with a lawyer – for example, attending the same church. Two had uncles who were lawyers, and another had an aunt, but those family members did not practice nearby. One more had a grandfather who served as a judge.

Four participants interacted with lawyers in a professional capacity: One saw her parents go through a divorce and she appeared in front of a judge when she was a child to share her custody preferences; another's father owned a large business that employed lawyers; and two more interacted with lawyers who did legal work for the family farm or ranch. One of these participants experienced interacting with lawyers as "stressful," but noted that the rural South Dakota lawyer who assisted his family with an intergenerational ranch transfer made house calls – actually coming to the family ranch to meet with clients in their own home. Of note, both participants who saw their parents hire lawyers to provide agricultural legal work joined the law firms that their parents used.

Finally, three participants were raised by at least one lawyer. Zach Pahlke grew up in Winner, where both of his parents were lawyers. After law school Pahlke returned to his hometown and began practicing in his parents' firm. Ryan McKnight grew up in Sioux Falls, where his father was a partner at one of South Dakota's biggest law firms. McKnight joined the program practicing on the other side of the state. Finally, Cody Miller was a child when his father attended law school at the University of South Dakota. Miller's father is a prosecutor in a small South Dakota town and has been the hiring attorney for two participants, but Miller joined the Rural Attorney Recruitment Program in a community several hours away.

In comparison to Landon's Missouri study from the 1980s, fewer of these rural South Dakota lawyers were raised by lawyers. Fewer than 10 percent of the program participants in South Dakota were the children of lawyers, but Landon found 16 percent of rural Missouri lawyers were the children of lawyers.[143] Interestingly, several of the mentor attorneys in South Dakota, who brought in these young attorneys, had gone into rural practice with their parents. Several multigenerational firms in South Dakota saw a change to new ownership with this generation – the children of the rural lawyers were not taking up the family business, and those rural lawyers had to look elsewhere to transition their firms. Robert Wuthnow argues that for generations rural families have encouraged children to leave rural areas for better job opportunities.[144] Some of the children of these retiring attorneys may have heard that message – from parents, from schools, from peers – and decided to seek greener pastures elsewhere.

GETTING TO LAW SCHOOL

A wide range of experiences, desires, and life circumstances led the thirty-two Rural Attorney Recruitment Program participants to law school. Their explanations of why and when they chose law school resonate and contrast with a 2018 study by the Association of American Law Schools ("AALS") called "Before the JD."[145] In that study, most law students considered law school before entering college, with a third considering law school even before high school. While some of the rural lawyers made decisions that early, these rural lawyers were more likely to decide later in their educational career.

---

[143] LANDON, *supra* note 7, at 20.
[144] WUTHNOW, *supra* note 31, at 7.
[145] *Before the JD: Undergraduate Views on Law School*, Ass'n Am. L. Schs. (2018), https://perma.cc/K5N8-M6KY.

Some participants could not even remember why they decided to go to law school, while a few only remembered that they just decided on law school as a kid. Amy Jo Janssen was eight when she decided to become a lawyer, even though her only real exposure to the law was through television. Mason Juracek was also inspired by watching television, but he was a high schooler with a penchant for true crime shows like 48 Hours. Juracek was "intrigued by the court stuff at the end" and knew he wanted to pursue a career in law. Casey Jo Deibert's interest was piqued as a child when her dad's employer ended up in litigation. No rural lawyer incentive program can manufacture these types of interests, but an incentive program can be available to bring these dreams to fruition.

Parents and teachers had a large impact on getting students into law school. Only one participant said he was driven to follow in the footsteps of a parent by becoming a lawyer, but several nonlawyer parents pushed their children to attend law school when they were floundering with career decisions. Only one participant felt negative about this parental interference; most appreciated the push their parents gave them. In general, rural parents are more likely to focus on good outcomes rather than elite credentials.[146] Following this trend, parents tended to encourage in-state public law schools because of cost savings.

Teachers and high school career counselors also pushed their students to become lawyers. A high school counselor connected a future participant with a lawyer to job shadow. Several other participants were encouraged by high school teachers to pursue law. Austin Hoffman had a reputation for arguing with his childhood teachers, and several told him he would make a good attorney because of his aptitude for arguing. Hoffman and Austin Schaefer both grew up in McPherson County, which has a population of only 2,420 and two lawyers (one being Hoffman). In this very rural county with few lawyers, both Hoffman and Schaefer were encouraged by their public school teachers to pursue law; both are now rural practitioners.

Whereas the AALS study found over half of law students first considered law school before college, in my study only a third considered law school before college. For several rural lawyers, college professors encouraged law school. A few students were enrolled in science degrees in college, but, after taking a required civics or government class, they realized their passion lay in the law. Good college professors served as career advisors, encouraging several of the rural attorneys to choose law school. Once, a more striking college event encouraged a career in law – Justice Clarence Thomas spoke at Victor Rapkoch's university and inspired him to pursue law.

Outreach to high school teachers and college professors might be a more successful path than reaching out to students directly because invested teachers can inspire decades of students to pursue rural legal practice. A couple of decades ago when I was involved in the high school and college policy debate world, the University of

---

[146] CURRID-HALKETT, *supra* note 72, at 198.

Kentucky hosted a summer debate camp for high schoolers. The high school kids were mostly well-resourced with parents who could afford summer camp. There was another camp running concurrently for high school teachers learning to coach debate. The teachers attending camp tended to be from low-income schools. The plan was for those teachers to return home with the skills to train students who would never be able to afford their own summer camp.

Those high school teachers were mostly from an urban core, but training teachers may be even more important in rural areas. Local schools play an important role in rural communities.[147] Schools provide services and can act as a community-centered core.[148] For example, a high school might be best positioned to identify potential future lawyers to connect with practitioners for high school internships. I think about this debate camp for teachers when I see law schools, including my own, put on programming to introduce high school and college students to law school. Perhaps there should be a day where law schools host high school teachers to build long-term relationships with the educators who are in daily contact with potential future lawyers. Teachers may fear encouraging their best and brightest to leave rural communities to obtain higher education, but if *rural practice* is understood as a viable job opportunity, then teachers may be more willing to encourage law school with the hope of those students returning.[149]

There remains, of course, an important role for outreach programs aimed directly at students. As one example, Amanda LaCroix decided on law school after attending Girls State during high school. Girls State is a week-long civics camp organized by the American Legion Auxiliary where LaCroix had the opportunity to do a mock appellate argument. This summer camp, where volunteer lawyers served as mentors for high schoolers, convinced LaCroix to become a lawyer. Years earlier, when I did the exact same program, the mock appellate argument gave me a taste of what a law career could be. It was a powerful enough experience for me that I now volunteer for the event every summer. There are many camps that can provide the same hook for students, and those camps should take care – like Girls State does – to recruit from rural communities.

There are also ways to do outreach in rural communities, rather than bring rural students to college campuses. Local lawyers can offer job shadowing to rural high schoolers. In fact, job shadowing days inspired some participants to consider law school. The local lawyers need not do everything alone. State bars and law schools can, and should, continue to do outreach events because they do make a difference in recruitment. It may return small numbers of lawyers, but even one or two lawyers

---

[147] Allison L. Ricket, Jacquelin Yahn & Emily Bentley, *Rural Community and Career Connected Learning: Impacts of High School Internships Prioritizing People and Place*, 39(3) J. RSCH. RURAL EDUC. 1 (2023).

[148] Schafft & Biddle, *supra* note 58, at 558–60.

[149] *Id.* at 562.

per generation in the smallest communities is enough. Too few attorneys are Native American, and the State Bar of South Dakota has recently taken special care to do outreach events in rural reservation communities.[150] Only time will tell how many future lawyers are inspired by these outreach events, but my interviews suggest that these types of events can make the difference for students deciding to pursue a legal career. Outreach events, though, certainly do not capture all potential lawyers, because those programs are generally aimed at students, not people already in the workforce.

Targeting college graduates looking for a profession is a more difficult prospect, but might be pursued. A third of the participating lawyers did not even decide to attend law school until after college. This is twice as high as the 16 percent of post-college decision-makers in the AALS study. Half of the participants worked between college and law school, though some workers had previously decided to attend law school. But a third of participants did not decide on law school until they were working in their first career. An educator felt burnout; a businessman realized a law degree would improve his business dealings and ability to facilitate charitable work; a former football player hoped a law degree would aid becoming a sports agent; several men had careers in law enforcement or were thinking about that option; one ranch kid could not find a bank job in his hometown. A couple of participants had even more interesting jobs: Jennifer English was a karaoke host on cruise ships before law school and Victor Rapkoch was running a shark-hunting business in Florida.

Interestingly, even though the rural lawyers I met tended to choose law school later, they delayed law school by taking a break after college at a lower rate than students in the AALS study. Several participants who went straight from undergraduate to law school told me they moved quickly to limit student loans and get, as quickly as possible, back to their rural communities. For lawyers set on going home, they found it better to get law school (and thus their absence from their rural communities) out of the way as early as possible to allow them to move back home. In the AALS study, by contrast, future law students were more likely to take time between college and law school in order to gain work experience.

For the participants who worked after college and only chose law school while in their first career, law school was a second career choice mostly driven by wanting a stable-income job. This explains the higher rate of postcollege choice with these rural lawyers than in the AALS study. The lawyers who had started with other careers found that good employment was hard to obtain in rural America. This is true on two fronts. The well-paid blue-collar jobs in manufacturing and agriculture are gone.[151] Well-paid white-collar jobs don't exist; instead, those are concentrated in urban areas. The job market is tough, especially for smart and motivated young

---

[150] Heather Lammers Bogard, *President's Corner*, St. Bar S.D. Newsl. 6 (Nov. 2023).
[151] Wuthnow, *supra* note 31, at 69, 73.

adults. But the beauty of encouraging the rural practice of law is that these young professionals do not need to *find* a good job – they can *create* one.

And thus, for these lawyers, professional education became key to stable rural employment. One lawyer who grew up on a modest farm in a rural area described law school as an opportunity for "mobility – both economically and geographically." A couple of participants saw law school as a flexible graduate degree at a time when they were not sure what a future career would be. For most, though, law school was a path to secure employment. As Cole Romey said, his wife "deserved more than a failed farmer." For many of these participants, law school would provide financial opportunities far greater than those they experienced in their childhoods. This is unsurprising. For several decades, poverty and unemployment have been higher in rural areas than in urban areas, while average incomes have been lower.[152] This is not to say that all of these participating lawyers came from poor or struggling families. In fact, some have family wealth – though often tied up in agricultural land.

Regardless of the path to law school, participants were commonly drawn to law because they wanted to help people. As Cassie Wendt explained, she wanted to help "the people who didn't have a voice." Amy Jo Janssen did not know much about lawyers as a child, but she knew that "lawyers helped people, and that's what I wanted to do." This sentiment is true of many students entering law school regardless of whether they enter rural practice. The AALS study found that, along with potential for career advancement, a primary driver for considering law school was giving back to others or society.[153] Thus, for the participants driven by a desire to help people, choosing law school did not necessarily mean choosing rural practice – that was a separate calculation.

A few participants decided on law school in order to have a rural practice. Cole Romey was looking for a job that allowed him to support his own family while ranching with his family. Kirby Krogman had a similar drive and explained: "I'm saving up money to buy land so I can keep ranching. That's all the reason I went to law school, so I can afford to keep ranching." Both Romey and Krogman provide important legal services to their home communities while actively ranching. Relatedly, two participants made career decisions to allow working where a spouse farms or ranches. In today's economy, those who farm or ranch often need off-farm income. Rural recruitment programs might consider pitching law schools to similarly situated individuals: Either people who want to farm or ranch themselves yet have economic concerns about doing it full time, or the spouses of those people. Regardless of who has the law career in an agricultural family, it offers off-farm income and a level of legal sophistication that can help with managing the family agricultural business.

---

[152] SHERMAN, PARADISE, *supra* note 70, at 5.
[153] *Before the JD, supra* note 145, at 32–33.

After all, law need not be a full-time job to make a difference to either a lawyer's financial status or the well-being of a community. In fact, many South Dakota towns have lawyers who only practice part time, but still fill legal needs. For example, one town in my study has a stay-at-home mom who only takes immigration cases. While she is not available for most legal needs in the community, she provides critical representation in immigration cases, taking pressure off the other attorneys in town. When a rural attorney decides to go part time and specialize, general practitioners can refer the specialized cases, allowing them to focus on other areas. Everyone benefits. A part-time practice is more justifiable when student loans are paid off, but that is a major benefit of the Rural Attorney Recruitment Program. It is also a benefit of low-cost education, which is more likely to come from a state school in a rural area.[154] By keeping their costs low, law schools can allow more graduates to choose rural practice, whether full or part time.

FROM LAW SCHOOL TO CHOOSING RURAL PRACTICE

Choosing to attend law school is just the first step – choosing to enter rural law practice is another. There is also a risk that comes with recruiting more rural students to higher education and law school. Historically, adults with higher education have migrated away from rural locations because they have gained access to the social capital that allows them to be successful in more urban locations. Meanwhile, adults with less education stay in rural areas, creating a base population without higher education. This is the brain drain we hear so much about.

The number of college graduates is substantially lower in rural than urban areas.[155] Older adults, who came of age when good jobs were readily available in rural areas, did not necessarily need higher education for good jobs.[156] But now that rural economies have moved away from a stable set of jobs in extractive industries, higher education is needed for stable employment. Yet higher education opens the door for those educated young adults to leave.[157] I see this happen all the time with my law students. Every year we bring rural students into the law school and ultimately graduate them away to jobs in cities and bigger towns. Most of my rural students do not enter rural practice. The lawyers who decide to go to rural America are bucking the trend of rural brain drain, making their reasons for returning to rural areas after receiving an advanced degree particularly worth understanding.

Only half of the participants entered law school with a plan of entering rural practice at the end. For these students, their interest in rural practice was not contingent

---

[154] 20 Most Affordable Law Schools 2024, supra note 56.
[155] Educational Attainment Improved in Rural America but Educational Gap with Urban Areas Grew for Bachelor's Degrees and Higher, US DEP'T OF AGRIC. (Mar. 20, 2023), https://perma.cc/3YEJ-2ZBE.
[156] BROWN & SCHAFFT, supra note 112, at 101.
[157] Id. at 103, 152–53; WUTHNOW, supra note 31, at 56–57.

on the Rural Attorney Recruitment Program. Rather, there was a general interest in working in a small town because they like small towns or wanted to live near their families. One established rural attorney explained to me that when he was in high school, the attitude was "get out of here. Do not look back. There is zero opportunity" if you stay in a rural community. He ignored that advice and went back to a rural community, but now in raising his own kids he sees a different attitude. An attitude that promotes the value of living in rural communities rather than just looking to escape.

A few participants were planning on the Rural Attorney Recruitment Program before they even entered law school: Dylan Kirchmeier was a high school legislative page in the appropriations committee meeting the day the program was pitched. Rachel Mairose was an undergraduate student when her mom saved newspaper clippings about the program. Only a minority of participants had knowledge about the Rural Attorney Recruitment Program before law school, in part because the first wave of participants was already in law school before the program was announced.

When asked about whether the program influenced their decision to choose law versus other professions, only two participants said the program played a role in getting them to law school in the first place. For Rachel Mairose and Kirby Krogman, the existence of the Rural Attorney Recruitment Program encouraged their choice to pursue a career in law. Both wanted stable careers that would allow them to live in rural South Dakota. Krogman would have been "more hesitant" about law school without the program, and for Mairose the program "helped solidify my decision to go to law school because I knew there was a financial incentive." For these lawyers, and others, law school is an advanced degree that offers the opportunity to go back to a small town.

For participants who already planned on going to law school, the program encouraged their attendance at the University of South Dakota. For Dylan Kirchmeier, it made sense to stay in South Dakota for school because he planned to practice in rural South Dakota. Victor Rapkoch is originally from Montana but was living in Florida when he decided to attend law school. Rapkoch learned about the program while applying to law schools: He chose South Dakota because of his interest in rural practice.

Participants who grew up in rural areas were more likely to enter law school with a plan to return to a rural area. Mostly, lawyers who grew up in larger communities or urban areas did not enter law school with plans for rural practice. For the most part, participants planning on rural practice from the beginning of law school were from rural backgrounds. For the participants who entered law school without planning to enter rural practice, about half were from rural areas and half from larger towns or urban areas.

About half of the participants entered law school without any particular plans to practice in rural areas. Ryan McKnight, who grew up in Sioux Falls (South Dakota's largest city), described his views of rural practice when entering law school as follows:

> I didn't even know [rural practice] was a thing. I mean, I had no idea. It never even came across my mind that that was even an opportunity. If you would have told me I was going to end up in Philip, I would have laughed in your face. I didn't even know where it was.

However, at his law school orientation McKnight sat next to a classmate who grew up near Philip. Three years later that classmate became his wife and they both were practicing law in the town of 736.

McKnight was one of several participants who were steered toward rural practice through relationships. McKnight and his wife began their legal careers in Philip, with McKnight participating in the program. Kathy Zenner, who entered rural practice years after graduating from law school, was looking for a legal job near her husband's employment. More decisions were driven by connection to land: Two lawyers began their legal careers near where their husbands farmed or ranched. Two lawyers wanted legal careers where they themselves could ranch part time; requiring that they set up their legal careers near their family ranches.

Several more participants chose locations near their families. Jackson Schwandt and Austin Hoffman had children born while they were in law school, and both wanted to bring their children back to their hometowns where they could grow up with extended family nearby. Hoffman also wanted access to the family farm and the local hunting opportunities, now living on the family's farm though he practices in town. Other participants simply wanted to raise kids in small towns even if not in their own hometowns.

For participants who were not driven by land location or raising children, two reasons for preferring rural areas dominated: the desire to serve communities and the lifestyle, including outdoor amenities. Rural areas supposedly have trouble attracting lawyers because rural areas are thought to be unattractive to young professionals. However, the group of lawyers who have participated in the Rural Attorney Recruitment Program show the opposite inclination. Many of these young attorneys actively desired the lifestyle available in small towns. When Jennifer Sherman studied rural communities on the West Coast, she found much of the same drive for rural: community, safety, slower-paced lifestyle, and the physical environment.[158] In a rural community in California, Sherman found a gender breakdown in why her subjects wanted to be in a rural community.[159] Freedom from regulation and outdoor activities – such as hunting, fishing, and camping – were primary drivers for men. For women, it was community and family. The lawyers I interviewed did not express their reasoning along such clear gendered lines.

When Chief Justice Gilbertson first contemplated this program, he looked at the existing makeup of the rural bar in South Dakota, noticing that most rural lawyers

---

[158] SHERMAN, PARADISE, *supra* note 70, at 6, 87.
[159] JENNIFER SHERMAN, THOSE WHO WORK, THOSE WHO DON'T: POVERTY, MORALITY, AND FAMILY IN RURAL AMERICA 42–44, 66 (2009).

were men who were hunting and fishing enthusiasts. Gilbertson figured it would be easiest to recruit a similar population, expecting mostly male lawyers to want to go rural. Gilbertson and the program administrator, knowing the makeup of the rural bar, made a special effort to recruit female applicants for the program. That recruitment was successful. Of the thirty-two participants, fifteen are women and seventeen are men. Of the eight who left rural practice, four are women and four are men.

The increased gender parity of rural practitioners is reflected in the legal profession as a whole. While women were historically excluded from the practice of law, in recent years women have been attending law school and entering practice at high rates. In South Dakota, women now make up over a third of the bar membership. Nationwide, over half of law students are women. In 2023, for the first time, women made up the majority of associates at law firms in the United States.[160] When narrowing down data to look only at parents working in law firms, mothers are more likely to work in small firms or solo practices rather than in large firms, data that bodes well for recruiting women to rural practice.[161]

There are economic forces that might drive more women to be rural lawyers. Several of the female lawyers are married to men who have blue-collar jobs, the exact category of men hit hardest by the decline in rural jobs. Sherman talks about how gender roles have changed in rural families, including that more women are taking on paid work because well-paid rural jobs for blue-collar male workers are in steep decline.[162] Other husbands are farmers or ranchers. Since World War II, economic forces in rural communities have led farm families to seek off-farm employment. These off-farm jobs have often been held by women, who are often limited to low-paid jobs and are often discouraged by giving up their careers.[163] There is probably an untapped pool of potential rural lawyers in the spouses of farmers and ranchers. For example, in the bush of Australia, many of the female lawyers are there because of husbands' jobs.[164] Encouraging law school as a career path could more productively use the skills of some rural women, providing families with a solid economic footing and giving more rural women satisfactory careers.

Another reason I am not surprised that almost half of the participants have been women is because of the long history of rural female lawyers in South Dakota.[165] The

---

[160] *Women Now the Majority of Associates in U.S. Law Firms, Make Record Gains in the Partnership Ranks*, N.A.L.P. (Jan. 9, 2024), https://perma.cc/4TR4-57BE.
[161] *Legal Careers of Parents and Child Caregivers*, A.B.A. 10 (2023), https://perma.cc/CBR6-9NPR.
[162] SHERMAN, WORK, *supra* note 159, at 143.
[163] Cynthia B. Struthers, *The Past Is the Present: Gender and the Status of Rural Women*, in RURAL AMERICA IN A GLOBALIZING WORLD, *supra* note 58, at 490, 494–96; WUTHNOW, *supra* note 31, at 20, 156–57.
[164] Reid Mortensen, *The Moralities of Australian Bush Lawyers*, in THE PLACE OF PRACTICE, *supra* note 61, at 20, 26.
[165] Lisa R. Lindell, *"Awake to All the Needs of Our Day": Early Women Lawyers in South Dakota*, 42(3) S.D. HIST. 197 (2012).

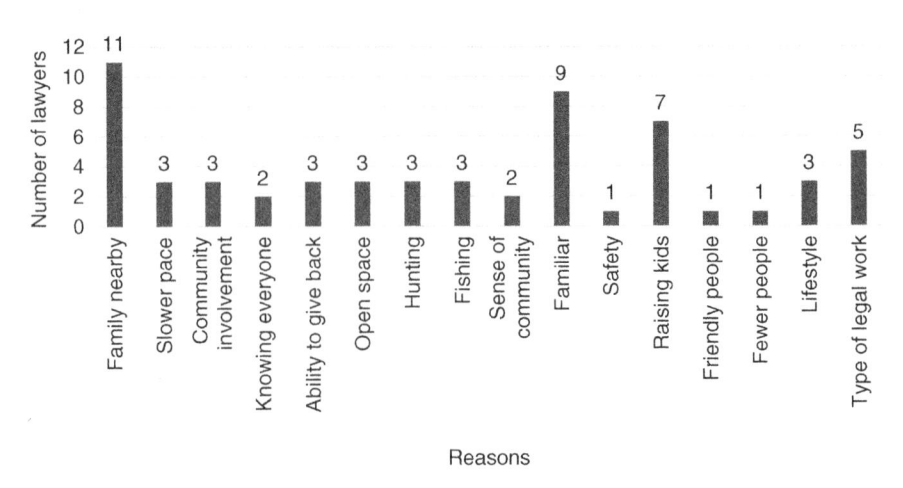

FIGURE 4.3 Reasons for choosing rural

Reasons (Number of lawyers): Family nearby 11, Slower pace 3, Community involvement 3, Knowing everyone 2, Ability to give back 3, Open space 3, Hunting 3, Fishing 3, Sense of community 2, Familiar 9, Safety 1, Raising kids 7, Friendly people 1, Fewer people 1, Lifestyle 3, Type of legal work 5.

first woman to practice law in South Dakota was a homesteader near Highmore, a community in central South Dakota. She began a legal career in 1882. One hundred and forty years later, Highmore had a female lawyer participate in the Rural Attorney Recruitment Program. Several more participating communities had early female lawyers: Grant County in 1893, Roberts County in 1896, and Haakon County in 1913. Lydia Johnson, who began practicing in Philip in Haakon County in 1913, was the first woman elected as a prosecutor in South Dakota in 1944, a job later held by a female participant of the Rural Attorney Recruitment Program. Rural female lawyers are neither new nor rare.

Figure 4.3 provides the reasons participants gave for preferring to work and live in rural areas. It turns out that men and women seem about equally interested in participating in the program and staying in rural practice. Both male and female lawyers hunt and fish, though more men do so, and men were more likely to identify hunting and fishing as a reason to prefer small towns. Beyond hunting and fishing, other benefits of rural areas for these participants include physical space, the slower pace, a sense of community, a feeling of safety, the ability to be involved in the community, and, perhaps most importantly, the ability to give back.

Research out of Australia about rural female lawyers found that women are attracted to rural practice because of the work–life balance it allows.[166] In my study, both men and women suggested that rural practice was attractive because of the lifestyle it offered, including flexibility in the job to facilitate spending more time with

---

[166] Trish Mundy, Women in "Rural" Practice: Opportunities, Challenges and Strategies to Thrive, in THE PLACE OF PRACTICE, supra note 61, at 64, 70–71.

children. Only one participant framed his interest in a rural community as *primarily* about the type of law he would practice, though a few others identified the type of law as one of several reasons to prefer rural. Generally, the type of legal practice followed geographic preferences. This is a good thing. When choosing a career in law, it is probably better to focus on day-to-day life than selecting a particular subject matter.[167]

This group of lawyers interested in small communities and moving to South Dakota, though, is likely different from the general population of law school graduates. After all, most of these lawyers chose to attend a state law school and look for employment in places that made them happy, rather than where the most prestigious jobs were available. Twenty-seven of the participants attended law school at the University of South Dakota. Three participants went to other public law schools (Ohio Northern, University of Minnesota, University of Nebraska) and only two participants attended private law schools (Oklahoma City and Stetson). The two who attended private law school had graduated from law school years before entering rural practice. These lawyers have not made career decisions seeking fame or fortune in the legal world; rather, they have sought a comfortable lifestyle in places they love. In other words, geography and lifestyle were important to these lawyers from the outset. Several participants applied to only one law school – the University of South Dakota – because they knew they wanted to practice in the state.

Michael Sandel writes about "the tyranny of merit" and how society has become sorted by education and prestige, including that students often "seek out the most selective college that would accept them."[168] Perhaps because of the more modest economic backgrounds of most participants, this was not true for the participants in the Rural Attorney Recruitment Program. Many of them chose to stay in South Dakota for law school in order to build relationships for their future practices rather than pursue educations at more elite institutions. Sandel suggests that people like these rural lawyers lose out in the "frenzy" of the tyranny of merit and find "a demoralizing world of work that offers meager economic rewards and scant social esteem to those who lack meritocratic credentials."[169] That depressing description could not be further from the truth for rural lawyers. Though only one graduated from a top-25 law school, almost all hold high social esteem in their rural communities – communities they chose to inhabit because they preferred the lifestyle and wanted to make a difference.

It turns out that the meritocratic obsession of elite education might not hold much sway in rural South Dakota where desperate communities and clients look for a competent lawyer who actually wants to help, rather than fancy credentials for the sake of fancy credentials. Urban institutions that use selectivity of educational

---

[167] *See generally*, Jonah Perlin, *How I Lawyer Podcast*, https://perma.cc/73T3-3T5J.
[168] MICHAEL J. SANDEL, THE TYRANNY OF MERIT: WHAT'S BECOME OF THE COMMON GOOD 175 (2020).
[169] *Id.* at 188.

institution as a proxy for applicant quality could learn a thing or two from rural communities that have accepted these lawyers.[170] As public policy professor Elizabeth Currid-Halkett concludes, "many rural people have found satisfaction and happiness in their lives without joining the meritocratic rat race."[171] None of this is to suggest that the education these lawyers received is less-than – in fact, I think the education these students received probably better equips them for legal practice than the "elite" legal education I received. But there also might be some bias – I taught twelve of them in my law school classes and feel confident that some could have competed at the highest level of legal education and employment.

In fact, quite a few participants were successful in other legal jobs before opening their rural practices. Ten of the participants worked other legal jobs before starting in the Rural Attorney Recruitment Program, including positions at firms and in full-time government employment.

Three lawyers completed one-year clerkships immediately after law school. One with the South Dakota Supreme Court; two for trial level courts in South Dakota. During law school, several participants served on *Law Review* and several were published – both important markers of academic success.[172] Upon law school graduation, some of these participants could have gone to higher-paying firms in the largest communities in South Dakota, but they decided to practice in rural areas. And it was that – a decision. Following the 2016 election, a political scientist argued that those rural residents who stay in their hometowns are "fearful, conservative, in the social sense, and lack ambition," but those who are "ambitious and confident in their abilities" leave rural areas.[173] This does not describe the rural lawyers in this study. These rural lawyers are ambitious, they are competent, they are hardworking, and they refuse to accept the narrative that their rural communities are destined to fail. In no way do these lawyers support the idea that rural practice is just for lawyers who cannot succeed in bigger legal markets.

For some, though, larger communities were tempting. Several interned and received job offers in bigger communities, where they would have started with guaranteed salaries and higher incomes. Some participants felt torn between career choices, and choosing to go rural was hard. Cole Romey, who clerked for the

---

[170] *Id.* at 177.
[171] CURRID-HALKETT, *supra* note 72, at 307.
[172] Sean Kammer & Ashley K. Hoffman, *Smoking Out Forest Fire Management: Lifting the Haze of an Unaccountable Congress and Lighting Up a New Law of Fire*, 60 S.D. L. REV. 41 (2015); Rachel E. Mairose, Note, *Aguilar v. Aguilar and Third-Party Custody Determinations: Examining the Definition of Parent from the Eyes of the Child*, 63 S.D. L. REV. 163 (2018); Cole Romey, Comment, *The Legal Landscape is Rough Country for South Dakota Ranchers Who Operate on Federal Lands*, 64 S.D. L. REV. 148 (2019); Thomas J. Horton & Dylan Kirchmeier, *John Deere's Attempted Monopolization of Equipment Repair, and the Digital Agricultural Data Market – Who Will Stand Up for American Farmers?*, C.P.I. ANTITRUST CHRON. (Jan. 2020), at 2.
[173] Thomas B. Edsall, *The Closing of the Republican Mind*, N.Y. TIMES (July 13, 2017), https://perma.cc/D5ZU-VX3J.

Supreme Court of South Dakota, felt like Justice Janine M. Kern was a mentor who kept him "on the straight and narrow." As Romey explains, having a Supreme Court clerkship opens up work opportunities at some of the state's biggest firms, yet Justice Kern "helped guide me away from [the big firms]. She knew where I'd be happy. She could read her clerk and knows what I wanted. She helped me turn down offers that were extremely enticing because when you get into law school, you go to *Law Review*, you get a clerkship, you're on the track" for the biggest firms. But Justice Kern encouraged Romey to enter rural practice because "she knew I wanted to have a small-town practice with my ranch and my baby and my wife out on the ranch."

Justice Kern epitomizes here what more mentors should recognize: The most money, the fanciest clients, and the biggest firms are not the goals for everyone. A very bright young attorney who *could* be successful in such places should not feel any obligation to seek those roles. In writing about America's obsession with meritocratic credentials, Sandel notes that "[t]hose who are affluent and those who are of modest means rarely encounter one another in the course of the day. We live and work and shop and play in different places; our children go to different schools."[174] The lawyers who have chosen small, rural communities have necessarily rejected this separation. These towns have one high school where students of different socio-economic backgrounds study together. These lawyers will work with a variety of clients and live in mixed-income neighborhoods. They are less socio-economically isolated than the world that Sandel describes, and perhaps they are better off for it. In fact, this mingling is a *benefit* of living in rural areas.[175] Those in cities can isolate themselves into precise social circles, but in rural areas everyone sees and interacts with everyone.

Certainly, some of the participants were more academically precarious, including several who initially failed the bar exam. One participant was working at a firm but was fired after failing the bar, then relocated home for rural practice. Yet these hiccups on the way to beginning a legal career have presented no long-term detriment. As with most lawyers, grades or first-time bar passage have little bearing as careers progress.[176] A more concerning aspect is when bar failure keeps potential participants from entering the program. One new graduate failed the bar and, instead of retaking, gave up on becoming a licensed lawyer. It was too expensive to stay underemployed in a rural area waiting for bar passage, and a rural lawyer was lost.

ARE INCENTIVES NEEDED?

The participants all had good reasons for choosing to practice in a small town, which raises the issue of whether the Rural Attorney Recruitment Program was needed to

---

[174] SANDEL, *supra* note 168, at 226.
[175] WUTHNOW, *supra* note 31, at 36.
[176] NEIL W. HAMILTON, ROADMAP: THE LAW STUDENT'S GUIDE TO MEANINGFUL EMPLOYMENT 10 (3d ed. 2023).

bring the lawyers to rural areas. Some participants were already dedicated to rural practice even without the incentive program, but the program was a way to increase their chances of success. Other participants, though, would not have chosen rural practice.

Several participants only ended up in rural South Dakota because of the program. Amanda LaCroix, originally from South Dakota's second-largest city, "would never have gone to Martin without the Rural Attorney Recruitment Program." Two participants with no prior connections to South Dakota entered the program because of national media coverage. Kristen Kochekian saw a news story on South Dakota's new rural attorney funding and applied the next day. Within a month, she moved to rural South Dakota where she has practiced ever since. Jennifer English read an article in the ABA journal about the program and called the program administrator, Suzanne Starr. For English, Starr was the "first person" who was "excited for me to be a lawyer." That excitement brought English to rural South Dakota.

For others, the program served as a nudge. Austin Hoffman wanted to move home to Eureka, but he "had no idea if I was going to be able to make enough money to put food on my table for my kids and wife." Without the program, it was too big a risk to start a solo practice in rural South Dakota, even in his hometown. Cody Miller, who also had a wife and children when he graduated from law school, similarly noted the risks of rural practice with "having family and kids to worry about" and how the program made his location choice "more possible." Kristian Ellendorf also had children and wanted to practice in rural South Dakota. When Ellendorf was a law student, the career service office at the University of South Dakota informed her of the Rural Attorney Recruitment Program, which started her on the path to her current job.

On the other hand, there are participants who wanted to work in their hometowns and viewed the program as a help, but not a necessity. For Elizabeth Steptoe, it made returning home "not as scary." For Jackson Schwandt, when the program became available "the stars aligned a little bit better" for him. For Zach Pahlke, the program made it "more feasible to come home because I think it's kind of intimidating and hard to get a start in a rural community." For Amy Jo Janssen, the stipend allowed her to "make it work" to start a practice in a new town. Jake Fischer explained that the program "wasn't the thing that made me come, but it was a thing that almost allowed me to come." For Cole Romey "it was icing on the cake" and made him think that rural legal practice is "where I fit." For Abigail Monger, it was a "hook" that helped solidify her choice to move to a rural community.

When I asked mentors about their ability to hire new attorneys, mentors were more likely to say the stipend was a necessity. Some mentors had tried and failed to hire previously. Recognizing that they cannot compete with bigger salaries in larger towns, some mentors never bothered to pursue hiring an associate before the stipend. As one said about hiring, "I never tried, because I didn't think I would really be successful." Others used the stipend to meet the salary demands of a new hire and perceived that they would have been unable to hire without the stipend. One mentor acknowledged that when the program was first announced, "I thought it was a terrible idea. I thought it was awful because if you're going to go to a small town, you better put on your boots and get to work, and that's just the way it's going to be." But then, she tried to hire "to no avail" and quickly came around to viewing the stipend as necessary to recruit. Another mentor simply described trying to hire a young attorney as "terrible" and that his rural lawyer friends had "scary horror stories about trying to find someone to come to little towns" before the incentive program was available.

For only a few participants did the program have no influence on their job choices. Two lawyers hired into full-time positions at a prosecutor's office received information about applying for the Rural Attorney Recruitment Program only after getting their jobs. Cassie Wendt moved home to Philip after a decade as a prosecutor in a different county and did not initially think she would qualify for the stipend because she had prior legal experience. Only after her move did Wendt apply for the program. Clay Anderson had already settled on returning to Miller when he was encouraged to sign up for the program. A few other participants were planning on rural practice even without the program, but it is hard to disentangle cause and effect. At least for those who attended law school in South Dakota, the participants already planning on rural practice were connected with program leadership during law school, further encouraging rural practice. Plus, the law school promotes rural practice through events and internship opportunities. No one could come through the University of South Dakota Knudson School of Law without having exposure to rural practice as a viable career option, though this is not true for all law students, even in other rural states.[177]

There is one more way that the incentive program might matter. To the extent that students are considering a move to a rural community, there are now substantially increased opportunities for remote work. Lawyers are moving to remote places, but not necessarily opening up local firms to serve the local community. There is a young Native American attorney in the heart of South Dakota's Indian Country who works remotely for a firm out of Omaha. Another Native American attorney, working in Indian Country in North Dakota, works remotely for a Colorado firm. Despite their remote jobs, both do keep at least some of their work local. A couple of participants unhappy with rural practice considered staying put and doing remote legal work, one even receiving a job offer to do remote discovery work. The increased ability to do legal work remotely from a rural community just creates one more competition – now, even if a lawyer wants to live in a rural community, they can do work for urban clients while living rural.

CHOOSING A RURAL LOCATION

For some participants, the choice of where to practice was obvious. Some wanted to be able to ranch with their families. Some wanted to be near their spouses. Some wanted to go back to their hometowns. For these participants, choosing a location

---

[177] Tomisich, *supra* note 53, at 87, 119.

FIGURE 4.4 Persisting placement based on distance from home county

was easy – they really had only one option and the question was whether they could make that location work as a new lawyer. Rural lawyer incentive programs must be flexible enough to help lawyers set on returning to a very particular place. No programmatic suggestions will change the desired locations for that type of participant, which makes broad geographic coverage important. My study shows that ties to a geographic place are important, as are different amenities for different lawyers. Rural lawyer programing should be broad. While it is important to make special efforts to encourage lawyers to go to communities with the greatest need, programs need not focus only on those communities.

While there have been thirty-two program participants, there have been thirty-three contracts because one participant left one placement and rejoined in another county. Of the thirty-three contracts, ten saw participants joining in their home county, seven in a nearby or neighboring county, and the rest were at least a few hours away from their hometowns. Figure 4.4 reflects where lawyers worked and whether they stayed.

Moving home is a good indication that participants will stay. Of the ten participants who joined the program in their home counties, none have departed during the first ten years of the program. For the seven participants who joined in nearby or neighboring counties, four have stayed as practicing lawyers and three have left. Even being in a contiguous county lessens the connections and commitment to a place: One lawyer in a contiguous county would prefer to be practicing closer to home and might make that transition in the future.

Of the sixteen participants who are not near their hometowns, six have left. Yet, that means ten lawyers have stayed in rural communities despite having few prior geographic connections. The reasons people chose those communities vary, and there is certainly evidence that a rural lawyer incentive program can play a large role in placement. Two participants ended up practicing in towns where their grandparents lived. Even though the participants did not grow up in those small towns, the generational connection was enough to attract them – one of those two lawyers left after the end of the stipend, but the other has stayed.

For the participants who joined away from their hometowns, something happened to draw them into their adopted rural communities. Kristen Kochekian, who heard about the program on television and had no prior connection to South Dakota, chose her community by looking at housing and hospital access. She continues to happily practice law in her rural community despite having no prior experience with the area. Jennifer English, who similarly had no prior connections with South Dakota, chose her community sight unseen and prioritized access to Sioux Falls and its amenities. English chose her location "experiencing it only through Google Street View." English's placement has been less successful personally and professionally, though she finished her five-year commitment and continues to have a law office in her rural community.

National media on South Dakota's incentive attracted Kochekian and English, but more participants were brought in through local networking and recruitment. Several participants met a program administrator early in their law school career, and she helped them join the program. The University of South Dakota Knudson School of Law career services office facilitated several connections, and rural lawyers have hired through the on-campus interview process. This is not to suggest passivity on the behalf of students who were connected through the career services office or the program administrator – most of them reached out with a goal in mind, and someone simply helped facilitate it. Amy Jo Janssen was more direct. Knowing she wanted to practice in a small town within a reasonable drive of her family, Janssen did cold reach-outs to rural attorneys in her targeted area of the state. Luckily, a lawyer wrote back, and Janssen has successfully taken over a rural law office in a one-attorney town.

Similarly, some practicing lawyers have taken the initiative to hire. One lawyer spoke at the law school about his community needing more lawyers, and a local student approached him about joining the firm. One rural law firm hired three participants, each one opening a satellite office. That firm recruited in various ways, including through on-campus interviews. Despite the strong recruitment by that firm, the mentorship and firm structure proved unsuccessful, and none of those three mentee attorneys stayed permanently in their placements. When Rachel Mairose was in law school, her parents happened to be meeting with their lawyer in rural South Dakota and mentioned to him that Mairose was in law school. That attorney reached out to Mairose "because he was getting close to retirement age at that time, and he didn't have anyone else in mind to leave the business to." That connected Mairose with her future employer, though it helped that Mairose "always had it in the back of my mind that I would do small practice, just because I'm not a city person." There are many ways to recruit and make connections, and most of them take effort.

LESSONS LEARNED

The lives of these participants – like the lives of all humans – are complex. Someone like Kirby Krogman, who was able to go home and practice near his family and spend time ranching, will probably never leave. He's happy and doing what he loves. I heard the same from other lawyers. Derrick Johnson said, "I love my job; I love being home." Dusty Ginsbach explained, "I always wanted to be here; I didn't really want to leave." For these lawyers and many others, rural was not a compromise or a fallback option, it was their affirmative desire.

But life is complicated. Children, death, marriage, and divorce have played a role in determining whether some lawyers would choose to go rural or would later decide to stay or leave. As anthropologist of law Michele Statz describes it, lawyers "are *in the midst of life*" as they work in rural communities.[178] Take children for example. Most participants with children have stayed because they strongly desire raising their children in small towns. But not all have stayed, and the parents who have departed did so because of their children: either for easier access to medical care, better health insurance, or easier access to extended family. The joys and sorrows of life will occur for these lawyers, just like everyone else, and sometimes lawyers will leave for reasons unrelated to their careers.

What concerns me the most is having rural youth who leave their rural communities without real consideration for *why* they are leaving. As one self-described "rural expatriate" wrote in her memoir, she "had not been deliberate" in leaving rural America, instead she "simply followed the migratory pattern of rural kids, moving to the nearest city."[179] In many ways, programs aimed at increasing rural lawyers simply have to fight against rural students leaving their communities without deliberation. Asking students to consider the rural practice of law is asking them to be deliberate about their departures from rural America. That thoughtfulness might encourage more lawyers to stay rural.

Even though the South Dakota data supports the idea that lawyers are most likely to stay in rural areas if they are from those rural areas, transplants have also seen great success and longevity. In fact, declining rural populations mean that rural communities need to retain and attract professionals.[180] Though recruiting at rural schools is probably the easiest, recruiting needs to also include outsiders and working adults who may see law as a way to stay in their rural communities while still having meaningful employment.

---

[178] Michele Statz, *The Scandal of Particularity: A New Epistemological Approach to Rural Attorney Shortages and Access to Justice*, 69 S.D. L. REV. 396, 402 (2024).
[179] MELANIE HOFFERT, PRAIRIE SILENCE: A MEMOIR 229 (2013).
[180] BROWN & SCHAFFT, *supra* note 112, at 165.

5

Entering a Rural Community

FIGURE 5.1 Cole Romey, William Hustead, and Austin Schaefer

William Hustead graduated from law school in 2018. Originally from Wall, South Dakota, Hustead wanted to have a career in a small South Dakota town. At the time, the South Dakota Rural Attorney Recruitment Program had not yet been expanded to cover small municipalities. Though Wall has only 700 people, it sits at the far eastern edge of the state's second-most-populated county. The county does not qualify because Rapid City, population 78,824, sits an hour away at the western edge. Hustead had to look for other options and found a law firm in Hot Springs, population 3,590, that gave him a job offer and promised mentorship.

Hot Springs is located in the rural county of Fall River, so Hustead worked toward joining the Rural Attorney Recruitment Program. Since local approval is required, Hustead appeared in front of the Fall River County Commission with program administrator Suzanne Starr, who regularly facilitated these contracts. The commissioners were intrigued, but not overjoyed with spending money on a lawyer. No formal action happened at that meeting, though Starr used it to give "her spiel" explaining the benefits a new lawyer brings to the community, including that lawyers "generate money, then taxes." Meanwhile, Hustead started working in a local law firm then came back to a later meeting. At the second meeting, the commissioners took a split vote – Hustead was not approved for the program. One of the commissioners in 2018 was antilawyer, saying to Hustead "more lawyers mean more lawsuits in the community, and I can't support that." Because the county refused to sign the contract, Hustead was not qualified to participate and could not get even the state portion of the funding. Though Hustead would never see a penny of the incentive money, he decided to stay.

Two years later, in 2020, Cole Romey graduated from law school. After a year of clerking, Romey was ready to find a permanent job in 2021. Originally from a ranch in rural Fall River County, Romey wanted to go home to practice. This time, the commissioners approved the contract. There had been changes on the commission; the antilawyer commissioner was gone. The process wasn't necessarily easy. Romey felt like he was in a job interview, even though he was originally from the county and was a known entity for the commissioners. The commission approved Romey's contract unanimously; Romey joined Hustead's firm.

Then, in 2022, Austin Schaefer, a law school classmate from a tiny town on the other side of the state, decided to join Hustead and Romey. Once again, they approached the commission. This time, some commissioners were hesitant to take on a second contract, especially with someone from out of town. Yet, the commissioners, wanting to attract more lawyers to their town, signed the contract.

Within a five-year period, Fall River County went from rejecting one contract to later approving two more. Now, three young lawyers work in the county seat. They take court appointments. They serve private clients. They are engaged in the local community. The firm purchased and moved into the historic Carnegie Library in town. The attorneys that hired Hustead have retired, and this new generation has taken over a long-standing firm in the community.

This chapter focuses on lawyers entering rural communities. Because the program requires a local government to sign a contract and provide funding, the local rural community was necessarily involved in the process of new lawyers setting up offices. The chapter starts by examining the contract process in relation to local government approval. Even once a local government signed a contract, new lawyers had to move to town and open law offices. This chapter includes a focus on actually moving to these rural communities – what it was like for lawyers to obtain housing and office space once a contract was signed.

THE RURAL COMMUNITIES

The old adage says that "if you've seen one rural place, you've seen one rural place." My study looks at only one program in only one state, but even within just South Dakota, the communities where these lawyers work vary greatly. The differences in community size, culture, and economics impact how these lawyers enter communities and their ultimate level of success. For context of understanding how the communities welcomed lawyers, I start by introducing the communities themselves.

Figure 5.2 shows all of the placements in South Dakota's program categorized by population of the town where the lawyer primarily practiced. Rural is relative, and one of the problems in trying to put rural experience into perspective is that what "counts" as rural in any particular study is wildly different. In South Dakota, the statute sets what communities qualify for the program, thus defining rural for my purposes. A county must have a population of 10,000 or less while a municipality must have a population of 3,500 or less.[181] Of the thirty-two contracts, most have been with counties. Only four contracts have been with cities.

Though most of the contracts are with counties, every lawyer has a primary place of business, and that town forms an important aspect of their legal practice. The South Dakota program has mostly targeted very small towns. Larger towns in South Dakota are also in need of attorneys, but not as desperately. Overall, Figure 5.2 shows that placements were concentrated in smaller towns, but so were departures.

Rural areas can be distinguished by their main economic activities. Of the rural communities I visited, one town is a bedroom community, with commuters driving to work in the state's largest city. Only Hot Springs, home to the trio of Hustead, Romey, and Schaefer, has a significant tourist industry. Fall River County, which includes Hot Springs, has even seen a modest influx of amenity-driven transplants

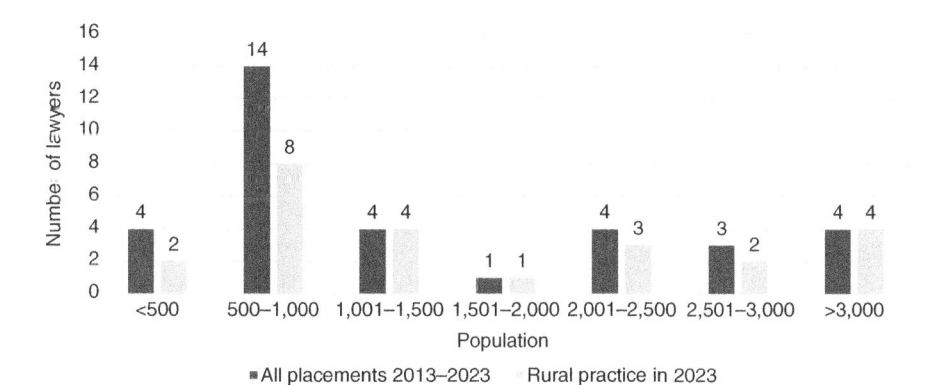

FIGURE 5.2 Lawyer placements by community population

---

[181] S.D. Codified Laws §§ 16-23-2.1 & -2.2.

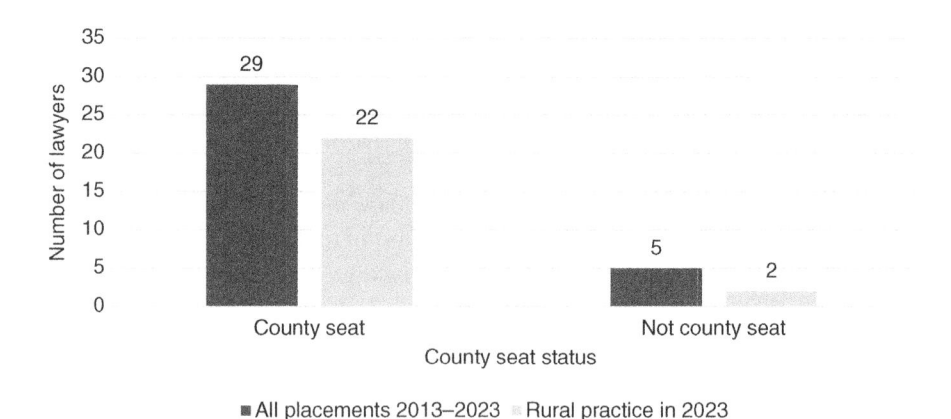

FIGURE 5.3 County seat placements and their persistence

from urban areas, especially from 2020 until the present. Hot Springs also has a Department of Veterans Affairs hospital while another town has a state university; both communities benefit from those government employers. All of the communities I visited rely on extractive industries, and for most communities that is their only real industry. In my study, these industries were farming, ranching, dairy, hunting, and oil.

The economic well-being of rural towns significantly influences demographic change.[182] Farming and ranching communities are mostly dwindling, in part because of limited employment opportunities. As I develop more in Chapters 6 and 9, the economic well-being of these particular rural towns influences how lawyers engage with work and the communities themselves.

Another factor in whether small towns – and their lawyers – will survive is whether those towns serve as county seats. Figure 5.3 shows placements and remaining lawyers in county seats.

County seats are often, but not always, the largest towns in South Dakota counties. As political units were being established leading up to statehood, towns fought for county seats.[183] In one case, that of Spink County, the militia was deployed after 300 settlers set out on a march at the end of a six-year debate about the county seat location. The end of the "Spink County War" left the county seat in Redfield, which now has two lawyers (including a Rural Attorney Recruitment Program participant) and a population of 2,188. Ashton, which lost the battle for county seat, tried another strategy – relocating to a railroad line. Even that wasn't enough – today Ashton has

---

[182] Jessica D. Ulrich-Schad, Megan Henly & Thomas G. Safford, *The Role of Community Assessments, Place, and the Great Recession in the Migration Intentions of Rural Americans*, 78 RURAL SOCIO. 371, 372–74 (2013).
[183] HERBERT S. SCHELL, HISTORY OF SOUTH DAKOTA 204 (4th ed. 2004); ROBERT F. KAROLEVITZ, CHALLENGE: THE SOUTH DAKOTA STORY 180–90 (1975).

108 people and no lawyers. That trajectory, of growth for county seats, and diminishment for other towns, has played out across many counties.[184] Today, county seats are more likely to have lawyers and more robust populations, and it is not surprising that most of the lawyers have worked in county seats where county courthouses are located.

Each rural community is unique. While it is helpful to think about lawyer viability through metrics such as population size, county seat status, amenity access, racial diversity, and poverty levels, there are also wide variabilities of these counties beyond measurable metrics. The culture of each community is different in ways I cannot categorize.

SIGNING THE CONTRACT

One of the distinctive features of the rural attorney program in South Dakota is the requirement that a local county or municipality sign a contract and provide 35 percent of the funding. When Chief Justice Gilbertson first began working on the structure of the program, he "was hoping that the state would fund it at 100 percent." But even as Chief Justice and administrative head of the state judiciary, Gilbertson did not have the power to create and fund this program without legislative approval. It was Senator Mike Vehle who sponsored the state legislation, and Vehle has strong opinions about localities providing partial funding.

Vehle explained to me that his personal belief is to require "skin in the game" for all programs benefiting local communities, meaning that local governments need to pay a portion whenever the state provides funding. When I asked more, Vehle was ready with a practiced quip: Local funding was "part of Mike's deal, in any bill." With nearly twenty years of experience in the South Dakota legislature, Vehle has had time to develop his perspective on local funding. For Vehle, localities need to chip in for infrastructure (like bridges), and the incentive program for rural lawyers was no different. To be fair, it wasn't just Vehle who wanted local buy-in, local funding was key to gaining the support of fiscally conservative Governor Dennis Daugaard.[185]

South Dakota law requires that participating local governments provide 35 percent of the funding, and that funding must be provided in order for a contract to be signed.[186] The statutes do contemplate potential cost-sharing, allowing local governments "to enter an agreement with any county, municipality, school district, or nonprofit entity to assist the county or municipality."[187] Either a county or a

---

[184] Paul H. Landis, *The Growth and Decline of South Dakota Trade Centers: 1901–1933*, 279 BULLS. 1, 32 (Apr. 1, 1933).
[185] Patrick G. Goetzinger & Robert L. Morris, *Project Rural Practice: Its People & Its Purpose*, 59 S.D. L. REV. 444, 456 (2014).
[186] S.D. CODIFIED LAWS § 16-23-6.
[187] S.D. CODIFIED LAWS § 16-23-7.

municipality may sign the contract, though only four of the thirty-two contracts have been with municipalities.

Putting a positive spin on the local funding burden, program supporters cite it as ensuring that local communities are willing to support the lawyers who come to town. And perhaps there is a benefit to this. Because the state law requires that a local government sign the contract, these lawyers – or a program administrator – had to attend county commission or city council meetings to seek approval. These meetings introduced the lawyers to rural communities, communities had the chance to tell a potential lawyer whether there was a need for another lawyer in town, and lawyers learned about the communities they would be joining. Law professor Rick Su writes about how little control local governments have and argues for giving them more control.[188] Asking local governments whether they want to support a new lawyer does exactly this, giving local communities more ownership of their decision-making process and expenditure. Plus, requiring local funding does mean the locality has an incentive to bring business to that new lawyer.

But there is also a major downside – some communities who desperately need lawyers will not participate in the program because of the financial obligations. In this way, the South Dakota program runs up against the same problems inherent in matching grants. Funding opportunities that require matching grants from local communities are a known problem for rural areas.[189] The poorest and most rural counties often need outside funds the most, yet those same places have the hardest time providing local funds for matching requirements. Some counties have said no to the Rural Attorney Recruitment Program because of the money; that means some lawyers are missing from rural communities because of the requirement for local funding. Sometimes, rejected lawyers have decided to keep trying, either in the same county or a different one.

Several participants appeared in front of the same county commission several times before getting approval. One county twice rejected a participant because of money and the perception that the town did not need more lawyers. Only after that participant found outside funding to cover the county's portion did the commission approve his contract. The first time a different county commission voted on an applicant, the vote was tied; the participant had to wait in suspense until the next meeting when the absent commissioner returned and broke the tie in favor of approval. Another county commission tabled a participant without voting until partial outside funding could be obtained.

Two lawyers were rejected by one county, then tried again in a different location. For one participant, the first county he approached was swayed by a local lawyer who convinced the county commissioners that it was not a good investment to fund

---

[188] Rick Su, *Democracy in Rural America*, 98 N.C. L. REV. 837, 838 (2020).

[189] Anthony F. Pipa, *Policy Lessons – and Surprises – From the 'Reimagine Rural' Podcast*, BROOKINGS (May 1, 2023), https://perma.cc/76XA-BKWP.

a new lawyer. That local lawyer was not ready to retire and saw the potential participant as a threat. Less than five years later, the local lawyer is retired, having left no successor. Now, the county is paying an out-of-town lawyer to drive in and serve as prosecutor. In a different county, the commissioners were "nice" but "weren't really receptive" to the program because they also did not see a need for more lawyers. Their position was more reasonable – that county seat has an active firm with multiple lawyers and is only an hour away from a larger town with several established firms. Not to be deterred, both of these initially rejected lawyers approached nearby counties and got approval. Both remain in their rural counties today.

Many counties reacted with skepticism, but approved participants. One participant described his meeting in front of the commission as more of a "sales pitch." Though the commissioners liked the idea of "young folks moving into the area" they were skeptical of subsidizing an attorney. Program administrator Suzanne Starr attended meetings with most participants where she was able to pitch the program to skeptical governments. Starr held the position until 2021, and there is a general sense that Starr and her ability to convince local governments to sign contracts was a major reason for the early successes of the program. As others associated with the program have written, "there would be no rural practice success" without Suzanne Starr.[190]

A few counties were open to subsidizing lawyers, even without direct connections or lobbying – simply because those counties wanted new lawyers. But in many of the counties where approval was easy, it was because someone was working behind the scenes. Several participating attorneys told me their approval was quick and easy only because an attorney in town had already convinced the county commission to approve the contract. For these attorneys, a vote by the county commission felt like a mere formality. One mentoring attorney desperate to hire an associate to take over his firm told his commissioners "that the list of young attorneys wanting to come" to their rural county "was pretty darn short, and if they had an opportunity to get someone it would be wise for them to participate in the program." As he explained to me, "fortunately, I represented all, or at least most, of the commissioners, and so it was no problem at all" to get them to sign the contract. The density of acquaintanceships in rural areas means established lawyers had the chance of impacting the vote, whether to encourage bringing in a new attorney or keep out competition.

In a few places, personal relationships helped get the county commission on board. A hiring attorney's son was a commissioner. A participant knew all the commissioners because her father had been on the commission for years. A participant's dad was cousins with a commissioner. A participant's grandfather was longtime friends with a commissioner. Several participants who went home knew all the commissioners, or at least the commissioners knew the lawyer's family name.

[190] Patrick G. Goetzinger & Robert L. Morris, *Project Rural Practice: Its People & Its Purpose – The Next Chapter*, 69 S.D. L. REV. 334, 334 (2024).

A few participants who joined away from their home communities worried about the lack of connection. One explained there was "nervousness" about him being "not from around here" because of the risk he would only stay for five years then leave. Another participant who relocated "was super nervous that day, because I didn't know any of them and that was the hardest part, because it feels like everyone here knows each other. And then there's this young couple that just pops up out of nowhere." But that nervous participant was approved right away, without any real pushback.

A few counties have become more concerned over time about the commitment of participants. For example, a participant started in one county then restarted in another. Yet that move created concerns for both the county she departed and the county where she rejoined. The first county gave "a small amount of pushback" when a new attorney asked to join, and they were "a little hesitant" to commit to a new attorney, though ultimately did so. The second county knew this lawyer had left a prior placement and "were a little bit leery" about whether the participant intended to stay, but did sign a contract. As another example, one county had approved a participant who then had issues becoming a member of the bar, and when another attorney wanted to join "they were skittish" about signing a contract. As the program continues on in years and more attorneys come and go, the risk grows that counties will feel burned, and thus unwilling to participate again.

Some counties, though, have become more receptive, not less, over time. For example, when Ryan McKnight approached Haakon County about joining the program, the county was skeptical and getting approval was an "uphill battle" even though there were only two lawyers in town at the time – one about to move away and one already eighty-five years old. The commissioners went so far as to ask about law school class rank, as if wanting to ensure they were getting a worthy new graduate. A year later, when McKnight and his wife Brittany Kjerstad McKnight left Haakon County, the county immediately began actively recruiting new lawyers to participate in the program.

Even when counties and cities were excited about having a new lawyer around, the requirement to pay created issues. There were several local governments that signed contracts only on the condition that they did not have to pay. Of the four cities that signed individual contracts, none paid the local government portion. For three cities, the county (which was too big to participate) paid. For the fourth city, the hiring law firm paid. Two counties had a similar condition, signing only when the hiring law firm paid. In four instances, the county asked to split costs with the host city. In three of those instances, both entities were agreeable. But in another, the city balked at covering half of the local government cost and, instead of providing money, the city provided office space at under market rent and installed air-conditioning. In that case, negotiations were so difficult the attorney was "willing to waive" the local government portion, but Suzanne Starr pushed forward to "make a deal." Another time, two counties and two cities agreed to bear the financial burden, easing the path to approval for the participant.

These local governments operate on shoestring budgets, so it is not surprising that funding requirements presented difficulties. Local governments signing attorney contracts in South Dakota have to balance questions about why lawyers, but not other professionals, get subsidized. One county refused to fund a lawyer because it needed truck drivers more than lawyers. In another county, a farmer spoke at the commission meeting against the program arguing that farmers were the ones who really needed financial subsidies, not lawyers. The county commissioner who told me about this farmer complaining that he had no government support was dismissive of his complaint. Despite the oddity of a farmer alleging no government support (when farmers are notoriously reliant on federal farm subsidies), the broader point remains that local governments have limited resources. This is the same problem that keeps rural communities from getting grants when there are matching requirements.

For local governments that agreed to sign but did not provide funding, the program is not operating as expected. Though state law allows cost-sharing agreements, sometimes the compromise has left the government entirely off-the-hook. A few hiring attorneys ended up paying the county portions, but often did so through "in-kind" donations of office space or secretarial help, leaving the participants with smaller monetary stipends. One participant whose firm decided to pay became a partner before the end of the stipend, which means he is actually partially paying his own stipend. These workarounds have made it possible to get more contracts, but at the cost of decreasing the stipend amount paid to the participant.

Having local governments sign the contract also meant they could promise or demand something extra from participants. The base contract requires that participants live in the county that signed the contract, take a pro bono case each year, and participate in a mentorship program. Though most governmental entities did not require their participants to agree to anything extra under the contract, two did. One locality required an annual report from the participant showing how much money the county had saved on travel. Another locality required the attorney provide a time sheet to show she was doing enough legal work in the community. Several more attorneys felt there was an unwritten understanding that they would either take court appointments or would serve as a prosecutor. All of the attorneys who had those unwritten understandings followed through because those understandings matched their career goals.

Governmental entities also had the opportunity to offer more in their contracts, though very few did. Most local governments did nothing extra for these attorneys beyond signing the contract and providing the stipend. One county purchased a set of code books for a new attorney. Another county agreed to modify its first stipend payment so that, instead of going to the participating attorney, it would go directly to pay for office furniture owned by two attorneys who had just left town. Four participants got free office space to use for government work and private clients. One county provided a free phone line to a participant. In Tripp County, which has now signed three contracts, a local economic development board offered an additional stipend of 5,000 dollars per year for the most recent lawyer to move to town. Of course, rural communities could offer this type of help without the program; in fact, a rural lawyer in Iowa told me she got free rent as a solo practitioner in a small town because the town wanted an attorney so badly. Small communities should consider sweetening the deal for rural lawyers, regardless of whether a larger incentive program exists.

PHYSICAL SPACE: HOUSING AND OFFICES

Despite the perception that housing prices and shortages are urban problems, that same crisis presents itself in rural areas.[191] Rural South Dakota is no different. Rural sociologists focus less on dollar amount when determining housing affordability and more on housing-cost burden, a ratio of income to housing costs. By that measure, housing in rural America is more unaffordable than housing in urban America.[192] As I spoke with attorneys about moving to their new communities, obtaining housing was a constant discussion. The difficulty with obtaining housing is compounded because the program generally requires lawyers to live in their contract county. While some lawyers were able to rent or purchase houses in town or in close proximity, not all were. Three attorneys purchased homes in nearby towns because nothing was available in their place of work.

Four participants started in mobile homes. And while living in trailer homes or manufactured homes is more common in rural than urban areas, the dangers and costs are the same.[193] Mobile homes offer affordable housing but come with faster depreciation and increased environmental exposure to weather events like tornados. Even if you own a mobile home, finding a place to put it is another hurdle, though family and other communities were quick to offer land for parking trailers. Two participants used mobile homes only temporarily until moving into bigger homes; two participants continue to live in their mobile homes.

Parents were critically important in providing housing to many participants. Four participants lived on the farms or ranches of their parents. Three participants lived on the family farms or ranches of their spouses. Two participants lived in homes purchased by their parents, while another lived in a home purchased by his grandparents. For some, living on the family farm or ranch was the dream. Austin Hoffman, for example, lived in town when he first moved home to Eureka,

---

[191] Stefan Kordel & Matthias Naumann, *The Rural Housing Crises: Analytical Dimensions and Emblematic Issues*, HOUS. STUDS. (2023).

[192] Katherine A. MacTavish, Ann Ziebarth & Lance George, *Housing in Rural America*, in RURAL AMERICA IN A GLOBALIZING WORLD, *supra* note 58, at 680.

[193] *Id.* at 678.

but has since built on the land that has been in his family since his great-great-grandfather homesteaded in the late 1800s. Cassie Wendt similarly built on the family ranch, only 200 yards from her parents' home. Living on the ranch was a driving factor for Wendt and her family to move home. For others though, living with family was a temporary state while they looked for housing. Ryan McKnight lived in a spare house on his in-laws' ranch, commuting forty miles until a house became available in the town of Philip. Rachelle Norberg could not find a home to purchase in Burke, so she lived with her parents for the first year before moving into town.

For lawyers without access to family help, things were a bit more complicated. Amanda LaCroix signed her Rural Attorney Recruitment Program contract as a first-year law student and – despite constantly looking – was unable to find a home to purchase until immediately before she moved to Martin. Another participant delayed her move by six months because she could not find housing. Kelly Kanaan was a recent law school graduate who intended to join the program. She moved to rural South Dakota with two dogs and could not find a long-term rental that would accept her dogs. For Kanaan, housing was a major reason she stopped pursuing rural practice.

But even those attorneys not moving home tended to have help – for example, hiring attorneys have taken an active role in providing housing, often through connecting participants with a real estate agent, but sometimes more directly. One hiring attorney sold his home to his mentee, another rents to a mentee, and one more even opened up a room in his own home so the new attorney had a place to live.

Even when housing was available, obtaining mortgages was difficult – especially for new graduates. For one participant, "no traditional bank would want to loan to a recent graduate with basically no assets and a lot of debt" who is self-employed, so she used a rural development loan. Another participant could only get a ten-year loan with a balloon payment, requiring that she use her stipend to pay down the principal. Yet another participant had so much student loan debt that his wife is the only person on the mortgage; his debt was too large to get a loan.

Three participants took advantage of a housing program called the Governor's House Program. Aimed at providing affordable housing to moderate- and low-income individuals, the program provides prefabricated houses built by prisoners and delivered to a lot prepared by a buyer. Unfortunately, the wait for newly ordered housing is now up to three years. Since 2018, no participants have attempted to obtain a Governor's House, likely because of this wait. South Dakota, on the whole, could improve life for those in rural areas by investing in more housing opportunities like the Governor's House Program.

The difficulty of finding housing is compounded by distance in rural areas, but is also complicated by the standard contract for the Rural Attorney Recruitment

Program requiring that participants live in their contract county. Requiring lawyers to live in their contract county makes sense. In Chapter 10, I extensively cover why lawyers are good for local communities, and that impact is greater when the lawyer lives locally. Without a contract requirement, there is a risk of rural lawyers living in larger places and commuting. In a study of rural Arkansas lawyers, 60 percent of rural lawyer respondents commuted from a more populous county.[194] In South Carolina, some lawyers are doing the same.[195] Residency requirements are a way to combat commuters using the stipend.

While it is ideal to have rural lawyers living in the communities where they work, it can make housing more difficult to acquire. Some counties have waived the residency requirement when negotiating the contracts. Haakon County temporarily waived that provision for Ryan McKnight, allowing him to live on his in-laws' ranch while he looked for housing. Dylan Kirchmeier negotiated a waiver because he originally thought he would be unable to find housing in the county, though he ultimately did so. Jake Fischer was able to live on the family farm only a half-mile over the county line and Elizabeth Steptoe was able to live where her husband farms. Cassie Wendt faced the opposite problem – she moved home to live on the family ranch in Jackson County and is contracted with Jackson County. However, she offices in Haakon County where her children attend school. Jackson County agreed to this arrangement because Wendt assured them she would be available to provide legal services to Jackson County residents and might open a satellite office in the county.

While the participants appreciated the flexibility in having the ability to live in neighboring counties, that choice might come with a cost. One participant who lived in one community and worked in another thought that his legal practice suffered because of his weak ties to the community where he worked. This may be why programs for rural lawyers focus on *residential* lawyers who live and work in the same community. South Dakota has this as a base requirement, as does Arkansas with its rural incubator program.[196]

Speaking of offices, office space has not always been easy to find. Participants who are prosecutors or joined a firm did not have to think about office space. Solo practitioners who were not serving as prosecutor had a harder time, though communities have been willing to help. A few counties provided free office space in the county courthouse for new solo practitioners. A couple of cities did the same. In one town, a community member paid for the first year of office space for a participant. When Cassie Wendt moved to Philip, several local community members jumped in to help her build out an office. While construction was ongoing, participant Stephanie

---

[194] Pruitt et al., *Hinterlands*, supra note 24, at 643.
[195] Chambliss, supra note 63.
[196] *Rural Practice Incubator Requirements*, U.A. Little Rock, https://perma.cc/D7RM-24L2 (last visited Mar. 24, 2023).

Trask allowed Wendt to share her existing office space. Jennifer English was never able to find affordable office space and decided to purchase her own building with her first stipend payment. Only one participant works out of a home, meeting clients in the front room of his mobile house.

LESSONS LEARNED

Senator Mike Vehle agreed to bring legislation in 2013, but insisted on local financial investment, similar to the matching requirements often placed on community grants. Vehle wanted local governments to have "skin in the game." It is not entirely clear whether Vehle's idea of local buy-in has been necessary to successful participation.

Overall, there has been no meaningful difference in the happiness or ultimate success of lawyers based on whether the municipalities paid, or someone else paid. In fact, some of the most successful participants who are least likely to leave are in locations where the county refused to fund the program. But perhaps we should expect this – the participants who persevered through complicated local government approval often did so because they were highly invested in returning to a particular community. The dedication to returning home helped some participants stay the course even when the local government balked at paying. Other counties, though, enthusiastically funded participants, only for those participants to quickly depart from the program.

What did become obvious from my interviews is that there are tangible negative impacts of requiring local government funding approvals. First, some lawyers have felt like they were not really wanted in their communities, and some still hold grudges against the local government even if they were ultimately approved for the program. Second, when a local government refused to pay, sometimes another entity paid instead, but other times the participant realized a lower stipend in their pocket. The fact that sometimes an unwanted participant has had a lower stipend only exacerbates the concern about community support, because the communities who refused financial support ended up with lawyers with a lower stipend amount, potentially threatening their ability to financially survive.

Finally, the poorest counties arguably have the highest need for new lawyers, yet the smallest ability to fund the program. Because county funds come mostly from real estate taxes, and because land held in trust is not taxable, counties with Indian Country are likely the most disadvantaged by the requirement to pay. As are counties with other nontaxable land, like state and federal grasslands or forests. Add in that those counties with small land tax bases are more likely to be persistent poverty counties with low populations, and suddenly it is hard for lawyers to make a living in the same counties that struggle to pay for the stipend. This problem is not unique to South Dakota – in general, some of the most rural counties have the smallest tax base and the biggest trouble providing resources to their populations.[197] To the extent that local funding is a requirement of such a program, there should be a way for the poorest localities to seek a waiver of the local support without the lawyer having to take a lower stipend. Just like matching requirements for federal grants hurt the poorest communities, so do local funding incentives here.

---

[197] Statz, *On Shared Suffering, supra* note 81, at 24.

6

Acceptance

FIGURE 6.1 Jennifer English

McCook County was having trouble filling criminal court appointments when a local judge approached the Rural Attorney Recruitment Program administrators suggesting that the county should participate in the program. Program administrators began recruiting and found Jennifer English, a new law school graduate from Ohio. English was graduating from law school at Ohio Northern when she read about the program in an ABA publication. When English spoke with program administrator Suzanne Starr, Starr was "the first person that I talked to that was excited for me to be a lawyer." English and her husband decided on Salem sight unseen, moving to town after she graduated from law school. English was excited to build a rural practice that would serve community needs and provide access to justice for those in the community. Yet when English moved to town, ready to join the program, the county commissioners were not convinced the county needed more lawyers. The commission first tabled English's request to participate until she had proof of bar passage, even though the contract itself already had a condition of being a member of the bar.

English passed on her first attempt, but the commission's insistence on delaying the contract approval meant that English waited in limbo for months to know if she would have the Rural Attorney Recruitment Program funds. McCook County did not want to pay the full local government portion – the city of Salem, where English set up her office, paid half. But, still skeptical, an extra condition was added requiring English to provide time sheets to the local government showing she had completed enough hours of legal work.

Even once she was approved for the program, English never felt welcomed to town. She started a solo practice rather than being invited to join an existing firm, and she found the town itself "very unwelcoming, to the point where most people that move here typically stay about five years and that's about as much as they can handle." Her experience was that "people don't help each other unless you've lived here for generations" and the town "doesn't want anybody" new to join the community. At times, and by some people, English felt that racism toward her Black husband came into play. For context, McCook County has a population of 5,809 and is 95 percent white. Whatever the cause, a disconnect emerged between English and her community. McCook County and its residents were less eager to participate and did less to welcome their new lawyer, which compounded to create one of the more negative programmatic experiences.

While writing about community in small South Dakota towns, I can't help but think about Kathleen Norris. Norris captures, better than any other writer, the reality of moving to rural South Dakota with an education and career. Norris, in her memoir, writes about the experience of moving to Lemmon, South Dakota, a rural and remote town where her grandparents lived.[198] Norris's observations, along with the sociologists who have written extensively about rural communities, provide ways of thinking about the community aspects of becoming a rural lawyer, especially in relation to community acceptance.

The contract-signing process, detailed in Chapter 5, can have an influence on the relationship between a lawyer and her community. With Jennifer English and a few other lawyers, the politicians' skepticism of paying for a lawyer soured relationships. But whether the politicians were unenthused did not necessarily determine whether there was community acceptance of that lawyer. Picking up after the contract is signed and the lawyer has moved to a rural community, this chapter speaks about feelings of community acceptance. This includes acceptance by the local community members and any lawyers in the town or region.

[198] KATHLEEN NORRIS, DAKOTA: A SPIRITUAL GEOGRAPHY (1993).

The community acceptance must be understood in the context of having lawyers like Jennifer English who walked into a new community unknown and had to start fresh as well as lawyers who started legal careers in towns where they grew up and everyone knew the participants and their families. The hometown aspect matters: Chapter 4, in Figure 4.4, shows that lawyers who joined the program in their home counties stayed at a 100 percent rate. Despite that, community acceptance has varied widely and is not necessarily predictable. Community arises several times in this book. For now, I address feelings of acceptance. Later, in Chapter 10, I cover how lawyers engaged in community service. Then, in Chapter 11, I address the feelings of attachment that played a role in whether lawyers stayed or left the program.

COMMUNITY ACCEPTANCE

The contract, the office space, the housing – these were all preliminary steps for lawyers entering rural communities. But the bigger, and more intangible, step was for those lawyers to integrate and connect with their chosen rural communities. Even with a signed contract and a place to live, these attorneys still had to begin their law practice, oftentimes in a new town. I asked each attorney whether the community welcomed them, whether local lawyers welcomed them, and whether the local community was willing to bring legal business. In general, the participants who returned to their hometowns were the most welcomed, while those without prior connections had a more mixed experience. There was no *significant* difference between the experience of acceptance by men and women, though a few young women felt like their age and gender played a role in whether they were accepted as lawyers.

When asked if the community welcomed them, over half of the participants said "yes" without qualification. The participants who moved home had no concerns about reintegrating back into their rural communities despite their years of absence to obtain higher education. In fact, only one attorney who moved home had any concerns about being welcomed by the community, and that was an attorney who lived at home and commuted to a neighboring county to work. Instead, the concerns about community acceptance were related to lawyers who were transplants – lawyers who chose new communities not where they grew up.

Jennifer English, as explained at the start of this chapter, has never felt fully welcomed into the town. Despite English's attempts to volunteer in the community, and despite her husband running a business in town, after five years in Salem she has yet to feel accepted. This is the experience we might expect for outsiders. Kathleen Norris says that it is "a truism that outsiders, often professionals with no family ties, are never fully accepted into a rural or small-town community. Such communities are impenetrable for many reasons."[199] I think Norris goes too far, because it

---

[199] *Id.* at 83.

turns out that many of the communities *are* penetrable. I heard from others that Salem can offer a strong sense of community, particularly tied to churches and high school sports. And while it might be hard to break into that community as an outsider, it is possible. Victor Rapkoch had a positive experience in his adopted town of Britton, where his family was "welcomed with open arms." Kasen Lambeth was so welcomed by his new town of Elk Point that even after leaving the program for a full-time job in a larger community, Lambeth later reopened an office in Elk Point. Both Rapkoch and Lambeth grew up outside of South Dakota, but both developed a South Dakota connection by attending law school in the state.

Many transplants noted how they became involved with the community in ways that increased their engagement – like having children in school or coaching local sports. For example, when Kristian Ellendorf moved to Howard, seventy-five miles away from her hometown, she and her husband already had several children – at kindergarten, at preschool, and in daycare – and having "all of our kids everywhere" allowed them to integrate into the community faster. But someone like Ellendorf started in a different situation than English – Ellendorf is originally from the state of South Dakota plus has kids in the local school system. A better comparison to English's poor experience is that of Kristen Kochekian, the only other person who joined the program with no prior ties to South Dakota.

Kochekian says "the community there has been amazing since day one" giving examples of community members assisting with a blown tire and providing help after she broke her leg. For Kochekian, "there's never been a time where I've been low or needed help from the moment I moved here that I didn't have both hands reaching out to help me in whatever way I needed." For Kochekian, that community help is "a tremendous benefit" to making the Rural Attorney Recruitment Program work – especially for transplants like herself. An important piece is that Kochekian was an active member of her community, volunteering in her community from the time of her arrival. Of the various volunteer work Kochekian has done, making fundraising meals of her New Jersey Italian food for hundreds to fund a church roof repair sounded the best to me. Kochekian, though half-Italian and full of East Coast energy, has managed to integrate into the community and fit the mold of what the community wants.

There was a sense, for a few participants, that if a lawyer did not fit the local mold, they would not be accepted into the community. Sociologist Robert Wuthnow writes of this: That rural communities exist around developed norms, so rural community means that people feel "an obligation to one another and to uphold the local ways of being."[200] English decided to move to Salem when she was a law student with purple hair; a white woman married to an African American man from Columbus, Ohio. When English moved to her rural community and knew she needed commissioner approval, she got rid of her purple hair and dressed conservatively. She

---

[200] WUTHNOW, *supra* note 31, at 4.

"consciously made that decision" in order to be accepted by the local community. By the time I met with her, English was near the end of her five-year obligation and was back to styling herself as she wants – bright blue hair welcomed me to Salem.

It was not just English who had fashion or style sense that did not fit the norm of rural South Dakota. Once a lawyer opined to me that the reason one participant left was because the young lawyer wore "super tight pants" and had "dyed hair" every other week. In the observer's opinion, the hair and pants made it hard for the young lawyer to attract and retain a clientele of ranchers. In other words, the young lawyer simply did not fit the community expectations. Because I did not interview those clients, I don't know whether the pants and hair dye were *actually* an issue for clients. The participant in question was a South Dakota kid who grew up on a farm and knew the culture. Yet knowing the culture is only the first step. Wuthnow suggests there is also a performative element – "to uphold the ways of being" in a rural community is an expected part of being a community member.

There is a performative element to being a lawyer as well. Lawyers are expected to look the part and dress the part. A 2024 job posting for a prosecutor in Hughes County (population 17,694) required applicants to "maintain professional appearance and demeanor."[201] This is not just a rural requirement. The legal profession generally expects conservative dress: dark suits, modest shoes, and traditional hair. When lawyers do not dress the part, there can be "significant career consequences."[202] To the extent that rural lawyers felt consequences from their personal styles, it is not clear they would fare better in legal careers in larger places. In fact, one of the benefits of rural practice for these lawyers was the more relaxed environment with fewer restrictions on dress and style. When I travelled around South Dakota doing interviews, the lawyers knew we would be taking photos for a book, yet very few wore suits. Norris describes this as a "relaxation of urban standards, as simple as the bank president not wearing a tie to work. We bend the rules; that's part of small-town charm."[203] It is not obvious to me that lawyers wanting "super tight pants" or "dyed hair" will suffer more professional consequences in rural rather than urban practices. The rural population is more conservative, but perhaps the ability to bend the traditional rules of professional clothing is greater.

It turns out, though, that most transplants who entered new rural communities entered with the goal of adopting and upholding the local culture. Chapter 4 talks in depth about why lawyers chose rural communities, and one major reason was a sense that rural communities were "familiar." I heard the word "familiar" from lawyers going home *and* lawyers heading to new communities. The new community itself may not have been familiar, but the culture of a rural community was, and the lawyers had an interest in living within the constraints of that rural culture.

---

[201] *Career Center, supra* note 110, at 62.
[202] Elizabeth B. Cooper, *The Appearance of Professionalism*, 71 FLA. L. REV. 1, 5 (2019).
[203] NORRIS, *supra* note 198, at 55.

Just because participants felt familiar with the culture of rural communities does not mean they were immediately accepted. Even when transplants came from other small towns, there were sometimes tensions. Kathleen Norris says that rural communities treat outsiders "with an uneasy mix of hospitality and rejection."[204] The professional mobility that allowed these lawyers to choose towns that fit their families and careers can also create a level of social isolation. Two lawyers who moved to new communities several hours away from where they grew up found their adopted communities skeptical at first. One noted the "typical South Dakota small-town issues where it's kind of a clique" and that "people are hesitant" to let new residents into their social circles "until they know that you've really put down roots and you're going to stay." Another attorney explained almost the same phenomenon: That community members "were never mean, or rude, or anything" but, after living in the town almost a decade, she still gets questioned about whether she is going to stay there, or whether her family will leave because she has no connection to the town. Becoming more involved with the community as her children grow has helped increase overall community acceptance, yet there remains some doubt.

Other transplants found acceptance, but felt their easy acceptance was because someone in the community actively helped them build connections. Abigail Monger found the town of Tyndall welcoming and thought "it was a lot easier to get to know people than I thought it would be." A part of her success was because her hiring attorney and the office secretary introduced her to locals. A legal assistant who had been in the office for forty years provided the same assistance to Amanda Work when she moved to Winner. Many hiring attorneys helped new lawyers build similar connections. One mentoring attorney explained that his town is "a pretty progressive community" and that "anybody willing to come in here and work is welcome." But that mentoring attorney also took care to introduce his mentee to the community. Introductions are powerful, even in communities craving more professionals.

For those moving home (or close to home), some community connections were easy to build. Mason Juracek grew up thirty minutes away from Winner where he practices, and he "had a lot of friends" when he moved to town. Rachel Mairose is practicing near home, and though she did not grow up in her new town of Plankinton, "a lot of my distant relatives came by to say hi" from nearby communities when she first came to town. Another participant who practiced law one county over from his hometown found less active community acceptance, noting that "nobody was sitting around waiting for me to show up." He worries that the press coverage of the Rural Attorney Recruitment Program might have been a mistake, but also notes that the community acceptance might have been greater had he decided to live in the town where he practiced, rather than commute from a different community.

[204] *Id.* at 7.

South Dakota's nine reservations contain approximately five million acres, and Native Americans make up around 9 percent of the state's population. For those on or in close proximity to reservations, acceptance by local tribal members was part of overall community acceptance. Border towns are often very racially diverse and several participants lived in communities that do not have a majority white population.

Only two lawyers have been placed in Indian Country. Dylan Kirchmeier works on the lands of the Sisseton Wahpeton Oyate. Sisseton, with a population of 2,479, is about half white and half Native American. Kirchmeier, who describes himself as "about the palest white dude you can find," realizes the difficult position he has prosecuting mostly Native American defendants. Within his first year as prosecutor, the American Indian Movement did a protest outside of the sheriff's office based on a no-prosecute decision Kirchmeier made with a Native American victim. Kirchmeier has felt accepted by the city officials and county officials. He has found the overall community reaction in Sisseton more mixed, though Kirchmeier has chosen to live in a nearby small town, perhaps slowing his integration into the town of Sisseton. Evan Hoel, who moved to Timber Lake on the Cheyenne River Reservation, did not stay long enough to develop deep community connections.

For lawyers who live near, but not on, reservations, Amanda LaCroix's experience is instructive. LaCroix joined the program in Martin, several hours away from her hometown of Rapid City. Martin sits in Bennett County, originally part of the Pine Ridge Reservation. In 1910, a federal statute transferred much of the land in Bennett County to white homesteaders, and the reservation eventually was held diminished, removing Bennett County from the lands of the Oglala Sioux Tribe.[205] Martin's current population of 938 is approximately half white and half Native American. LaCroix, who is white but was married to an Oglala tribal member, felt the community was "very excited" in the beginning and overall "pretty supportive." After LaCroix established her law practice, LaCroix and her husband purchased the local hardware store in town, which was popular around town because the young couple was "making this even bigger commitment to the community." LaCroix explains that "we had more support from the community – and especially the tribal community – when we bought the hardware store than they ever supported my law office." Though LaCroix ultimately left Martin, it was not because the town or tribal community did not accept her.

While buying the hardware store with her husband was a key piece of community acceptance for LaCroix, nearly the same situation did not help English. English and her husband purchased the local thrift store, with her husband running that store for his employment. As a business it basically breaks even and, in many ways, is about serving community needs rather than turning a profit. But even that thrift store did not turn the tide for community acceptance for English.

[205] U.S. ex rel. Cook v. Parkinson, 525 F.2d 120 (8th Cir. 1975).

One final aspect of community acceptance was mentioned by the two attorneys who moved to rural communities where their grandparents had made their lives. This is what Kathleen Norris did. Norris herself did not grow up in Lemmon, South Dakota, but her mother did, and her grandparents were lifelong residents. Norris described herself as both an "insider by virtue of family connections" and an "outsider" because she spent her "formative years away" from the community.[206] Yet her family history helped her forge connections in the local community, exactly like the two lawyers who moved to their grandparents' towns. For both participants, their last names were familiar and a certain amount of the community felt personal ties because of those grandparents. Recruiting more lawyers who have extended family, especially grandparents, in rural areas provides an opportunity to bring in outsiders with an inside connection.

Though community acceptance varied, a few factors helped in gaining traction into a new community. Being from the community originally was the best indicator that a lawyer felt welcomed. For those who were transplants, extended family nearby helped, as did having children integrated into the local schools. For most participants, increased community involvement through volunteer work (addressed later in Chapter 10) helped with community acceptance.

LAWYER ACCEPTANCE

In addition to integrating into the community where they live and work, these participants were integrating into a local legal community. In rural practice, the law can be collaborative and sometimes informal. Having strong networks with other lawyers is critical for all rural practitioners, but especially those new to rural practice needing to learn about local norms. Scholarship on rural practitioners in Australia described solo practitioners as building "alliances" with other rural lawyers in order to improve their own practices.[207] Landon described rural Missouri practice as expecting "attorneys to be cooperative rather than contentious; trustworthy, not tricky; reasonable, not radical."[208] A 1992 article about rural practice in Kansas described that "all the lawyers in town have to work together" and "there seems to be a consensus among the attorneys not to 'personalize' professional behavior."[209] Rural practice is driven by collegial relationships where lawyers know they will have repeated interactions across decades. The participants of the South Dakota program recognized the importance of building connections with local and regional lawyers,

---

[206] NORRIS, *supra* note 198, at 86.
[207] Trish Mundy & Amanda Kennedy, *Rural and Regional Legal Practice*, in THE PLACE OF PRACTICE, *supra* note 61, at 46, 59–60.
[208] Donald D. Landon, *Clients, Colleagues, and Community: The Shaping of Zealous Advocacy in Country Law Practice*, 1985 AM. B. FOUND. RES. J. 81, 109 (1985).
[209] Nina W. Tarr, *Two Women Attorneys and Country Practice*, 2 COLUM. J. GENDER & L. 25, 52 (1992).

and the acceptance by those lawyers played prominently in the way the participants viewed their success in the early years of practice.

An unfortunate number of participants felt at least some of the local bar did not welcome the new attorneys for fear of competition. South Dakota is small, and the legal community is even smaller. The participating attorneys were hesitant to speak ill of local lawyers – especially by name – but it was clear that not all existing lawyers were okay with the next generation entering their geographic areas. As one participant explained, while most attorneys are welcoming and happy to help, some "would rather see you fail" because they fear competition. A different participant noted that "lawyers are very territorial" and "don't like competition." One participant, loathe to say anything negative, merely described the local attorneys as "cordial," but clearly would have preferred more colorful terms. The nicest thing another participant could find to say about the local attorney was "he wasn't hostile." Young lawyers, especially women, sometimes felt excluded from the social scene of local lawyers. In a 2023 study on rural lawyers in Wyoming, one young female attorney struggled with the "good ol' boys club" in her community.[210] Some young women in my study felt similar exclusion.

Sometimes the relationships with existing lawyers were difficult, not because of malice, but because of personality or communication difficulties. I heard about aging local lawyers who struggled to communicate through email, which the younger attorneys preferred. I also heard about difficult personalities in older lawyers that made it challenging to build relationships, but not because of animosity toward the new lawyers.

Most participants listed nearby attorneys they could call for help and noted general acceptance by the local bar. For those without local mentors, there were attorneys statewide invested in mentoring new rural attorneys. In a few instances, once a participant decided on a place to practice, they reached out to local lawyers. The reaction was mixed – sometimes those local lawyers were "immediately distrustful," for example asking a new attorney, "Why are you here?" One local lawyer told a newcomer there wasn't enough business, but when the participant approached a different attorney in town it was a different story. A few participants were told by one attorney in town to stay away because no new lawyers were needed, while another attorney in town was actively recruiting.

Overall though, local lawyers were supportive. After all, most of the participants joined existing firms, stepping into offices where at least one attorney was dedicated to seeing them succeed. Some non-hiring attorneys were also very helpful. There were attorneys who sold their offices and firms at low cost (but there were also some who tried to charge too much). There were established prosecutors who gave up their elected positions to provide stable income and work to participants (but there were some who refused to share well-paid prosecutor positions). There were plenty

---

[210] Tomisich, *supra* note 53, at 117.

of lawyers who took reduced court appointments to ensure that new lawyers had a chance (but there were some who fought hard to keep their entire court appointment load, even if it meant that counties paid more for them to travel). The sacrifices of local lawyers are explored more in Chapter 8 about mentorship, but there was a split between existing lawyers who were actively involved in welcoming new lawyers and existing lawyers who were hostile (sometimes very openly) to the competition.

CLIENTS

There is also the issue of the local community bringing legal work to these new lawyers. Norris posits that professionals moving to rural America will struggle. In her view, "[s]mall-town people are often suspicious of the professionals who move to the Plains; 'if they were any good, they'd be working in a bigger place' is how the reasoning goes."[211] That concern was not felt by the lawyers I interviewed, though some felt other hesitation from the local community in bringing business to the new lawyer in town. This type of acceptance, about whether local community members would bring business to new lawyers in town, also brought up the most blatant discussions of sexism that I heard during my research.

One participant explained that business was slow in the beginning. Not because the locals were skeptical of him, but because "old farmers are going to go with who they know." In other communities, clients were "hesitant" but "pretty quickly the fact that I'm right here outweighed any concern" that the rural attorney was less qualified than those in larger towns miles away. One attorney said it was "hit or miss" whether locals would bring him legal work. Another attorney who describes herself as an introvert was never able to bring in enough clients to sustain a civil practice, and she, against her preferences, had to take criminal appointments to survive. As one participant said, "if you are an introvert, rural practice might not be for you." A very extroverted lawyer, on the other hand, told me that "you definitely have to like people" to be a successful rural lawyer. This is an ever-present facet of rural practice: A Georgia lawyer explained that rural lawyers are "in the people business."[212] Most attorneys simply noted things were slow at the beginning, but it did not take long to have a full caseload. Very few attorneys felt any long-term hesitancy by the local community to bring them business.

For attorneys joining existing firms, the senior lawyers in the firm generally took care to hand off appropriate clients and refer new clients to the new lawyers, thereby creating a sufficient book of business to sustain the new lawyers. Clients might question a new attorney about qualifications, but being able to say that "I've spoken with my mentor who you used for years" might be enough to get skeptical clients to bring business to a new lawyer. A few attorneys brought into firms have lost clients

---

[211] NORRIS, *supra* note 198, at 32.
[212] LEAPHART, *supra* note 60, at 9.

because of the history of the firm. One lawyer mentioned there are "some people who won't come in because of things [the hiring attorney] has done in the past." Another lawyer explained that "this firm has been around for a long time, and so it's got some enemies." As one lawyer said, it is unsurprising that "a firm that's been suing people in town for seventy-five years" has "some people that don't like it."

One attorney noted that when she arrived – "as a young female having no connections" – she worried what would happen when her hiring attorney retired and left her the office. A few of his clients left, but most stayed, and people in town are very willing to bring her business. She notes that her "town is very loyal to local business and that's just a huge thing here." That loyalty, in addition to word-of-mouth referrals and referrals from the local Register of Deeds and Clerk of Courts, keeps her busy. The word-of-mouth referrals can cut the other way as well – someone from Salem explained to me that Jennifer English perhaps had trouble getting clients because there are two lawyers in town who are "well-known" and "well-established" and anyone who is knowledgeable about the community will likely go to one of those established attorneys rather than English, who is still perceived as being new even though she has been in town for over five years.

While attorneys practicing in their hometowns had an easier time with broad community acceptance, they did sometimes struggle to bring in clients as a new professional. One attorney who practices in his hometown said that, in the beginning, he got "a lot of dog cases," but then high school classmates, members of his church, and other connections in town started to bring him more business. That family connections and local ties help build a book of business is unsurprising; Elizabeth Chambliss found the same thing with South Carolina lawyers.[213]

On the other hand, and as another lawyer explained, working in a hometown fresh out of law school "can kind of be a bad thing." For that lawyer, local residents will come to her office and say, "I remember when you were in kindergarten," and the lawyer fears that "I said something I should not have as a five-year-old kindergartener that can haunt me forever." A retired lawyer told me something similar, that the "toughest part" about beginning rural practice was "convincing people I wasn't the young brat that I used to be in high school." Senator Dale Bumpers expressed this same feeling in his memoir. Writing about his small-town law practice, Bumpers said: "Returning to one's small hometown to practice a profession dealing with people's lives and property can be a bad idea. Too many people think of you as the towheaded kid they watched grow up."[214]

A more common concern expressed with regards to clients trusting the lawyers was about sexism. One male attorney told me that "there was a stereotype" that "you can't do rural practice if you're a woman." And though he described that stereotype in past tense, he explained that "there's still people today who would not go

---

[213] Chambliss, *supra* note 63.
[214] BUMPERS, *supra* note 59, at 127.

to [a particular female participant] because she's a woman." Though this attorney thought that the "era" of sexism "is done" he saw the sexism as "still present" in his rural area. The participating lawyer he was speaking about did not identify sexism as a barrier in her practice, though other women did.

The three female lawyers who raised sexism all tied it to age. It was not just being a female lawyer; it was being a *young* female lawyer serving an older clientele. One woman told me, "I always thought that going into a rural area as a young female was maybe an additional challenge." Her clientele is mostly older male ranchers, and "there are times when people talk to me, and I just want to say, 'if I were a male right now, would you be treating me the same way?'" She has felt that some clients used her only reluctantly because no male attorneys are nearby and that she has needed to prove to her clients that she knew what she was doing. In all, "being a young female, I think you just have to really hold your ground and prove that you can do and will do it. No matter what [the clients] say or do, you gotta be stubborn." Another young female lawyer explained that "most sixty-five- to seventy-five-year-old farmers don't really want a twenty-five-year-old woman telling them what they should or shouldn't do." That aspect made her nervous, but she has been surprised by how busy her practice is. A final woman noted that "being a younger woman attorney" has an impact on her practice because she is not seen as an authority on legal topics and clients think she is "too young to know" the business. She thinks this perception has kept older male clientele from bringing her business and incentivized more complaints about hourly rates. One young female lawyer who felt disrespected by older male clients quit representing those problematic clients about four years into rural practice, and saying "no" to the problematic clients has been freeing.

LESSONS LEARNED

Mismatches are inherent in a program that is sending professionals into rural areas. When I interviewed English for the first time in November of 2017, she had just been sworn into the bar. She was idealistic – a new rural practitioner optimistic about the way she was going to impact her community. Driven to rural practice by the idea that she could serve the public good, English was excited about her new town and new career. Five years later, that optimism had worn off. The rural practice of law was not what she expected. She felt pushback from the local lawyers, the local politicians, and the local business leaders. There were times when she felt that some community members interacted with her in ways driven by racism on accord of her Black husband. She felt that in order to financially succeed she needed to take cases that she did not want to take. Rural practice was nothing like she expected; living in a rural community was stifling, not inspiring. But others who entered rural practice have felt welcomed and embraced.

There is no magic recipe for ensuring that new rural lawyers will feel accepted. While going home helps with community engagement, it does not guarantee acceptance as a professional. And plenty of transplants have made permanent homes in rural South Dakota towns through this program. Acceptance is critical because of the nature of rural practice. Chapter 11 picks up on what one mentoring attorney called the "intimate" nature of rural practice. That is, lawyers are deeply connected with their local communities. Amanda Work, a participating lawyer, summed up the community involvement aspect well: "You have to be ready to be all in within the community. Figure out your community. That's just something that's part of" rural practice. Stephanie Trask, another participating lawyer, cautioned that "the community that you decide on is a massive consideration because" even lawyers who are competent at legal work but in a mis-matched community will struggle.

7

Legal Work

FIGURE 7.1 Cassie Wendt

Cassie Wendt graduated from law school in 2012 and started her legal career as a prosecutor in Butte County, South Dakota, where she worked for a decade. Butte County has 10,456 people; its county seat of Belle Fourche has 5,617. To Wendt, who grew up on a rural ranch, Belle Fourche was "a big town." Then, Wendt lost her thirty-eight-year-old brother to cancer, prompting her, her husband, and her three kids to move home to the family ranch in Jackson County. Wendt opened a solo practice in the closest town, Philip, in Haakon County. Both Jackson County and Haakon County are rural. Haakon County has a population of 1,872. Jackson County has a population of 2,806 and over half of its land lies within the Pine Ridge Reservation belonging to the Oglala Sioux.

As Wendt planned for her new career as a solo practitioner, she ran for a part-time prosecutor position in Haakon County but lost in the 2022 primary. Not dissuaded by the loss, Wendt moved home, opened her law firm, and joined the Rural Attorney Recruitment Program. When I visited Wendt, she was adjusting to new practice areas after a decade as a full-time prosecutor. She was doing court-appointed defense work in six counties, though primarily in Jackson County, the county that signed her rural attorney contract. Wendt also does civil work, including family law, business law, and estate planning. Almost as soon as Wendt opened her doors, she started doing free and reduced cost legal services, writing off fees when she knows clients cannot afford them. In 2025, after my study had completed, Wendt became State's Attorney in Haakon and Jackson Counties but has been able to continue her part-time private practice.

Wendt is, in many ways, typical of the rural lawyers in my study. She does a combination of government and private work. She practices in a variety of subject areas. She regularly reduces or writes off fees for poor clients. This chapter surveys what types of services the Rural Attorney Recruitment Program lawyers have provided to their rural communities. Every participant has done criminal law – either prosecuting, defending, or both (when they do both, it is in different counties). Accordingly, I start with that criminal work, then move to other government work before addressing private civil work. These lawyers also engaged in substantial pro bono work, though I save those details for Chapter 10 when I further discuss the contributions these lawyers make to their rural communities.

By the time of my interviews, the longest-serving lawyers had been in their communities for almost ten years, and a number of lawyers had changed jobs. Eight lawyers had left rural law practice, putting all of their work in the past tense. For those who have stayed, many have shifted their work priorities – for example, beginning or ending prosecutorial work. Some of these changes occurred because lawyers figured out they had preferences for certain types of work. Other times, lawyers initially did whatever work their hiring firm already did or they took particular cases because others in the firm did not want those cases. Over time, as colleagues, jobs, and legal needs changed, so did the practice area focuses of these lawyers.

Almost all of the lawyers have managed multiple practice areas and jobs at one time. One theme that runs through this chapter is conflicts and potential conflicts that these lawyers face in their rural legal practices, especially because they wear different hats at the same time. Never once during my interviews did I perceive that a lawyer was acting unethically or violating the rules of professional conduct.

92   *Legal Work*

Accordingly, the discussion in this chapter about conflicts is not directed at the acts of particular South Dakota lawyers, but rather at the *risk* created by the types of practices.

PROSECUTORIAL WORK

Sixteen lawyers, or exactly half of the participants, have been prosecutors in their rural placements, and this section addresses those sixteen lawyers. In South Dakota, each county has an elected "State's Attorney," a licensed attorney who is on the ballot each general election.[215] When counties are willing to provide funding, one or more "Deputy State's Attorneys" may be appointed by the State's Attorney to serve as an additional prosecutor in the county. State's Attorneys are responsible for prosecuting crimes in their county and providing opinions and advice to the county commissioners and other civil officers in the county. Accordingly, even a full-time State's Attorney will do non-prosecutorial work serving as counsel to the county.

Larger counties must have a full-time State's Attorney, while smaller counties are allowed part-time prosecutors. Though full-time State's Attorneys are prohibited from engaging in private practice, part-time State's Attorneys can supplement with private work. Generally, a State's Attorney must reside in the county where they are elected to office, but in counties with populations under 5,000 a State's Attorney candidate can run for office if they live in a contiguous county.

Of the sixteen participants who have served as prosecutors in their rural communities, six have served only as Deputy State's Attorneys. The other ten have served as the primary State's Attorney for their county, though most State's Attorneys started as deputies. Almost all have part-time prosecutorial positions and also operate a private law practice for the remainder of their time; only three have had full-time prosecutorial positions. These prosecutorial positions raise a number of issues for the lawyers and the program itself.

The first issue raised by prosecutorial work is that the three full-time prosecutors are the only three full-time government employees in the entire Rural Attorney Recruitment Program. All other lawyers are doing private practice with some part-time government work. Unsurprisingly, the counties that have hired full-time prosecutors are larger. In fact, all three full-time prosecutors work in counties that are too large to participate in the program.

Roberts County, which has one full-time prosecutor in the program, is barely over the 10,000-person threshold with a population of 10,163. Since the county is too large to participate, the county seat of Sisseton signed the contract, though the county pays

---

[215] The laws governing State's Attorneys are found in S.D. CODIFIED LAWS §§ 7-16-1 to -31.

the local government portion of the stipend. Dylan Kirchmeier, the lawyer in Roberts County, started as a Deputy but was elevated to the State's Attorney position mere months after becoming licensed to practice. There are legitimate reasons why Roberts County needed the help of the program to recruit a prosecutor. With its former prosecutor ready to retire, the county was under pressure to recruit. The county lies within the disestablished reservation of the Sisseton Wahpeton Oyate, and with substantial untaxable trust land the county struggles to fund a competitive salary. Kirchmeier, who took the job, cared deeply about the incentive when he was considering the position. He now carries a heavy caseload, mostly of drug cases, and navigates prosecuting in a county that is partially Indian Country. Since Kirchmeier has taken over, the county has authorized the hiring of a full-time Deputy State's Attorney, a position that took years to fill, and in the meantime Kirchmeier was the only prosecutor in the county. Without the stipend drawing in Kirchmeier, it is unclear how a prosecutor would have been hired.

Union County, with a population of 16,811, is the thirteenth most populated county in South Dakota and located near several population centers. The county seat of Elk Point has a population of only 2,124, qualifying it to participate as a municipality. Twice, full-time Deputy State's Attorneys signed contracts with the city of Elk Point, with Union County paying the stipend. One left; the other is active in the program now. Both explained that they took the job *then* considered the program, which sets them apart from other participants, including Kirchmeier in Roberts County, who targeted rural practice specifically. It is far less obvious that Union County needed financial support to bring in Deputy State's Attorneys.

Full-time government employees see benefits that do not accrue to lawyers in private practice. Only full-time employees are eligible for Public Service Loan Forgiveness, a benefit that encourages lawyers to seek public interest and government work. Full-time positions are guaranteed employment benefits. The counties who are hiring full-time employees are necessarily larger, and generally better funded, than the rural communities most often served by the program. Recently, the Unified Judicial System has excluded full-time prosecutors from the program. The three full-time prosecutors who have entered the program will be the only three. That option is now gone.

All of the remaining prosecutors have done their prosecutorial work on a part-time basis. These part-time prosecutors have part-time private practices. Many of them estimate their prosecutorial work at about 50 percent of their legal work, with the smallest estimate at ten hours a week and the highest part-time estimate at thirty-two hours a week. The rhythm of prosecution is different in rural communities where court may happen only once or twice a month, but attorneys generally appreciated this aspect of basically having two part-time jobs.

And this leads me to the second concern with these prosecutors. Part-time State's Attorneys face serious conflict of interest problems in their legal practices. There is a substantial body of caselaw, ethics opinions, and academic literature about the conflicts of interests that part-time prosecutors face, including specifically about South

Dakota part-time prosecutors.[216] Some of those ethics concerns were raised by the lawyers I interviewed.

Some part-time prosecutors spoke about the difficulty of being a general practice attorney in the same small community where you prosecute. Lawyers lost private clients who hold grudges about prosecutions. Lawyers serve clients who have been previously prosecuted. Several prosecutors have had to criminally charge a private client. Often, the charge is relatively minor, but it still creates a conflict and forces attorneys to either recuse from prosecution (sending it to a nearby State's Attorney) or withdraw from the civil case.

Clients, though, may not want to lose their private attorney. One lawyer had a long-term client who "got in some very minor trouble and they just came in and I didn't even have to call them, you know, just walked in the door." And the client said to the lawyer: "Hey, here's what happened. I'm going to come in. I'm gonna plead guilty. Whatever you gotta do you gotta do. I'm good with it." The client was willing to plead guilty instead of fighting a criminal charge in order to stay as a civil client of the lawyer. That might work for very minor trouble, but not for serious criminal charges.

And yet, despite the downsides of part-time prosecution, one of the shining successes of South Dakota's program has been recruiting rural prosecutors to some of the state's smallest counties. Like other rural states, South Dakota has had trouble filling all of its prosecutorial positions with local lawyers.[217] Marty Jackley, who served his first term as Attorney General of South Dakota from 2009 to 2019 and started a second term in 2023, advises local State's Attorneys. Jackley thinks that an ideal situation is to have a local prosecutor in each county, though he acknowledges that it is impractical because of a lack of lawyers in the smallest counties. From Jackley's perspective as Attorney General, the Rural Attorney Recruitment Program can play an important role in recruiting more rural prosecutors, and he (or future Attorneys General) can provide mentorship. Having an Attorney General who wants to recruit and train local prosecutors helps the Rural Attorney Recruitment Program find and place new local prosecutors.

Jackley wants local attorneys, but he also wants each county to have its own prosecutor. From Jackley's perspective, having one prosecutor in two counties risks conflicts, especially in the role of advising the county commission. Giving me just one example, Jackley noted that State's Attorneys in two neighboring counties might have a conflict over a road maintenance contract. Two participating lawyers have already been State's Attorneys in multiple counties, having to balance these conflicts.

The recruitment and retention of prosecutors has been strong. No participating attorney serving as State's Attorney has left the program or their rural community. Another way to view this success is looking statewide at the sixty-six counties. As

---

[216] Margaret Raymond, *The Other Half: Challenges of the Part-Time Rural Prosecutor*, 69 S.D. L. REV. 504 (2024) (discussing South Dakota and citing many other sources on part-time prosecutors); Timothy W. Bjorkman, Comment, *The Part-Time State's Attorney in South Dakota: The Conflict between Fealty to Private Client and Services to the Public*, 27 S.D. L. REV. 24 (1981) (same).

[217] Quinn Yeargain, *Sharing Elected Prosecutors*, 69 S.D. L. REV. 523 (2024).

of early 2024, twelve South Dakota counties have a Rural Attorney Recruitment Program participant serving as State's Attorney. Almost 20 percent of South Dakota counties are currently served by lawyers who have taken part in the program.

With rare exception, most of the State's Attorneys started out as Deputy State's Attorneys working under someone else for training purposes. Sometimes those mentorship relationships were in the same firm, and sometimes the participant was a solo practitioner who was hired as a Deputy by an outside lawyer. Sometimes Deputy State's Attorneys are only there to help a permanent prosecutor, not take over. Lawyers in this last category have been more likely than not to leave rural practice. One participant who left after serving as Deputy State's Attorney explained she would have stayed had she been able to take over the State's Attorney position with its higher income.

All of the participating attorneys serving as State's Attorneys have graduated from law school in the last decade. Most of them are young. A few have gone straight from undergraduate to law school, assuming their prosecutorial roles in their twenties. Given that some of these participants are working near their home communities, they might be prosecuting their peers. Several young State's Attorneys told me about prosecuting high school classmates or other people they knew from childhood. Two attorneys who are prosecuting, but not in their home counties, see being from outside the area as an advantage. One explained he was a better prosecutor because he did not come in with biases from it being his hometown. Another explained that "personal relationships might get ruined" if he were prosecuting in his home county. One lawyer noted "it's very difficult to raise your kids in a community that you prosecute in – especially in a small community because everybody knows who your kids are."

Rural prosecutorial work comes with the issues discussed above, as well as more conflicts for the part-time prosecutors who also serve as criminal defense attorneys. Despite these challenges, rural prosecutorial work is crucial for half of the lawyers in the program.

DEFENSE WORK

Of the thirty-two attorneys who have participated in the program, all but five have done criminal defense work. The five who have not done rural criminal defense include the three full-time prosecutors, who, by statute, cannot practice law outside of their prosecutorial role. One participant, Evan Hoel, planned to take criminal defense appointments but left his rural community before accepting any cases. Abigail Monger, a part-time State's Attorney, has never taken criminal defense cases. For Monger, her lack of criminal defense is not ideological, it's practical – her husband is a state trooper, creating too many conflicts to make a criminal defense caseload worthwhile.

Other than those five, every lawyer in the program has done defense work in their rural communities, handling court-appointed defense cases at some point.

South Dakota had no statewide criminal defense system at the time of my interviews, and even though a state office now exists, criminal defense is still mostly handled on the local level.[218] None of the rural counties have public defender offices, so attorneys in my study did their defense work through individual court appointments. A few attorneys who now serve as prosecutors have taken very few court appointments, but they have had at least one. Most participants also take retained criminal defense clients, though those are rare in many of these economically depressed rural communities. Only a few had a significant number of retained defense clients. Participants located near tribal courts also take criminal defense cases in tribal courts.

For a few participants, court-appointed criminal defense work was their primary source of income. Before he took over as State's Attorney in two counties, Kirby Krogman relied on court appointments as his primary source of revenue. A majority of Derrick Johnson's legal practice is criminal defense appointments. Before leaving her rural community to take a full-time job as a federal public defender, Amanda Work took criminal defense appointments in seven counties, describing the work as "a lot" of her legal practice early in her career. Cassie Wendt was taking court appointments in six counties. Two more attorneys took appointments in four counties, quite a few in three counties, and several in two counties. Some participants only take court appointments in the counties where they live or a single nearby county.

Getting these appointments was not guaranteed. A county might sign a contract hoping that a local lawyer will take defense appointments and save the county money on travel. But the county commissioners do not get to appoint defense counsel, the court does. Not all magistrate judges were on board with giving the new local lawyers court appointments. Magistrate judges sometimes gave only misdemeanor cases to the new attorneys, or they refused to give many cases to a new lawyer because the lawyers driving from other counties relied on those court appointments. Once, a county commission wrote to a local judge asking for the participant to get more appointments. Twice, Chief Justice Gilbertson of the South Dakota Supreme Court intervened to encourage magistrates to appoint the new lawyers to more cases. The competition for court appointments in these few counties was abnormal.

In most rural counties in South Dakota and across the rest of the United States, the problem is that there are insufficient lawyers available to appoint in criminal defense cases.[219] Law professor Pamela Metzger has written extensively about how rural lawyer shortages impact the criminal legal system and now leads a center at

---

[218] Brooklyn Bollweg & Neil Fulton, *The Future of Indigent Defense in South Dakota*, 69 S.D. L. REV. 551 (2024).

[219] Daniel Beekman, *WA's Public Defender System is Breaking Down, Communities Reeling*, SEATTLE TIMES (Feb. 25, 2024), https://perma.cc/SJ7N-RDZM; Sarah Lehr, *From "Serious" to "Dire:" DAs Offices Across Wisconsin and the Country are Struggling to Hire Prosecutors*, WIS. PUB. RADIO (Feb. 8, 2023), https://perma.cc/2PLH-XC9S.

SMU Dedman School of Law dedicated to studying the topic.[220] In South Dakota, the difficulty in appointing criminal defense counsel became a rallying cry for the substantial changes to the criminal defense system that were instituted in 2024.[221]

The Rural Attorney Recruitment Program has worked to lessen this shortage. Ashley Anson felt like the local judge "treated my rural contract as a criminal contract, and I was getting almost every appointment." For the six years that Casey Jo Deibert practiced in northwest South Dakota, she "was the only one that lived up there, so they were trying to get me appointed to pretty much everything so the counties wouldn't have to pay the mileage." The reason program administrators recruited Jennifer English to McCook County was because the local judge was having trouble appointing lawyers in criminal cases. Allowing the part-time prosecutors to take defense appointments helps too.

At the same time, counties cannot hire a full-time public defender. As English explained: "Rural communities don't have that many court appointments. Even if I took every single court appointment that's in this county, I still probably wouldn't make a decent living." The reason these counties use appointments is because the caseload is not high enough to hire a full-time public defender. The low volume of local criminal defense cases led many attorneys to take cases in multiple counties, which worked for some and caused frustration for others. Several attorneys who drove to very small counties commented the paycheck was not worth the time. A sense of obligation, though, keeps some attorneys taking court appointments even when they need to drive.

For some participating attorneys, a sense of obligation is also what has them taking criminal defense appointments in their own county. Cole Romey wants to build a career doing civil litigation and estate planning. Romey takes court appointments only in his home county, and he does so "just to save this county money, because otherwise they have to hire others, and I feel that's my duty, even though it's not in the contract" for the Rural Attorney Recruitment Program. Romey regularly carries about "half a dozen or more of criminal files just to save the county money." Other participants similarly commented about taking court appointments in their contract county to save the county money. When lawyers are local, counties save on travel and criminal defendants have easier access to their lawyers.

This feeling of obligation has not always extended past the contract period for all attorneys. One attorney who regularly takes criminal defense appointments plans to stop when her five years in the program ends, though she has no plans to leave her community. Two lawyers who felt obligated to take appointments during their contracts

---

[220] Pamela R. Metzger, *Rural Criminal Justice Reform*, in TRANSFORMING CRIMINAL JUSTICE: AN EVIDENCE-BASED AGENDA FOR REFORM 242, 242–43 (Jon B. Gould & Pamela R. Metzger, eds. 2022); DEASON CTR., https://perma.cc/BC8H-XUEM (last visited Apr. 5, 2024).

[221] 2024 *State of the Judiciary*, S.D. UNIFIED JUDICIAL SYSTEM (2024), https://perma.cc/AUN4-N4X8; Indigent Legal Services Task Force, *Final Report and Recommendations*, S.D. UNIFIED JUD. SYS. (Oct. 1, 2023), https://perma.cc/BVW7-BPV6.

stopped after their five-year commitment. There are a variety of reasons for this: not liking criminal law, time constraints or conflicts for higher-paying civil work, and feeling inadequately trained to do criminal work. It is not surprising that as lawyers age, they move from a more varied practice – including criminal law – to a practice that focuses on a particular specialty, especially if there is space for an estate planning practice. On the other hand, there are still past participants taking criminal defense cases, several who mentioned a sense of obligation to their rural communities as a reason.

PROSECUTING AND DEFENDING

There are thirty-two attorneys, twenty-seven who have engaged in criminal defense lawyering in rural communities and sixteen who have prosecuted in rural communities. Necessarily, this means that eleven overlap and have prosecuted and defended in rural communities, some at the same time and some at different times. Figure 7.2 shows the breakdown of criminal work done by these attorneys in their rural placements.

Law professor Margaret Raymond has written about the challenges that part-time rural prosecutors face, including when part-time prosecutors also do defense work.[222] The concerns are legion, though have not erupted into issues for the rural lawyers in South Dakota. It helps that in South Dakota, criminal cases are clearly demarcated by county line, so a part-time prosecutor would never defend in the same county where they prosecuted.

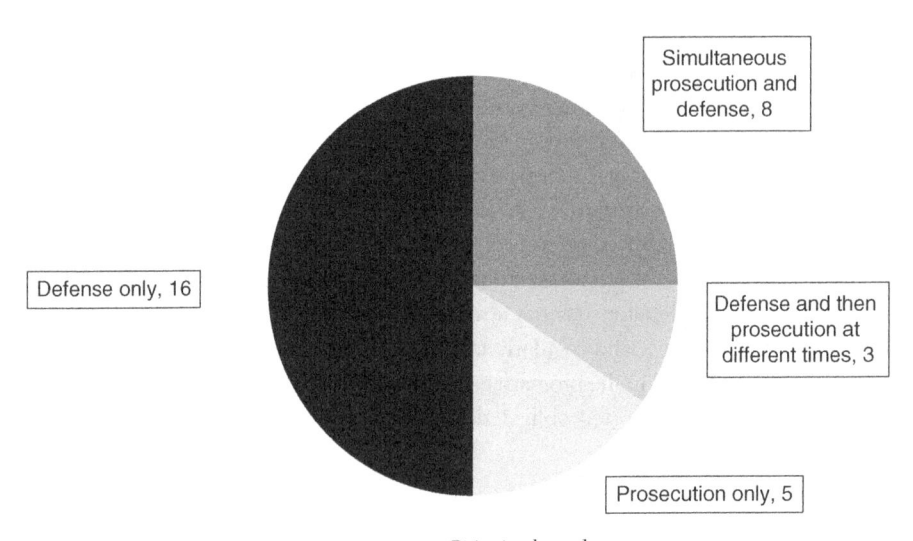

FIGURE 7.2 Criminal work

[222] Raymond, *supra* note 216.

There can still be conflicts for lawyers prosecuting and defending even in different counties. A part-time prosecutor may end up wanting to bring charges against a current or former defense client who has travelled across county lines with their criminal activity. One attorney described this exact scenario to me – a court tried to appoint her to represent a criminal defendant, but before she accepted the appointment the defendant was arrested in the county where she prosecutes.

There are also less noticeable conflicts.[223] A part-time prosecutor may not be willing to intensively cross-examine officers as part of their defense work for fear of ruining relationships that are critical to their prosecution work. A part-time prosecutor may be in a position of arguing a different interpretation of the same statute or rule depending on whether the lawyer is prosecuting or defending. None of the lawyers I interviewed raised these as concerns, though there is a separate concern that lawyers may not even realize they face these conflicts.

The lawyers in my study seemed unconcerned with conflicts. Only three State's Attorneys have stopped doing defense work. Two are too busy. Only one stopped because of perceived conflicts. He was the only participant who expressed concern about both prosecuting and defending at the same time. He likes "to keep to one side" by only doing prosecution work, preferring to communicate with other State's Attorneys without worrying about any compromised communication due to taking criminal defense cases. That attorney did limited defense work when he first entered rural practice, but has since moved entirely to prosecution.

Other lawyers did discuss the oddity of prosecuting and defending in front of the same judge. Because South Dakota judges ride circuit and appear in different counties, many of these lawyers are appearing in both capacities in front of the same judge. Stephanie Trask served as State's Attorney in Haakon County, her contract county, and would take defense court appointments in other counties. Trask explained that she would "drive over and defend in the morning in Jackson [County], and then, along with the caravan of the judge and the court services and all of the attorneys, come here and prosecute in the afternoon." Brittany Kjerstad McKnight had a similar experience. Kjerstad McKnight would "have court with the judge in the morning, and then the same judge would come over for court in the afternoon in Haakon. So, I would go from defense in front of that judge to prosecutor in front of the same judge" in the same day. The lawyers who played both roles in front of the same judge did not perceive that their practices were harmed by doing both, though it is easy to see how a lawyer in this position could end up making contradictory legal arguments.

For the eight participants who have regularly engaged in both prosecution and defense simultaneously, none expressed concern that it hampered their ability to do their job. There is a sense among some of these attorneys that doing both defense and prosecution work makes you better at both. One attorney who was new to practice at the time of our interviews was purposefully taking defense cases at the start of her

---

[223] *Id.*; Bjorkman, *supra* note 216, at 37.

career with a plan to begin serving as a prosecutor soon, explaining that she thinks "it's better to have some experience in the defense side before you just go right into being a prosecutor." Another lawyer expressed that doing both has taught her she prefers to prosecute because criminal defense clients are "harder to please" than the state.

Though prosecuting and defending creates potential and actual conflicts, it also keeps lawyers from getting siloed. Zach Pahlke noted that prosecutors in South Dakota are "fortunate" they can take criminal appointments in other counties to supplement their income. Pahlke explained that other states are more restrictive "because there is a strong sentiment among many prosecutors that defense attorneys are the enemy, or vice versa, and you have to keep them separate." Pahlke "wholeheartedly disagrees" with that perspective and thinks it is beneficial for lawyers to do both. As one mentoring attorney explained, prosecuting and defending is "a good perspective to have" because "it keeps your skills sharp" and "makes you look at cases just a little bit differently."

Despite the potential downsides to simultaneous prosecution and defense work, there are reasons that it is necessary in rural places. The State Bar of South Dakota once considered, but rejected, a rule to prohibit State's Attorneys from taking any criminal defense appointments.[224] Prohibiting part-time prosecutors from all defense work would immediately harm some of the most rural and remote counties that rely on nearby prosecutors to take court appointments. In short, there are too few lawyers in rural South Dakota to remove all of the part-time prosecutors from taking defense cases.

Run-of-the-mill defense cases would not even be the worst hit; multidefendant cases and abuse and neglect cases that require multiple appointed attorneys would create substantial problems. Across the country, court systems do not have enough lawyers to appoint, creating delays for parents seeking return of their children.[225] Several of the prosecutors who take court appointments in other counties try to limit those appointments due to driving and time constraints, but find themselves taking abuse and neglect cases where three or four attorneys are often needed, and sometimes more. Zach Pahlke is one of those lawyers, and though he prefers to limit his travel, he feels obligated to take abuse and neglect cases because of the severe lawyer shortage. If for no other reasons, the abuse and neglect proceedings are reason enough to justify having part-time prosecutors available for court appointments.

GOVERNMENT WORK

Because lawyers are working for the government when they do prosecution and court-appointed defense work, every participant has worked for the government in some capacity. But there is also other government work, including for involuntary

---

[224] *44th Annual Meeting*, St. Bar S.D. Newsl. 12, 13 (July 1976).
[225] Josh Keefe, *Lack of Attorneys Keeps Parents Waiting in Child Removal Cases*, Me. Monitor (Apr. 14, 2024), https://perma.cc/62V2-RLZ8.

commitments, serving as counsel to municipalities, and serving as counsel for other government entities. Absent was work for tribal governments, though at least one participant sought tribal government work and was turned down. Tribes often have full-time employees or contract with specialists in bigger, often urban, firms.

In South Dakota, each county has a Board of Mental Illness, the entity in charge of involuntary mental health commitment proceedings. In rural counties, local lawyers play a critical role in the involuntary commitment process. Each board must be chaired by a licensed lawyer, but the State's Attorney may not serve on the board because they represent the petitioner.[226] Four participants have served on the Boards of Mental Illness in their counties, with several serving in many counties. For example, Rachelle Norberg is currently the chair in six contiguous counties, including Todd County, home to the Rosebud Sioux Tribe. There is a separate process for involuntary commitments for drug and alcohol abuse, which is now about 90 percent of Jennifer English's practice.

Thirteen of the lawyers have served as counsel for at least one small community in South Dakota, either under an individual contract or a contract through their firm. South Dakota has cities, towns, townships, and even one village. The predominant way that these lawyers refer to their work representing municipalities is as a "city attorney" even if that municipality has a different legal structure. City, here, does not indicate larger communities – several of the "cities" represented by these lawyers have only a few hundred people.

Of the thirteen attorneys who have represented municipalities, most serve as the city attorney for their own community – only two who do city attorney work are not representing their own small towns. One because another law firm in town has the contract. Another who declined the opportunity, saying: "I've already told the city that it's not something I'm going to do" because "being in the town, living in the town, where you're city attorney – I don't think it's a good idea, frankly. I think that it should be somebody who is removed." None of the eleven lawyers who represented the town in which they practice raised concerns with doing so. But this is clearly conflict-riddled work; a few lawyers have taken conflict work from cities when the contracted city attorney had a conflict of interest in a particular matter.

Stephanie Trask, who serves as city attorney for six communities near her home base of Philip, raised a different type of conflict concern. Trask represents cities in three different counties, several of which have joint law enforcement between the county and the city. In Jackson County, which has joint law enforcement agreements, Trask is conflicted out of taking court-appointed defense work because she represents cities responsible for the law enforcement. She has stopped taking court appointments in Jackson County because "there were several that I got appointed and then, once I got into the facts," she realized she had a conflict and had to withdraw.

---

[226] The laws controlling county Boards of Mental Illness appear at S.D. CODIFIED LAWS §§ 27A-7-1 to -11. The role of the State's Attorney appears at S.D. CODIFIED LAWS § 27A-11A-4.

Trask is one of two participants representing six municipalities, the highest number, but several more represent three or four communities. The contract obligations and payments differ for the towns and lawyers. Some attend all city meetings; others only when asked. Some lawyers are helping their cities with major public works projects. Derrick Johnson has assisted Springfield with a new water treatment plant in his capacity as city attorney. When Amanda Work was the city attorney for Winner, she was almost full time, in part because Winner has its own municipal electric company, which required more legal work. Similarly, Kristen Kochekian is counsel for a town that owns its own hospital, meaning she basically serves as corporate counsel for the local hospital as part of her city attorney duties.

There are also entities in rural communities that provide critical services but are not cities. For example, Cody Miller serves as counsel for sanitation districts and road districts. Jackson Schwandt does legal work for the local school. Just like Derrick Johnson's work on a water treatment plant and Amanda Work's work with the electrical services, Miller's work with sanitation and road districts is critical to ensuring that rural communities have infrastructure, and Schwandt's work strengthens local schools.

Between these services and the advising role that prosecutors play for the counties, these lawyers are highly involved in advising local governments. Sociologists Kai Schafft and David Brown argue that: "Local government is the primary institution of rural governance. It is the nexus through which services are produced and delivered, municipal functions administered, and development strategies planned and executed."[227] These services are important. During my research, I was able to attend a city council meeting in a town of about 500 residents. The participating attorney I interviewed that day was attending the city council meeting in her role as city attorney. During even just one meeting, I watched the lawyer provide meaningful advice on several legal issues, including changes to the city plat and a more fraught topic – a request by a resident to install a new fence on his property. My former student was a confident advisor to the city council, giving them compliance advice in the moment. She talked the council through strategies about dealing with issues and what was legally allowed, or not. These lawyers serving as city attorneys are making differences in their communities and ensuring that communities can continue. This help with compliance advice, with special projects, with day-to-day operations, means that these tiny municipal governments can continue to function.

PRIVATE CIVIL WORK

Program participant Austin Hoffman's "big three" for civil work are "probates, real estate, and estate planning." That trifecta of cases is the dominant civil practice for

---

[227] BROWN & SCHAFFT, *supra* note 112, at 92.

the lawyers participating in the Rural Attorney Recruitment Program, though participants take a broad array of cases. This section describes the areas of work, noting a few particularly relevant aspects of the private civil work that participants are doing.

Estate planning – wills and trusts – was the most common practice area. Almost all lawyers do some estate planning. A few are trying to specialize in estate planning – especially trusts – for their long-term career plan. Many of those same lawyers do probate work, which is the process of distributing property after death. A law practice focusing on transfer of assets upon death makes sense, especially in rural areas with aging populations. From a financial position, estate planning and probates are good practice areas. This has been true across time and place for rural attorneys. Estate work was the dominant practice for rural lawyers in Landon's study of Missouri.[228] A 1992 article quoted a lawyer explaining "the real bread and butter for a firm in rural Kansas is estate planning."[229] More recent information from rural Australia finds the same.[230]

Next in popularity was real estate work. Most attorneys draft contracts for the sale of land and write deeds. South Dakota is a title plant state, requiring that abstractors own a full copy of recorded instruments. Rachelle Norberg is an abstractor and the only participant who owns a title plant, though Ryan McKnight was planning to purchase a title plant before leaving the program. In the western part of the state, lawyers work with mineral deeds. Other property issues, like easements, covenants, adverse possession, and lot line disputes have made their way to these lawyers.

One reason that the Rural Attorney Recruitment Program received support in South Dakota was on the premise that attorneys are good for local business. Many of the attorneys serve businesses – they draft documents to form companies and nonprofits; they structure the buying and selling of businesses; they represent businesses. They also do general litigation, including debt collection and civil defense. Yet they also hold businesses accountable. One attorney is building a practice representing plaintiffs in construction contract disputes, another helps their clients obtain insurance payouts. Still more are drafting contracts and doing general civil litigation. Several participants file income taxes for individuals and businesses. Doing business work is widely accepted by these attorneys as a core part of their job.

Family law, which arguably is just as critical to rural life as business law, has not been viewed as a core part of many rural lawyers' jobs. Family law includes divorce and custody determinations. Broadly construed, it also includes guardianships and name changes. Several attorneys do not handle divorces but will do guardianships or take appointments in abuse and neglect proceedings. Others will accept noncontested family law matters, such as adoptions or name changes.

About half of the participants take family law cases, simply viewing them as part of their practice. At least some general practice rural lawyers have long seen divorces

---

[228] LANDON, *supra* note 7, at 30, 72.
[229] Tarr, *supra* note 209, at 38.
[230] Mundy & Kennedy, *supra* note 207, at 30.

"as an unpleasant by-product of representing otherwise lucrative clients in their business dealings."[231] A few lawyers I interviewed noted that though they take family law cases, the parties can be difficult and the cases can be draining. Several lawyers perceive family law clients as needy: calling frequently, complaining about immaterial problems, and generally taking more time than it is worth to represent them, especially when "there's no winner" in these cases. One lawyer ultimately reached an equilibrium with her family law practice – she only takes one family law case at a time because "any more than that is too much drama, and I can only handle one piece of drama at a time."

About half of the participants expressed at least a general hesitancy – if not an outright distaste – for handling divorces. One attorney is willing to do simple divorces, but not complicated ones because "they can spiral into something else real quickly," and he wants to avoid the headache. Austin Hoffman "used to do divorces" but now says "I'll never do them again." Hoffman is not alone. Several attorneys tried family law and then decided to quit taking any more cases. As Casey Jo Deibert said about her short foray into family law cases: "And that was enough. I quit doing those." At the beginning of her contract, one attorney thought the contract required her to take on everything in order to meet her obligations to the community, but once she realized the Rural Attorney Recruitment Program did not require her to take all cases, she quit doing any confrontational family law cases. Another lawyer, the only female attorney in town, gets referred every family law case on the assumption that a woman wants to do family law cases, and because the established male attorneys do not want them. In the beginning, family law was the bulk of her practice, but now she no longer takes family law cases.

Some lawyers refuse divorce cases entirely. One lawyer "wasn't going to touch that with a ten-foot pole." Another tries to avoid "family law at all means." Several other attorneys stated that they have never done family law and never will. One attorney does not want to be involved in the local politics of representing divorcing spouses. Another explained she did not want to create conflicts with the estate planning work she preferred. Conflicts for part-time prosecutors are relevant here as well. Multiple prosecutors explained they avoided divorces because of their prosecutorial work, worrying about conflicts developing if they brought domestic violence charges involving divorcing spouses. Allegations of domestic abuse and child neglect can arise during divorce cases, both of which would be prosecutable and create conflicts. These scenarios have gotten other lawyers in trouble before, so at least the South Dakota lawyers are realizing potential conflicts in advance.[232]

This refusal to take family law cases exists in the older generation of lawyers as well. One mentoring attorney explained that he was thankfully able to stop taking family law cases once elected to a State's Attorney position. Several attorneys were

---

[231] Tarr, *supra* note 209, at 43.
[232] Raymond, *supra* note 216.

hired by firms where the existing lawyers did not take family law cases, and the new lawyers decided to add it to the business. One lawyer moved to a county where all other lawyers would not take divorces, allowing her to quickly pick up divorce cases because there was no local competition. Yet even those wanting divorce cases discussed the struggle of large cases, especially with farming and ranching assets. Two attorneys brought up how difficult it was for lawyers raised without agricultural knowledge to handle agricultural divorces. Several attorneys told me they only take "simple divorces."

The way these rural South Dakota lawyers choose to take, or not take, family law cases is similar to what happens in other rural areas. In rural Kansas, there are so few lawyers that the lawyers who remain "can be choosy," often limiting family law cases "that can be lengthy and emotionally involved."[233] More rural lawyers in any community could take more family law cases, especially if there were enough lawyers to create competition for other practice areas. Right now, some participants are referring family law cases to attorneys in bigger towns, who are often swamped and not able to take more divorce cases. Even if lawyers in bigger places accept the referrals, rural clients must drive substantial distances to access legal services or communicate with their attorneys remotely.

While it is regrettable that the family law needs are not being filled in rural areas, this does indicate these rural lawyers have enough other legal work to allow them to reject cases they do not want. Several attorneys told me that initially they took everything but have been able to start turning away undesirable cases as their practices become established. Quite a few attorneys told me they take anything that walks in the door, though nearly everyone followed up with at least one or two exceptions. One attorney is turning away potential clients from bigger cities with the type of work he wants to do, simply because he is too busy. Other attorneys also mentioned that they could have more work if they wanted. One attorney became licensed in Nebraska, then realized he had enough local work without expanding to Nebraska. For some lawyers who are part-time prosecutors, they might not do "enough private practice to fully justify the additional office work and expenses that come along with it." While civil work would be available to those lawyers, they might choose court appointment work in other counties to round out their legal work rather than operate a private firm.

In her study of private practitioners in South Carolina's poorest rural counties, Chambliss found that personal injury work was a significant source of income for most lawyers.[234] In rural South Dakota, personal injury work was not a significant portion of any lawyer's practice. One mentoring attorney expressed concern with taking personal injury cases because of the unknown aspect of whether you would get paid. From his perspective, "instead of taking plaintiffs' cases, hoping for a big

---

[233] Najmabadi, *supra* note 80.
[234] Chambliss, *supra* note 63.

payday, I would sell a ranch" on commission when he needed additional revenue. The stark difference in rural lawyers focusing on personal injury work between South Dakota and South Carolina is startling and needs further explanation. The size of communities, the density of population, the poverty rate, and the frequency of owning valuable agricultural land probably play a major role.

While new attorneys often take in all sorts of cases, more established attorneys start specializing. Chambliss found high levels of specialization in South Carolina, especially as attorneys gained more experience. The South Dakota lawyers I interviewed were more likely to be generalists, but that might be because of their newness to rural practice. Even within the new lawyers I interviewed, most have chosen a few areas of law in which to specialize. Victor Rapkoch explained the process of specializing well. As a new rural attorney he accepted everything, but quickly started thinking about the types of cases he wanted to do. From Rapkoch's perspective, as a rural attorney you can "narrow your practice" to areas you want. And while it might take significant time to be viewed as an expert, it is very possible to build those reputations, even in small towns. This is a double-edged sword – a specialist can make more money, but at the cost of not serving as many clients in as many areas of law. However, in my interviews I almost always heard two things. First, that specialists still did pro bono work. And, second, that the lawyer shortages are so stark that even in communities with an established specialist in one area, new lawyers could still carve out significant practices in other areas. A judge from rural Iowa told me that the rural lawyer shortage means that the lawyers "who remain become very picky about what they can take – because they can." At least right now, most of rural South Dakota is so short on attorneys that if one attorney begins to specialize, it simply opens up more space for another lawyer to engage in general practice or another specialty.

TRIBAL COURT

South Dakota's largest minority population is Native American and approximately 12 percent of the state's land is Indian Country. None of the participants do primarily Federal Indian law, and none of them serve primarily Native American clients. However, a fair number interact with the tribal court systems or otherwise provide legal services in Native American communities. The level of engagement is tied very closely to geographic proximity to tribal lands.

Zach Pahlke serves on the governing board of the Sicangu Oyate Bar Association, the bar association of the Rosebud Sioux Tribe. Pahlke is one of several participants who are members of this bar. Pahlke practices some in the Rosebud Courts and does most of his pro bono work for the tribe "because they have an even more dire lawyer situation than the state." Pahlke, like other prosecutors who serve in counties bordering reservations, interacts frequently with the federal government and tribal police about jurisdictional issues. A few lawyers take criminal defense appointments in tribal courts. One lawyer told me she would have liked to take them but knew "it was not going to be advantageous for any client" she had in tribal court because she was an outsider.

The estate planning work in Indian Country tends to be more complicated and less profitable. While no lawyers specialize in this work, several have taken part in providing pro bono services for estate planning on reservations. Other attorneys have taken pro bono appointments in tribal court or for tribal members. Part of the reason that these attorneys have not taken tribal cases is because lay advocates, who are likely more affordable, can practice in tribal courts. Another is that none view themselves as specialists in tribal law or Federal Indian law. There are such specialists in rural America, but none in this group of attorneys.

THE REMAINING JUSTICE GAP

There is skepticism about whether incentive programs like South Dakota's actually solve the access to justice crises in rural America. One criticism is that lawyers cannot do everything – there will never be enough lawyers and their services are too expensive for many rural residents to afford.[235] Another is that programs should look for ways to directly subsidize legal services for low-income clients. I suggest policies can take a broad approach at getting more lawyers to rural America, while also paying attention to access to justice concerns. Chapter 10 details the pro bono work that these lawyers do, and, while substantial, it does not fill all of the legal needs of rural communities. I look at the value of a lawyer recruitment program like South Dakota's from a different angle, asking whether a full-time attorney provides services that are worthwhile. The answer to me is clearly yes – more legal needs are met when more attorneys live in rural communities.

A 2022 report on legal needs in South Dakota found significant shortages in clients having their legal needs met.[236] Add in that South Dakota ranks dead last on a 2021 Justice Index for having the nation's worst policies for access to justice, and the situation looks dire.[237] Undoubtedly, South Dakota would be better off if rural lawyers were paid to serve low income clients, either through legal aid providers or through onsite legal assistance at local courthouses or tribal agencies. The problem is sustained funding to pay lawyers to do that work.

The justice gap continues in rural communities, but every lawyer in a community helps to close that gap. This section does not show that a new rural lawyer can take all cases, serve all clients, or close the justice gap. Instead, it shows that rural attorneys can make a difference.

---

[235] Page & Farrell, *supra* note 99.
[236] *South Dakota Legal Needs Assessment Report*, ACCESS TO JUST. (2022), https://perma.cc/A4BU-UAS4.
[237] *Justice Index*, NAT'L CTR. ACCESS TO JUST., https://perma.cc/RCL9-QWE8 (last visited Apr. 2, 2024).

LESSONS LEARNED

Rural lawyers improve their local communities. Cassie Wendt, even in just her first year practicing in Philip, has taken important cases, including indigent criminal defense cases in several rural counties. The Rural Attorney Recruitment Program has not directed Wendt or any other lawyer about what type of legal services she needs to supply. And that freedom is appropriate. Any rural lawyer program cannot micromanage the day-to-day operations of the lawyers; rather, it should be flexible enough to allow participants to chart their own paths. The program requires one pro bono case a year, but every single one of these lawyers does more than that. The paid legal services these lawyers provide help their communities. They form and advise nonprofits. They file paperwork to create small businesses. They provide legal services for community members who get to avoid long drives.

But these lawyers cannot do everything. Tribal courts remain underserved. Family law cases too often come to court with no lawyers. This is not just because potential clients cannot afford legal fees, but also that rural lawyers can be selective about what cases they take. Competition is low, so rural lawyers can decide to specialize in a certain area or reject certain kinds of cases. Potential clients are still in need of legal services and lawyers cannot do everything. Conflicts, in particular, hamper the ability of any one lawyer to do too much in a community. What I heard from South Dakota lawyers reflects rural practice in other places: That rural lawyers are more likely to face representation conflicts.[238] Those conflicts not only put rural lawyers at risk of discipline, they mean that some clients will not be able to access legal services. When there is only one attorney and that attorney has a conflict, the client has few options.[239] Yet despite the widespread opportunities for disruptive conflicts, the small and interconnected nature of the legal community keeps lawyers acting ethically because they know the other judges and lawyers will see them again and again.

---

[238] Romero, *supra* note 53, at 28 (Wyoming); Mortensen, *supra* note 164, at 42 (Australia).

[239] Helen McGowan, *The Ethical Setting: Conflicts of Interest, in* THE PLACE OF PRACTICE, *supra* note 61, at 81, 85.

8

Mentorship

FIGURE 8.1 Zach Pahlke

When Zach Pahlke moved home to Winner, South Dakota, in 2014, he joined both of his parents in their law firm. Pahlke's parents opened doors for him, and Pahlke got experience through the firm with private practice and in helping his dad with prosecutorial work. Pahlke's dad later stepped down from his elected State's Attorney role, allowing Pahlke to become State's Attorney in Tripp County. Pahlke also took on the State's Attorney role in Mellette County. A few years later when Kirby Krogman joined the Rural Attorney Recruitment Program in Mellette County as a solo practitioner, Pahlke brought Krogman on as a Deputy State's Attorney so Krogman could learn to prosecute. Once Krogman had enough experience, Pahlke stepped out of the Mellette County State's Attorney role, giving

Krogman the slot. Pahlke's sacrifice of that steady income means he has to travel more to take defense appointments in several counties, but Pahlke thinks that sacrifice is worthwhile.

Pahlke believes in the Rural Attorney Recruitment Program and in the power of mentorship. Not only did Pahlke help program participant Krogman, but Pahlke has also taken on summer interns in his role as Tripp County State's Attorney; several have expressed the desire to enter rural practice after working with Pahlke. One of those interns has already entered the program – Mason Juracek is working in Winner as a Deputy State's Attorney with Pahlke. Pahlke's mentees in the program – Krogman and Juracek – speak glowingly about Pahlke as a person and a mentor.

Pahlke thinks nothing of it. To him the mentorship provided to new rural attorneys is well worth the effort. As he explained, helping new lawyers is "paying it forward" for all the mentorship he received. Pahlke is right to make this investment, because good mentorship turns out to be one of the most significant indicators of success for new rural attorneys.

This chapter looks specifically at the mentorship that program participants received along with the particular challenges of mentorship. The majority of participants worked under an attorney, walking into an office on day one where a built-in attorney mentor was ready to help them. Some, though, started solo. This chapter first divides the participants into three groups to discuss their rural law practices: the solo practitioners, the lawyers who joined an existing firm in a satellite office, and the lawyers who worked in an office with other attorneys, whether as a law firm associate, through an office-share agreement, or as a full-time prosecutor in an established office. Only Ryan McKnight does not fit well into any of these categories because he opened a law firm office with his wife, also a new attorney. Even though they worked as a team, I categorize McKnight as a solo practitioner because he was not working with an established attorney.

The structure of how lawyers joined affected the mentorship that participants received. Figure 8.2 shows the number of attorneys who joined in each category and how many stayed in their rural jobs. As Figure 8.2 reflects, there has been an extreme outcome for satellite lawyers, with all four satellite lawyers leaving rural practice. Lawyers working at law firms were most likely to stay, with solo practitioners and full-time prosecutors falling in the middle. Some participants have transitioned to different work environments over time; the categorization here is based on first placement.

The chapter also discusses mentorship more broadly, identifying failures and successes. To do so, this chapter relies both on interviews with the thirty-two participants and interviews with many of their mentoring attorneys. Not every mentoring attorney spoke with me, though I conducted interviews with eleven mentoring attorneys and exchanged emails with several more.

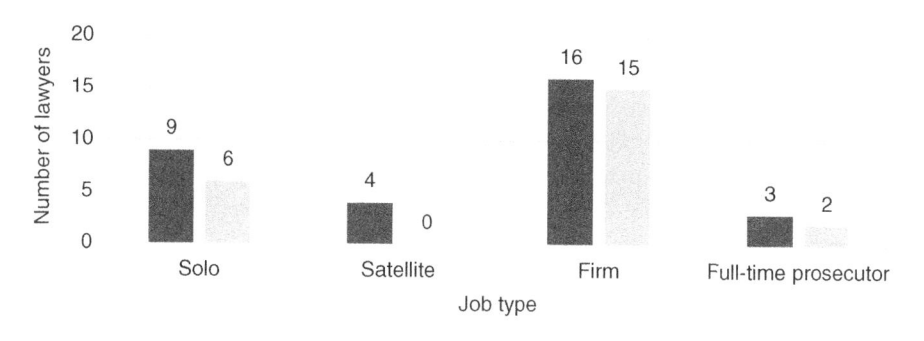

FIGURE 8.2 First hiring situation and persistence

GOING SOLO

Nine of the thirty-two Rural Attorney Recruitment Program attorneys started the program by opening their own rural law offices, with six remaining at the ten-year mark. The attorneys who started solo practices did not have built-in mentorship, but they created and nurtured various forms of mentorship.

Two solo practitioners entered rural practice after having obtained prior legal experience, easing their transitions. Stephanie Trask worked at a law firm for two years before opening a solo practice in Philip. Before Cassie Wendt also opened a solo practice in Philip, she was a prosecutor for ten years with prior experience as a paralegal doing civil legal work. When Wendt moved to Philip, her physical office was not ready and she used a room in Trask's building, which allowed Trask to mentor Wendt during her early months in rural practice. Trask was also one of several solo practitioners who had an experienced paralegal (in Trask's case, the paralegal was Wendt's mom), which also helped with the transition into rural practice.

Law school internships helped several solo practitioners prepare for rural practice. For example, Amanda LaCroix signed her contract as a first-year law student and knew for two years that she would be opening a solo law office in Martin, a town with no other practicing lawyers. During law school, LaCroix worked for a solo practitioner for two-and-a-half years to prepare for her future solo practice. Not only did the attorney provide hands-on training to LaCroix in a variety of cases, but she also accepted court-appointed criminal defense cases to give LaCroix experience in an area of law LaCroix expected to practice.

Ryan and Brittany Kjerstad McKnight opened a law firm in Philip without a local mentor. McKnight's dad, though, was a partner at one of South Dakota's largest law firms. When McKnight needed help, he would call his dad, who would then refer McKnight to someone inside the firm who could help. The model of an *entire law firm* serving as a mentor to new rural attorneys is enticing. No attorney in the firm was overburdened, yet the McKnights had access to experts in many different areas. That system of mentorship has not been replicated, but perhaps it should be.

Three solo practitioners worked as part-time Deputy State's Attorneys with established prosecutors. Two of those lawyers had part-time prosecutor positions from the beginning of their rural practice, providing some level of mentorship from day one. Kirby Krogman started solo without the benefit of a Deputy State's Attorney position and the beginning was hard for him. He had very few clients and very little work. When Krogman went to watch court, the clerk helped him get assigned to simple criminal defense cases. Slowly he started getting estate planning cases, calling up a law school professor to review his earliest work on wills and trusts. Then, one day, he got a call from Marty Jackley, South Dakota's Attorney General.

At the time, Jackley, while serving as Attorney General, had taken over a prosecutor position in a county with no local lawyers and offered to have Krogman serve as a Deputy State's Attorney. Krogman worked directly with Jackley, learning best practices on how to prosecute. Krogman also connected with Zach Pahlke, and Pahlke had Krogman work as a Deputy State's Attorney in another rural county. Krogman eventually became the State's Attorney in both of those counties, each of which has only one resident lawyer and which are two of South Dakota's lowest-population counties. For Krogman, the mentorship from Jackley and Pahlke was career changing. Jackley believes that training new rural prosecutors is something that the Attorney General's office should do and has helped that happen in several instances. Pahlke would call the Attorney General's office for help when he was a new State's Attorney. Brittany Kjerstad McKnight, who was a part-time State's Attorney during the year that she and her husband were in rural practice, explained that the Attorney General's Office was "very helpful" by "understanding that I was fresh, and they actually sent people down from Rapid City to come and just sit with me and go through everything." From Kjerstad McKnight's perspective, "I don't know what I'd have done without them."

The solo practitioners working as prosecutors had institutional support; the defenders did not. Until 2024, South Dakota had no statewide public defender office, leaving appointed defense attorneys without organized support.[240] It is important for rural practitioners that the new statewide defender office does not strip local attorneys of appointments. Rather, that statewide office will be providing mentorship and oversight of rural attorneys doing court-appointed defense.[241] Since all lawyers engaged in criminal work, having statewide mentors available to both prosecutors and defenders will ensure that all new solo practitioners have at least some mentorship.

---

[240] *Indigent Legal Services Task Force*, *supra* note 221.
[241] Andrew Davies & Alyssa Clark, *Gideon in the Desert: An Empirical Study of Providing Counsel to Criminal Defendants in Rural Places*, 71 Me. L. Rev. 245, 269 (2019); Bollweg & Fulton, *supra* note 218.

Overall, solo practitioners had to work the hardest to get mentorship, often needing to find different aspects of mentorship in different places. While some of the solo practitioners have used a paralegal or other administrative help, most solo practitioners have stayed truly solo – not hiring a secretary or paralegal. While this means they do their own administrative work, it keeps costs low. These lawyers were most likely to forgo traditional Main Street offices in favor of cheaper options. Krogman offices out of the front of his trailer home. A couple lawyers used free office space in the county courthouse. Beginning as a solo practitioner was not easy, but several of the solo practitioners are now firmly imbedded in their hometowns with strong rural practices.

A final thought about solo practitioners is due. The solo practitioners entered towns where there had previously been a well-known and well-established attorney, but that attorney was either unwilling or unable to create a successful transition plan before their retirement. If more established lawyers were able to recruit and mentor a successor *before* retirement, fewer new lawyers would need to start solo. Had Kirby Krogman been a few years older, he could have joined Mick Strain, a long-time lawyer who died the year that Krogman started law school. A few years before his death, I had the opportunity to visit Strain in his White River office and watch him practice in federal court. Strain could have offered so much to a young attorney, but the timing was off. There is a lesson here: When one-attorney towns lose their only attorney, there is an uphill battle to find a replacement. For example, a young Native American attorney who grew up on a rural reservation in South Dakota told me that one reason he did not go home was because there was no lawyer to join. Even a three-year gap between Strain and Krogman left White River starting entirely over with a new solo attorney. Krogman was willing to do it, but often the prospect of starting solo will deter new attorneys from going rural.

SATELLITE OFFICES

Early in the history of the program, four attorneys joined the program in law firm satellite offices. No satellite office placements have occurred in recent years. In communities with no existing lawyers, the idea of satellite offices is promising. A new lawyer opens an office in an underserved rural area while a distant law firm provides mentorship and otherwise eases the transition by providing secretaries, trust account management, and other law firm basics. In reality, satellite offices have not been successful for South Dakota's Rural Attorney Recruitment Program.

The four attorneys in satellite offices were associated with two different firms. One rural law firm hired three lawyers through the program and placed them in satellite offices. Jake Fischer, the very first program participant, opened a satellite office in Douglas County. Ashley Anson did the same in Aurora County and Amanda Work in Tripp County. Both Fischer and Anson opened these offices in counties near their childhood homes. Work, who grew up in rural West Virginia,

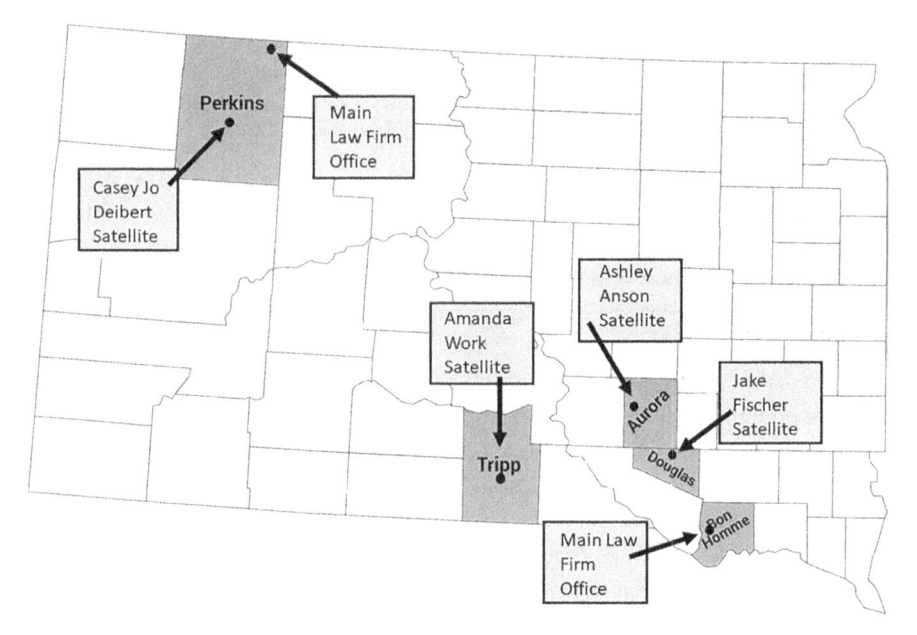

MAP 8.1 Location of satellite offices[242]

moved to a community that was entirely new to her. In the opposite corner of the state, Casey Jo Deibert, working with a different firm, opened a satellite office in Perkins County. Map 8.1 shows the physical distance between the satellite offices in this program.

None of the four lawyers are practicing law in those rural counties today. Deibert, Work, and Fischer are the only three participants who left their rural communities after completing their five-year commitment. Ashley Anson stayed in Aurora County for a year-and-a-half, then restarted the program as a solo practitioner in her home county. Even though Anson stayed in rural practice in her second placement, she does not think of herself as a success story and is working to transition away from legal practice.

These departures do not necessarily mean satellite offices should be thought of negatively moving forward. The right hiring attorney, who can provide the right mentorship and services, could likely make this a success. In fact, in South Dakota's case, there may be reasons beyond the satellite structure for these failures. The managing partner at the southeastern South Dakota law firm who had responsibility for bringing in three of these attorneys was disciplined by the State Bar of South Dakota in 2020 and again in 2021.[243] To be very clear, none of the three attorneys associated

---

[242] Created under A Creative Commons Attribution-ShareAlike 4.0 International License at mapchart.net on April 4, 2024.
[243] 939 N.W.2d 855 (2020); 955 N.W.2d 753 (2021).

with the Rural Attorney Recruitment Program were involved in the disciplinary cases. Yet, in the disciplinary cases, the South Dakota Supreme Court describes a high level of turnover and turmoil in the firm during the time period that all three attorneys left. Unrelated to the Rural Attorney Recruitment Program, I was assigned by my employer to work with the law firm on a project in 2019. The associate I worked with was not a Rural Attorney Recruitment Program participant, but my own interaction with the firm was one characterized by poor communication and planning; I felt the associate assigned to work with me had insufficient information to accomplish his tasks. The law firm declined to comment on its perception of the program, leaving questions unanswered about the workability of the satellite model.

In looking outside of South Dakota for a successful satellite office model, I found one in North Dakota with an attorney working and living on the Standing Rock Reservation who works remotely for a Colorado law firm. That attorney was a solo practitioner when she joined the firm hoping for mentorship and firm support. For her, the satellite model has been a success and has improved her rural practice. Even acknowledging success is possible, there are special problems to consider with satellite offices. Office space becomes a concern, and potentially bigger expense, when law firms open a satellite office. Whereas cleaning out an old office in the same building is essentially free for a rural firm, acquiring a new building or office in another town is more expensive. Casey Jo Deibert was able to office in the courthouse, preventing issues there. The law firm that hired three rural associates acquired office space for all of them.

Mentorship will naturally be more difficult in satellite offices, with mentor attorneys needing to work harder to provide mentorship remotely. Of the four participants in satellite offices, Jake Fischer had the best mentorship experience. Fischer was unique because he started in the main law firm office, allowing him to build a close mentorship relationship before moving to a satellite office. Fischer also had the advantage of prior legal experience before joining the firm. Amanda Work's office was farthest from her home firm, and she found more mentorship with local attorneys than with her hiring firm. The difficulty of distance mentorship is no secret for the mentors or the mentees – Shane Penfield, who brought on Casey Jo Deibert in a satellite office, told me about the difficulty he had in providing mentorship to Deibert when she was so far away. Mentorship in satellite offices is not inherently doomed to failure: Think of Fischer who left rural practice having had a good experience with both the program and the firm. Satellite mentorship, though, takes more work.

Distance can also complicate the provision of services to the attorney. Things like secretarial help, answering phones, and managing trust accounts will be more complicated in satellite offices. Though not impossible to overcome, there is a natural barrier for a new attorney to use the services provided in the home office. In one instance, a satellite office opened with an established paralegal, easing the administrative burden on one participant. That sort of structure is possible, but expensive.

As new lawyers consider embarking on careers in satellite offices, care must be taken to ensure there will be adequate support and mentorship, otherwise the benefits of starting associated with a firm may end up being minimal.

JOINING AN OFFICE

Most of the participants in the Rural Attorney Recruitment Program connected with an existing attorney and worked in the same building as their mentor. Three attorneys joined prosecutor offices as full-time employees with salaries paid by the county. One full-time prosecutor left, but the other two stayed. Sixteen attorneys joined private practice firms either as employees or in an office-share agreement, and all but one has stayed in the rural practice of law.

The sixteen lawyers who joined a firm's main office constitute exactly half of the program participants, and the experiences they had vary wildly. Most new attorneys joining an existing firm started with a base salary, some with a low base salary supplemented with a commission based on what they earned. A few others started in an eat-what-you-kill model, then paid a percentage of their proceeds to the firm to cover overhead costs. The model of paying into the firm makes more sense for attorneys in an office where they benefit from physical space and administrative assistance than, say, a satellite office where it is hard to take advantage of office support. A couple of attorneys started with an office-share agreement, though were not technically associated with the firm. Mentors expressed a concern about taking on the expense of a salaried associate because a firm might not break even with paying an associate a salary. Especially for solo practitioners, losing money on an associate is a difficult prospect.

The mentors who brought in these new attorneys made different levels of sacrifices to make the new lawyers' rural practice possible. Most hiring attorneys directed business to the new rural attorneys, sharing clients in a way that would give the new lawyers sufficient work and build experience. A few examples of mentoring attorneys assisting their new attorneys are worth sharing. Herb Sundall brought Amy Jo Janssen into his Kennebec firm on salary, and she remained salaried for three years. Then, when Sundall was ready to retire, Janssen took over the firm, having her rural attorney stipend begin once she was no longer on salary. Greg Protsch brought Kristian Ellendorf into his Howard firm on salary with a five-year plan to make her self-sufficient. But after only a year he proposed they go fifty/fifty on the firm, a deal that continues today. Kent Lehr brought Derrick Johnson into his Scotland firm on salary. Johnson first transitioned to merely sharing office space and sharing a secretary, and during this time Lehr did not charge Johnson rent. Then Johnson opened his own office in a different town, but Lehr continued to mentor Johnson from a distance.

Many other lawyers were similarly helpful and supportive of their new associates. The level of sacrifice and dedication provided by many of these mentors is particularly notable because many of them were not looking to hire another attorney. Rather, they opened their doors when a new attorney showed up in town interested in opening a practice. Several times, a new rural attorney assumed they would have to open a solo office, but when they went to meet local attorneys, someone offered a spot in their firm. That happened for Victor Rapkoch when he met Dana Frohling. I was struck when I learned that Frohling ran for State's Attorney only because he was bringing Rapkoch into his firm and Rapkoch wanted to prosecute. When Rapkoch was later ready to become State's Attorney himself, Frohling gave up his position for Rapkoch to assume the role. When Kristen Kochekian relocated to South Dakota to participate in the program, Paul Gillette offered to help in any structure Kochekian wanted, whether he would just serve as a local mentor, whether she would be solo but rent an office from him, or whether she would join his firm. Kochekian decided to join Gillette's firm, where she remains today, almost ten years later. In a few other instances, local lawyers made offers to incoming lawyers and, even when the new lawyer declined the offer, the local lawyer remained as an important mentor.

Not all law firm mentorship situations were good, and occasionally they sounded almost extractive. Underpaying salaries. Collecting a percentage of earnings without providing administrative support or substantial mentorship. Leaving town immediately once new attorneys passed the bar, providing no real mentorship. Asking new attorneys to take over law office management duties too soon while the mentor phased into retirement. Never making time to answer questions.

Joining an existing office is not a panacea, but it has mostly worked better for participants. Only one participating attorney who joined a firm has left the program, and that participant left to be a teacher. That participant, Elizabeth Steptoe, had only positive things to say about her hiring attorney, and her hiring attorney had only positive things to say about Steptoe. They remain in touch, both mentoring a new rural lawyer who joined the Rural Attorney Recruitment Program and the firm after graduating from law school in 2024. Every other lawyer who has joined a firm's main office has stayed in rural practice. Several lawyers who joined an existing firm have left that firm to start their own solo business, but none have left their rural communities.

THE MENTEE'S PERSPECTIVE

Mentorship comes in different forms. Participating lawyers spoke glowingly of different types of mentors – attorneys who hired them, other attorneys in the region and state, and even nonlawyers, like a trusted paralegal. Probably because of the small size of the South Dakota legal community, very few participants were willing to say *negative* comments about the attorneys who hired them, though it is clear that some mentorship relationships were better than others. The various types and qualities of mentorship are surveyed here, though I do so very broadly in the hope that individual experiences do not eclipse the more important message that mentorship is *one of the most determinative factors for attorneys to succeed in a rural area.* In her dissertation on rural lawyers in Wyoming, Ashli Tomisich concluded that mentorship and an independent spirit are the two most important attributes for success in rural practice, and that having an experienced lawyer in the same office was particularly crucial.[244] I agree with those conclusions, only adding that the independent spirit, perhaps best labelled as having grit and determination, was particularly important for new lawyers without good mentors.

There are ways to receive mentorship other than being hired into a firm and receiving mentorship from those hiring lawyers. For lawyers who started solo practices, or who were hired by lawyers uninterested in hands-on mentorship, other forms of mentorship emerged. But it was always important for mentorship to exist. Law school only does so much; law schools are not producing lawyers who are ready to practice without mentorship. Everyone understood this – mentors and mentees alike. Because the legal profession relies on "learning by doing," workplace mentors are crucial.[245] In the Wyoming study, every new lawyer interviewed felt unprepared for actual practice.[246] It wasn't quite that bad in South Dakota, though only because several participating lawyers sought out practical experience during law school.

Several attorneys interned with rural lawyers during law school to get rural practice experience. While most spoke glowingly of their summers in a rural law office, not all experiences were positive. One participant had such a bad experience in her summer internship that she decided against rural law practice, and it took years to come back around to the idea of making a career as a rural lawyer.

Several attorneys started at their law firms before passing the bar, getting experience under the limited practice rules available for recent law school graduates. A few more had worked in law offices *before* law school, giving them at least a general idea of how to manage cases. Three clerked for judges in South Dakota after law school but before beginning rural practice. That was particularly useful for Rachel Mairose who clerked in the same circuit where she practices. Mairose noted that "the first time I had to appear in court" as a prosecutor "it just took half the stress out of the matter, having already been in the courtroom several times and already knowing the judge, so all I could be stressed out about was just the cases themselves."

For the attorneys who came from prior legal jobs, the previous legal experience was vitally important. Stephanie Trask is typical in describing the importance of her prior firm work, saying "I probably would have been too terrified to even consider solo practice without those two years under a firm and guidance and support." Overall, "those two years were extremely useful to me figuring out how to start off and run a solo practice with no onsite resource of any kind."

---

[244] Tomisich, *supra* note 53, at 79, 110.
[245] Jeff Giddings & Michael McNamara, *Constructive Supervision in Regional, Rural and Remote Legal Practice*, in THE PLACE OF PRACTICE, *supra* note 61, at 219.
[246] Tomisich, *supra* note 53, at 61–62, 113.

For a few of the attorneys – especially those in solo practices – mentorship from paralegals was important. When Ryan and Brittany Kjerstad McKnight purchased a firm in Philip, the paralegal stayed and helped them get up-to-date on cases and learn local rules. That same paralegal worked with Stephanie Trask when Trask started her solo practice in Philip. Trask noted "she brought a wealth of experience with her to me that I drew heavily on." When Dusty Ginsbach took over as State's Attorney, the paralegal stayed. Ginsbach noted "she showed me everything that I needed to do, and without her I couldn't have done it." When Victor Rapkoch left the firm that had hired him, his transition to solo practice was easier because a secretary came with him. When Rachelle Norberg took over a firm, all three staff members agreed to stay through the lawyer transition for at least two years so Norberg would not have to train any more staff right away. Plus, their "institutional knowledge" was "invaluable" as Norberg began practice. Other participants in firms talked about the importance of support staff.

Local clerks of courts and judges provided forms of mentorship. Participants noted the tips they received from clerks of courts, including prompting to take certain court appointments. One participant described his local judge as "kind of a hard ass" but "that being said, [the judge] made me a better attorney" because the judge would tell the young lawyer when he did something wrong. Other participants had judges who would tell them after a hearing how to do better the next time. Once, a judge connected a struggling solo practitioner with a firm in a larger town that had legal work to share.

Lawyers outside of participants' firms played a critical role in mentoring these new attorneys. Some participants said the mentorship they got from other South Dakota attorneys was more useful than the mentorship they received inside their firms. In most instances, local lawyers would "go out of their way" to involve the new attorneys. Nearby attorneys reached out to new lawyers offering to provide forms or other assistance. Many lawyers across the state responded to requests for assistance. Kristen Kochekian, licensed to practice in North Carolina and Virginia before moving to South Dakota, found the South Dakota bar to be much more supportive and giving than in the larger states where she had practiced. Zach Pahlke found mentors "from all over the state" who helped of their own good will. Lawyers were generally giving of their time, choosing to help other lawyers improve rather than worry about helping a competitor. Yet the discussion in Chapter 6 about the degree of acceptance by the local lawyers shows that not all new lawyers were able to rely on professional mentorship.

Not all mentors are equal. One solo practitioner "felt like I had no idea what I was doing, and very limited means to figure that out" even though local lawyers said they would help. Some participants noted that their mentors were busy with "their own lives, their own practices" and had limited capacity to provide real mentorship. Some attorneys would try to get help from their hiring attorney but would never get a full explanation of how to handle a case and were given only limited time. Some attorneys had mentorship assignments through the state bar, but those mentors were sometimes "not very helpful at all." One lawyer described her mentor as "great," but "super, super busy," which meant she could not return phone calls or emails in a timely fashion. Some mentors genuinely tried, but they just were not good teachers.

For the attorneys who had a good mentor, it was really good. One participant met with her mentor every day for two years and still consults with him frequently. Another participant says her hiring lawyer's mentorship is "something I cherish more than anything – I mean, he became my family." Another participant says she "couldn't have picked a better person to practice with." Another participant will be "forever grateful for those five years because going straight out of law school, you know jack squat as far as regular practice." Another participant said "I couldn't have done it on my own" without the mentoring attorney, and that sentiment was widely shared by participants hired into firms. I count four mentors who gave up elected State's Attorney roles to give their mentees the chance at the stable income and benefits that come with the position, which is a major sacrifice.

THE MENTOR'S PERSPECTIVE

The mentors I spoke to were mostly happy with their experiences in bringing in a new lawyer, though few thought the process was easy. As one said, law school does not teach "how to practice law on a day-to-day basis" and that is left to on-the-job training. Most mentors recognized that their mentorship was critical to getting new attorneys established, and so they were willing to give of their time. This was especially true of mentors who had been trying to hire. Some mentors desperately wanted to hire to ensure they could hand off their practice instead of closing down at retirement.

The only mentors who thought the process was easy were mentors who took a hands-off approach. As one mentor said it, the mentee "has pretty much done it on her own." Yet mentees in those situations generally craved more hands-on mentorship. A few mentors thought handing off forms, files, and office space was good enough. That is better than nothing, but it isn't enough. Good mentorship takes supervision.[247] One successful mentor told me that a year minimum of daily contact is probably needed for a successful transition, though several less-successful mentors provided far less time than that. One mentor, who did a fast hand-off, explained that his firm provided "too much work for one, and not enough work for two," which made it difficult to execute a transition.

Mentorship of new attorneys, like many things, takes time and effort. There is a skill set to mentorship.[248] Almost all of the hiring attorneys in this program were hiring for the first time in their careers. They had mostly been solo practitioners or

---

[247] Giddings & McNamara, *supra* note 245, at 222.
[248] HAMILTON, *supra* note 176, at 62.

had been the most recent hire into their firm decades earlier. These mentors had no experience mentoring new lawyers; no template for the best ways to train someone into the practice of law. This lack of experience was especially acute for established lawyers who were not really interested in hiring a new associate but ended up doing it anyway because a new lawyer showed up in town.

There were plenty of successful mentorship relationships even where the mentor was not necessarily looking to hire. One mentor said the attorney "just showed up" in town and he decided "to help him out" by bringing him into the firm. Greg Protsch hired Kristian Ellendorf after "she called me out of the blue." Though Protsch was not looking to hire at the time, he now says that phone call was "the best thing that's ever happened to this law firm."

Mentors carry a heavy weight of wondering if they have recruited someone who will stay. There is a fear of hiring an attorney, providing training and experience, then having the young attorney leave for a bigger city. This is a widespread concern in rural hiring, appearing not just in my interviews, but also in the South Carolina study and a survey of rural attorneys in Oregon.[249]

When I spoke with the mentoring attorneys about how to get more aging lawyers to take on mentees and hand off their firms, specific ideas were lacking. Several suggested financial incentives for the older lawyers, though it is hard to imagine a program finding money to pay a well-compensated senior attorney. Plus, most saw mentorship as something a program could not really incentivize. One explained that for lawyers the willingness to mentor "lies within themselves as how they feel about their career, about their clients, who become friends quite frankly. That's best within the senior attorney, and their kind of character." This idea, essentially an "intrinsic desire to 'pay it forward,'" is a crucial part of successful mentorship and appeared throughout my interviews with mentors.[250] One mentoring attorney told me that having someone take over his practice "doesn't help me" at all, but he still did it because it helped the new attorney. Many of the mentoring attorneys took a wider perspective on the value of handing off a practice, thinking of it as an investment in the community. As one said, he has a clientele and it would "be hard to shut the door."

For attorneys wanting to retire, either immediately or after a couple of years, the predominant method of handoff was that the mentor did not sell the practice, but instead sold or rented the building and its contents to the new attorney. The established lawyers who ended up mentoring, and thus gave me interviews, were lawyers willing to come up with reasonable transition plans. Participants walked away from other established lawyers trying to sell a practice for profit. For the attorneys convinced that their practice is worth money, it is hard to convince them to give it away for free, especially if they must sacrifice time and money to train an associate.

---

[249] Chambliss, *supra* note 63; Collins, *supra* note 53, at 19.
[250] HAMILTON, *supra* note 176, at 66.

For some older lawyers, it does take convincing. Even mentors who were excited to hire new attorneys found it "burdensome to pay salaries." One lawyer described it as a "double whammy" in losing money – the established attorneys not only pay the young attorneys but also give time to mentorship, reducing their own income-earning potential. Because good mentorship is time intensive, it will always cost the mentor something, a concern that appears elsewhere in studies of rural lawyers.[251] One attorney near retirement told me that for many of these older rural attorneys, "the practice of law is not just what they did; it's who they are" and that in order to convince them to do a handoff, "they need to be convinced that they are doing what's right for the community that supported them, and built their life for them during their entire practice." If we fail to convince aging lawyers to transition their practices, "all you've really done is just made things worse and made it harder on the community."

PAYING IT FORWARD

Mason Juracek was the last participant to join the program before the ten-year anniversary. His entry into the program may become emblematic of the future. Juracek is working with Zach Pahlke, a prior participant in the program. Pahlke not only brought Juracek in as a law student intern, then as a newly licensed attorney, but Pahlke also was actively engaged in figuring out Juracek's contract with the county and the type of employment Juracek would have. From Juracek's perspective, it was a lot easier to take the rural attorney job knowing that a young lawyer was there to serve as mentor. Pahlke's success – and willingness to pay it forward – is opening doors for another rural attorney.

Most of the participating lawyers are invested in bringing more rural attorneys into their communities. Many participants have had interns. I heard about high school, college, and law school interns in these rural practices. Some of those interns joined or plan to join the program. Those internships are critical in recruiting the next generation of rural lawyers, and hosting interns will get easier with recently announced funding for law student internships.[252] While a high school student will provide little actual help to a lawyer, a lawyer can change a high school student's career trajectory by exposing them to the legal profession. Local internships allow students to understand local career opportunities.[253] If rural students know that a professional job is available in their rural community, perhaps they are more likely to pursue an education that will bring them back home.

Participants have also opened their offices to new rural lawyers. Two participants work together in a firm; two participants share office space; one participant works

---

[251] Giddings & McNamara, *supra* note 245, at 229 (Australia); Tomisich, *supra* note 53, at 79–80 (Wyoming).
[252] *Rural Internship Incentive Program*, St. Bar S.D. (2024), https://perma.cc/GZ98-RZ97.
[253] Ricket, Yahn & Bentley, *supra* note 147, at 14.

as a Deputy State's Attorney for another participant. Another participant has hired associate attorneys. Several participants would add a new associate attorney to their firm if they could find an interested lawyer. One participant entered into her contract knowing a law student wanted to do the same – during the presentation to the local government, the first participant made known that another attorney would be coming who they should also support. One attorney who saw resistance at his county has actively worked on developing a relationship with the commissioners and now thinks he can "get them on board" for another contract. With the commissioners on board, he's actively working to recruit to his rural community. In short, these lawyers are very open to more rural lawyers.

Outside of hiring, there are other attempts to create pathways to rural practice. One county hosts "Government Days" for its high school seniors, where the students come and watch court. The attorneys explain their jobs and how being a rural attorney is a viable career choice. As one participant noted, Government Days might be more successful in recruiting high school students to the law if there are at least some youthful lawyers on display.

Two attorneys who left the program recruit in their teaching jobs. Elizabeth Steptoe stayed in her rural community after leaving the program and is now teaching middle and high school. Steptoe finds herself talking to her students about what it was like to be a lawyer and has even arranged job shadowing for interested students to spend time with local attorneys. Ryan McKnight now teaches at South Dakota State University, the state's agricultural college. When the university recruited McKnight away from rural practice, a faculty member told McKnight "we actually have quite a few kids from Western South Dakota" and that perhaps McKnight can "help them get to law school and go back and help out [their] communities." For McKnight, this made him realize that college teaching and "getting kids excited about law school" was his "calling." He now regularly mentors students heading to law school and realizes he can make the biggest difference encouraging rural practice in the next generation.

LESSONS LEARNED

Mentorship is important. Zach Pahlke is one of several participants who have already demonstrated their willingness to help the next wave of lawyers. These lawyers help each other. When I asked about mentorship, many of the participating lawyers told me about other participants they call for help on particular types of cases. Sometimes they send referrals, but other times just call for advice.

Mentorship is an essential component for success in a rural lawyer program, and the program in South Dakota has realized this. In 2022, the Rural Attorney Recruitment Program changed its standard contract to require that participants sign up for a state bar sponsored mentorship program to mitigate concerns about mentorship. Whether this formal requirement makes any difference is yet to be seen, and there are reasons to doubt that a formalized mentorship requirement will make the difference. While some assigned mentors were wonderful, some failed to make themselves available.

Many of these new attorneys were scared when they started. Law school taught them the law, but not everything they needed to know in practice. Meeting with clients and answering phone calls was fraught – there was a fear for some attorneys that being unable to answer a client question in the moment would be a problem. Thankfully, most participants had mentors who helped them settle into rural practice. For some participants, the lack of mentorship has hampered their ability to form successful practices. A few participants told me about the hours they wasted early on in their practices, digging through legal research when a senior attorney probably could have immediately answered the question. Several participants told me they turn down cases they would take if they had better mentors to guide them. This is bad for the participants and bad for the local clients who cannot get their legal needs met in their own communities. But when there is good mentorship, it can be really good: Some of the mentorship stories I heard during the interviews powerfully demonstrated the value and importance of solid mentorship for a new rural lawyer.

9

The Finances of Practice

FIGURE 9.1 Rachel Mairose

Rachel Mairose comes from a large farm family, the sixth of ten children. Mairose graduated from a private college in Iowa, then did well in law school at the University of South Dakota. Among other things, Mairose was an editor on the *South Dakota Law Review* where she published an article about third-party custody of children.[254] Following law school, Mairose clerked for one year for a trial court in South Dakota, living in her parents' basement for her clerkship year. Then she joined a law firm in Plankinton, population 778. The firm she joined had two lawyers, a husband and wife, though only the husband was really practicing by the time Mairose arrived in

---

[254] Mairose, *supra* note 172.

2019. John Steele, the practicing lawyer, started Mairose as an employee, paying her 4,000 dollars per month the first few months, with the understanding they would soon begin a partnership. In January 2020 they formed Mairose & Steele with a 5,000 dollar buy-in. With the new firm, the two lawyers began to earn a percentage based on how much work they do. Each lawyer takes home 35 percent of their gross earnings each month, then at the end of the year they make an additional distribution if excess funds are available after covering overheads. Steele continues to own the building, which the firm rents.

Mairose's first stipend payment arrived in the fall of 2020, after one year in private practice. In 2020, her first full calendar year in private practice, and her first year as a partner in the firm, Mairose only took home about 23,000 dollars from her private practice. That year, the stipend "mattered a lot." That first year-and-a-half, Mairose was stressed – even answering the phones was hard because she "felt so uncomfortable not being able to answer someone's question." But then, Mairose became more comfortable in her practice, she survived the "substantial learning curve," and, in 2021, Mairose almost tripled her earnings, taking home closer to 70,000 dollars from private practice. Even by year two, the stipend "didn't matter as much – it was more like a bonus." During that same time frame, Steele moved closer to retirement, even leaving Plankinton for Sioux Falls. Mairose raised her hourly rate by 25 dollars an hour from 125 dollars to 150 dollars and was able to take on many of Steele's clients. Mairose still calls Steele for help, though she is now mostly a solo practitioner with one staff member.

There is no typical financial situation for these rural lawyers, but Mairose's story shows a few trends. First, even just one year of clerking likely helped Mairose become self-sufficient sooner. Lawyers with prior practice experience did better early on in their rural careers. Second, Mairose joined a firm and was initially paid as an employee, giving her stability right at the beginning of practice. Then that stability gave way to higher earning potential when Mairose became a partner. Third, like many participants, the first year was scarce. Mairose increased her income more quickly than many others, but the general trend holds – Mairose earned more in her second year than her first, showing the importance of early financial support.

Throughout this book, I hope I have made the case that rural lawyers are serving rural clients and rural communities. But even if this is true, it does not necessarily mean rural communities are a good place for lawyers to make their careers. The financial viability of rural practice is a critical piece of analyzing whether rural lawyer incentive programs are worthwhile. After all, policies should neither doom lawyers to poor wages nor waste government incentive money on unsustainable jobs. With that said, in general the lawyers in the South Dakota program have been satisfied with their financial situations in rural practice, though a few have found their income insufficient.

There is very little data available to draw comparisons for how the South Dakota rural lawyers are doing. Current data on lawyer salaries does not take into account rural/urban differences, though it can provide some insight based on firm size. The few studies of rural lawyer incomes differ in time and place, though studies of rural lawyers in Missouri in the 1980s, Australia in the 2010s, and South Carolina in the 2020s provide some insight.[255] Scholarship on the broader context of rural economic decline is important to understanding how rural lawyers operate but does not provide direct data about lawyer salaries. Needing to rely more on individual reports of financial stability, this chapter shows that, with a few exceptions, rural law practice has proven to be financially viable for these new lawyers.

EARLY FINANCIAL HARDSHIPS

The beginning of rural practice was financially difficult for most attorneys. A variety of factors play into why the first year was so hard. Solo practitioners had a tougher start than those who were hired into firms. Even for those joining firms, the pay structure made a difference. Some attorneys were given a salary and benefits; other new attorneys were in an eat-what-you-kill environment, immediately responsible for their own income. Sometimes hiring lawyers provided free overhead costs, other times hiring lawyers took a percentage of earnings. Even lawyers lucky enough to receive a paycheck did not necessarily have it made – one lawyer earned 20 dollars an hour as a new attorney; another lawyer earned a Deputy State's Attorney salary of 1,600 dollars a month for working thirty hours a week. Being hired into a firm was not a guarantee that the first few years would be financially easy. There was a general sense that "no one makes a lot of money their first year."

For the lawyers who had to take the bar multiple times, the delay in a bar license caused financial setbacks, making the first few years harder. Before bar passage, I heard of 18 dollars an hour hourly work and a 40,000 dollar salary. One hopeful participant left after she failed the bar because she could not afford to stay and try again. Most lawyers stuck it out in their rural areas, retaking the bar if needed and suffering decreased income while they powered through a second or third attempt. The delay in licensure made the early years harder but has not impacted long-term satisfaction with earnings.

The financial difficulty at the beginning of practice led to the stipend being vitally important for most new lawyers. Most lawyers thought their economic survival would have been impossible in the beginning without the stipend. Some lawyers felt stable after a year, for others it took two or three. Only four lawyers did not see the stipend as particularly important, but all four had other sources of income – two had other careers and two had husbands with stable employment. For most, though, the stipend was hugely important. For a few, the stipend was not enough. Many had to live frugally, often relying on the financial support of family members. One solo practitioner commented that "the information surrounding this program

---

[255] LANDON, *supra* note 7, at 31; Caroline Hart, *Entrepreneurship and Innovation in Regional and Rural Law Practice*, in THE PLACE OF PRACTICE, *supra* note 61, at 104; Chambliss, *supra* note 63.

needs to be a lot more transparent in what you're getting into because I was not prepared to live in poverty for basically two years."

South Dakota has spread incentive payments over five years, but other states have concentrated payments earlier on to combat the difficulties of that first year of practice. Incubator programs, like that of Arkansas, focus on start-up costs. The Illinois stipend provides half the money right away and half after the first year. South Dakota provides no funding until the first year is complete. One participant, when she set up her solo practice, thought she would receive the stipend payment immediately, rather than at the end of the year. The wait was problematic.

Considering that there is a year wait before the first incentive payment, the possibility exists for an improved incentive program to play an increased role in making sure there is early economic stability, especially for solo practitioners. Several participants said the delay left new lawyers with insufficient support. Several floated the idea of having payments monthly rather than annually; others mentioned there should be a separate pot of money to help solo practitioners set up offices. A few participants arranged to get part of their stipends early if the county (or the law firm paying on behalf of the county) paid up front. For new solo practitioners, an initial payment more akin to an incubator program would help.

Even without moving to an incubator format, a program can do more work to ease the transition for rural lawyers. When Ryan and Brittany Kjerstad McKnight moved to Philip, the Project Rural Practice leaders supported them and the community knew in advance. Importantly, the clerks of court in the region "were nothing but fantastic out there. As soon as they found out we were coming, they put us on the list" for court appointments. McKnight notes they were not getting "a big felony case," but were getting "all these misdemeanors nobody else wants just so they can actually start making some money." The first paycheck for their indigent defense cases felt like a major victory, and it only took two or three months to get in a groove with court appointments. Advanced communication and planning, as happened with the McKnights, could make the earliest days in practice easier.

Two separate lawyers, using nearly the same verbiage, described the stipend payment the first year as critically important, but as time went on the stipend began to feel like "a bonus." That tracks for most participants. For one, the stipend had a "huge impact on my family," for another "it was from heaven to get it," for another it was a "huge help" for the first three years, for another "it was very helpful," for quite a few lawyers "it mattered a lot." Some clarified that because of other streams of income – whether spouses or parental help – they likely would have survived in their rural communities without the stipend, though it would have been harder. Others think they would have left without the stipend. Austin Hoffman thinks he likely would have worked at a firm in a larger community, though now he is "doing very well" and has to turn away work. Several others think they would have walked away from rural practice without the stipend, and several more say the only reason they survived was because of the financial support provided by their hiring firm.

South Dakota's stipend lasts for five years. The participants used their stipends for various expenses. By far the most popular use for the stipends was to pay student loans. Several more used the stipend to pay for houses or land; one bought a commercial building with her first stipend to house her law firm; there were also payments to the business loans used to operate law firms. A couple of participants who were solo practitioners described the stipend as a direct coverage of their overhead costs. A couple of participants used that money to hire an employee for the law firm. Another, worried about the lack of retirement benefits, puts all of the stipend funds into retirement accounts. There were also other payments – of college tuition for a child, of airplane tickets to visit family out of state, of medical procedures.

The precarity of financial situations varied greatly. Six had some other form of employment during their time as a lawyer. Two rely on ranch work for income, and several more help with farming or ranching duties. There are several veterans and three lawyers in the National Guard. Military service comes with pay and health insurance, cutting down on the monthly costs of operating a law firm. One participant drove to a larger community to work at Starbucks early on "to make ends meet," though that was not permanently necessary. Then, there is Dusty Ginsbach, who has a different work relationship with the legal field than any other participant.

When Dusty Ginsbach graduated from law school and passed the bar, he fully intended to move back to northwest South Dakota. He was open to various communities in the region, even interviewing at several offices and getting a job offer from a small firm willing to pay 35,000 dollars a year in salary. After running into a high school classmate making almost twice that working in the oil fields of northwest South Dakota, Ginsbach took a full-time job with an oil company, working not as a lawyer but in the field monitoring drills. Pretty quickly after that, Ginsbach got a city attorney contract, then later became State's Attorney – all the while continuing his full-time oil job. Ultimately, Ginsbach signed with the Rural Attorney Recruitment Program. At various times, Ginsbach would ramp up his legal practice, anticipating a departure from his oil work, but every time he did so, the oil company offered him a raise. For the five-year period of the program, Ginsbach essentially worked two full-time jobs. The stipend mattered less for Ginsbach than almost any other participant, and since the program ended for Ginsbach, he now maintains a part-time law practice and his full time oil job. Ginsbach and his wife also ranch and own real estate; I spent the night in their newly remodeled hotel.

Perhaps for some, the idea that a lawyer took a stipend then ended up in only part-time practice looks like a failure, but I disagree. Ginsbach is the *only* lawyer in Harding County, which is in a very isolated part of the state. Harding County borders rural portions of North Dakota and Montana, which don't exactly have spare lawyers. In South Dakota, Harding County borders Perkins County, with two lawyers, and Butte County, with thirteen. The two Perkins County lawyers are ninety-eight miles away from Ginsbach, and the Butte County lawyers are seventy miles away. Without Ginsbach, a corner of South Dakota is empty. Yet when Ginsbach started – despite the huge legal need in that part of the state – he was unable to financially take a legal job. The fact that Ginsbach is available as a part-time lawyer is a testament both to his work ethic (which is incredibly high) and to why financial assistance programs are needed.

Ginsbach slowly entered the legal world, and he always had other sources of income. Most lawyers don't. Other than Ginsbach, the lawyers who moved to rural areas started their rural practices right away or as soon as they passed the bar. They did not have a few years to warm up to the practice of law, and they did not have the financial security of a second job. New lawyers face a steep learning curve and need hands-on experience. Think about Rachel Mairose. She entered rural practice with a year of trial-level clerkship experience but was still hesitant to answer questions on the phone during her first year of private practice. No stipend can take away the stress of the first year of practice because there will still be a steep learning curve and high levels of responsibility. What the stipend can do is mitigate the financial risks associated with starting in a rural location. Even if the timing of the first stipend payment can be questioned, the value of the stipend itself cannot.

GOVERNMENT PAY

Chapter 7 establishes that every participant has worked for the government in some capacity. Government work is a critical component to the financial viability of these rural lawyers. A few things come into play with government work. To begin, some – but not all – of the State's Attorneys are receiving employment benefits – most notably retirement and health insurance. None of the public defense work in these rural communities comes with those benefits because there is no salaried defense work – it is all done on appointment at a set hourly rate. However, guaranteed income on government contracts – whether from prosecutorial work, defense work, city representation, or mental health boards – was important for many lawyers. One participant who had a substantial city contract noted she was financially stable because she knew "X amount of money was going to be paid, and then anything else" she billed was on top of that solid baseline.

While the participants taking court-appointed defense work do not get employment benefits or a set guaranteed salary, they do have a stable source of income based on a set hourly rate. I have previously written about the problems that arise when states set their court appointment rates too low.[256] To the envy of most places, South Dakota's court-appointed hourly rate increases automatically with any cost-of-living increase received by state employees.[257] When this policy was established

---

[256] Hannah Haksgaard, *Court-Appointment Compensation and Rural Access to Justice*, 14 U. ST. THOMAS J.L. & PUB. POL'Y 88 (2020).

[257] *Court Appointed Attorney Guidelines*, 1-Presiding Judge Policy-19 (Nov. 4, 2022) (https://perma.cc/JMU2-A37R).

in 2000, the rate was 67 dollars an hour. In 2023, when I finished interviews, it was 107 dollars. In 2024, it increased to 115 dollars an hour. Of course, this is lower than the hourly rates charged by these lawyers, but not so low it cost them money by not covering overhead expenses.

South Dakota's hourly rate stresses county finances but provides sufficient hourly income for the lawyers taking cases. One attorney who did almost exclusively criminal appointments says she "made a pretty good living" on that rate, though she also ran entirely solo, not even having a secretary. Kristen Kochekian explained it well: "The boons from criminal appointments is at least you know you're getting paid by the county – it's a reduced hourly rate, but you're going to get paid at the end of the day." Derrick Johnson similarly noted, "that check's going to clear the bank" and added another benefit – taking cases paid by the state "saves a hassle of running [clients] down when I know they don't really have a ton of ability to pay." For Casey Jo Deibert, criminal defense "was my main money maker." These criminal defense appointments were bread and butter work for many participating attorneys and without that guaranteed income many of them would have been substantially worse off in their rural practices.

There are plenty of critiques to make against court-appointed defense systems.[258] There is growing support for moving criminal defense from local lawyers to statewide offices, including in South Dakota where the first statewide office for indigent defense opened in 2024.[259] Calls for full-time, state-funded defense counsel get at some of the problem, but without recognizing the impact on sustaining local rural lawyers. Appointed defense work has been critical to the economic survival of many of these lawyers. Taking away court-appointed defense work would cripple some lawyers, likely leading to departures from rural practice. South Dakota's new statewide office will provide mentorship without removing too many cases from local attorneys. Instead of taking cases away from local attorneys, a statewide office should focus on educating those local attorneys, ensuring constitutionally sound defense at the local level.

In South Dakota, rural prosecutors are doing financially better than rural defense attorneys because the job comes with a salary and, often, benefits. There is a statutory minimum for what counties must pay their elected prosecutors, though no corollary requirement for Deputy State's Attorneys. The State's Attorney mandatory minimums are set by state law, though they do not increase automatically like defender pay. Instead, the state legislature periodically reviews them. Table 9.1 shows the current statutory minimums, which were last updated in 2013 and went into effect on January 1, 2015.[260]

---

[258] Eve B. Primus, *The Problematic Structure of Indigent Defense Delivery*, 122 MICH. L. REV. 205 (2023); Maybell Romero, *Lowball Rural Defense*, 99 WASH. U. L. REV. 1081 (2021).
[259] The laws governing state-level indigent legal services are found in S.D. CODIFIED LAWS §§ 23A-51-1 to -14.
[260] S.D. CODIFIED LAWS § 7-7-12.

TABLE 9.1 *Prosecutor minimum salaries*

County population	Minimum salary ($)
Below 5,000	34,554
5,000–9,999	37,673
10,000–19,999	44,492
20,000–49,999	47,728
Full time, regardless of county size	71,534

At least for full-time State's Attorneys, the salary is in line with what many new graduates are earning; the median starting government income for 2022 graduates was only 70,000 dollars.[261] Yet only one lawyer in the program is a full-time State's Attorney operating with a guaranteed income above the national average for new government lawyers. Most attorneys are either Deputy State's Attorneys with no salary minimums or they are part-time State's Attorneys with much lower minimums. The part-time lawyers not only earn less, they may not get health insurance. Plus, counties may or may not provide separate funding for a secretary or office space, which means that a prosecutor in private practice often "donates" their secretary's time and their office space to the county.

There is a general recognition that these part-time State's Attorney jobs are the plum jobs in rural South Dakota. The assumption in my interviews was that if a new attorney could get a part-time State's Attorney job, they "could make it" in rural practice. One mentoring attorney worked as a part-time State's Attorney for thirty-seven years, which provided him a steady paycheck, health insurance, and state retirement. After he hit retirement age and hired a participating attorney, he did not seek reelection, letting his mentee have the job so she could accrue the same benefits. Several mentors specifically handed off their elected State's Attorney positions understanding that the salary and benefits would make rural practice work for the next generation.

Despite the better financial position for prosecutors, the system is not perfect, and it's arguably under threat. In the 1990s, the South Dakota legislature created the opportunity for counties to create regional prosecutor offices to get away from part-time State's Attorneys. While counties have not yet moved toward this model, there are periodic calls for greater "professionalization" of the prosecutor position, pushing for full-time positions in the name of expertise and efficiency.[262] If counties gave up their local prosecutors, for, by way of example, having one full-time prosecutor cover several counties, a lot could be lost. I've already addressed in Chapter 7 the risks of conflicts when each county cannot sustain its own prosecutor. But there's

---

[261] *Jobs & JDs, supra* note 42.
[262] Yeargain, *supra* note 217; Steve Young, *Full-Time Prosecutors Needed in Big Cases, Some Officials Say*, ARGUS LEADER, Dec. 6, 1999, at A7.

an additional problem, which is that the smallest communities may not be able to sustain a private practitioner if that lawyer is not working part time for the government. Take away the part-time rural prosecutors, and you might lose estate planning lawyers, defense counsel, and family law attorneys.

Even with state mandatory minimum salaries, State's Attorneys can be underpaid. It has been a decade since the legislature last increased the mandatory minimum salaries. Plus, State's Attorneys not only prosecute, they serve as counsel to the county. Some counties have much larger workloads than others, population size notwithstanding. For an attorney who is part time, the minimum salary might not account for how much work they really do, thus opening the possibility of counties underpaying. The more troubling aspect has been the underpayment of the Deputy State's Attorneys.

A repeated issue I heard was counties underpaying Deputy State's Attorneys because of the stipend. Not all counties did this, but enough tried to underpay that it is a concern. One county is counting the stipend as the actual salary paid to a Deputy State's Attorney. In another county, a Deputy felt she was being paid "like a secretary." Two other prosecutors told me the county did not use the program to justify a lower salary, but both had expectations of a salary raise at the five-year mark to cover the lost income. One said the county "will still pay me in accordance with what I would have gotten with the grant." This certainly seems as though the county is taking the stipend money into account when setting salaries for their prosecutors. A couple other prosecutors felt the stipend was directly used to reduce their salaries. One explained, "I almost certainly know that it was used as a way to reduce salary." Another said, "I think the reason that I was paid so minimally for the State's Attorney work that I did was because of the stipend."

When counties reduce salaries because of the program or when larger counties participate without really needing the help, it goes against the goal of the program. Those decisions are a short-sighted approach that takes advantage of a program that otherwise does a lot of good. When entities take advantage, they look like the farmer who told anthropologist Luke Bessire that he tries to "farm the government too" in an attempt to "get in every program and get every dollar I can."[263] There is a difference between taking advantage of programs versus using them for good.

One mentoring attorney, reflecting on how to encourage new lawyers to go rural, pontificated that "maybe those local governments need to make it worthwhile" for new lawyers to move to town. There is truth to this, both in the current system and the system I imagine where there are more opportunities for part-time salaried jobs with benefits. When local governments try to shortchange lawyers, those lawyers may not stay. Yet when counties provide fair wages and health insurance, lawyers don't leave. Under the current system, the salaried part-time prosecutors

---

[263] Luke Bessire, Running Out: In Search of Water on the High Plains 44 (2021); see also Ashwood, supra note 69, at 133.

enjoy more stable income along with employment benefits, and the next step may be creating other part-time salaried positions that come with benefits. The easiest to imagine is the government hiring a part-time public defender as an actual government employee, providing salary and benefits. But the sky is the limit: A tribe could employ part-time counsel. A legal aid organization could hire a part-time lawyer. A city could hire its attorney as a part-time employee rather than on contract, a practice already normalized in South Carolina.[264] A county could even pay a part-time salary and provide benefits to have a lawyer provide free walk-in services a certain number of hours a week.

The success of the part-time State's Attorneys proves that rural lawyers do not need full-time employment to stay. It is enough to have employment benefits and a part-time salary for part-time work. Lawyers can then supplement that guaranteed income with their own personal practice. Lawyers may even be willing to take on more pro bono or low bono work. For the most rural and most impoverished communities, the mentoring attorney is correct: If local governments want local attorneys to serve clients and improve the business climates in their small towns, they "need to make it worthwhile" for attorneys to come by figuring out how to provide benefits and part-time salaries. After hearing about the broad-ranging practices of the rural lawyers in South Dakota, I'm more convinced than ever that rural lawyer incentives should be broadly targeted to capture as many rural lawyers as possible. Perhaps larger counties or well-established firms could have funded a new lawyer without the stipend, but participants in all types of practices found the stipend crucial for their success. I do, though, agree with one argument for more targeted funds: Direct subsidization for providing services to low-income clients is a component that local governments and nonprofits should consider.

RUNNING A BUSINESS

These lawyers must make many business decisions, including setting their hourly fees, whether to charge for consultations, and how to handle billing. In writing about rural law practice in Australia, Caroline Hart stresses the entrepreneurial nature of being a successful rural lawyer.[265] Her observation that rural lawyers suffer stress, anxiety, and discomfort by having to set fees and bill clients is just as true in rural South Dakota as it is in rural Australia. Even the simple decision of whether to try to charge for consultations was fraught. Generally, the South Dakota lawyers I interviewed do not charge, but at a large cost – they often end up providing free legal assistance. Interestingly, in South Carolina, Chambliss found rural lawyers charging for the same thing.[266]

---

[264] Chambliss, *supra* note 63.
[265] Hart, *supra* note 255, at 105–6, 117.
[266] Chambliss, *supra* note 63.

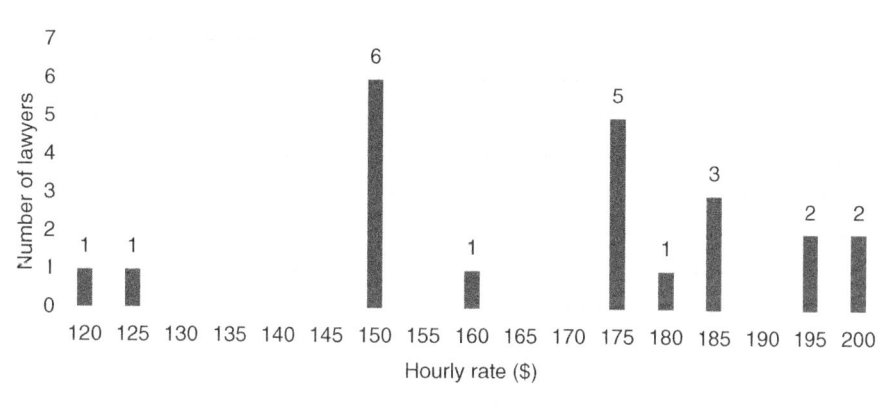

FIGURE 9.2 Lawyer hourly rates

In my interviews with lawyers in 2022 and early 2023, I collected hourly rates for those in rural practice at that time. Figure 9.2 reports their main hourly rate but does not reflect every way they charge. These hourly rates do not include that lawyers might charge higher rates for specialty items, like probate or mineral deeds, or charge some legal services in flat fees. As legal ethic rules allow, rural lawyers might also offer unbundled legal services under different pay scales. Figure 9.2 reflects what lawyers were charging at the time I met with them, though several disclosed plans to increase their hourly rates with the rising inflation of the time. Only one lawyer did not give a number, explaining his fees were too variable to quote a single rate.

The range is large, from 120 dollars to 200 dollars per hour. Though 150 dollars is the most common rate charged, the average hourly rate among these rural attorneys was 168 dollars an hour. It turns out this is not terribly far off the state average of 189 dollars in 2022, though the state hourly rate jumped to 199 dollars in 2023.[267] The differences in hourly rate among the rural lawyers cannot be explained by years of experience, gender, location, or even whether a lawyer is solo or joined a firm. Most attorneys who joined a firm had their rate set by the firm, but otherwise the array of hourly rates has no simple explanation.

A couple of these rural attorneys almost sounded apologetic for their rate – some for charging too much, and others too little. One lawyer charging 195 dollars noted she *could* charge more, but "in an area like this" she thinks "195 dollars is a lot easier to sell than 225 dollars." Another explained that at 185 dollars he knows he's "a little bit lower" than other attorneys, but that "he wants to keep [clients] local" and charging 200 dollars or 250 dollars would drive clients to bigger markets. On the other end of the spectrum, one attorney was charging clients 200 dollars, but had already

---

[267] *Hourly Rates of Lawyers in the United States from 2020 to 2023, By State*, STATISTA (Dec. 2023), https://perma.cc/JUP8-LXWU.

decided to move up to 250 dollars, noting that attorneys in Sioux Falls are charging 300 dollars, and "I'm like – screw that – I don't want to work that hard anymore."

Another aspect of business management and finances is whether lawyers take retainers and operate a trust account. For attorneys in firms, the default position was that retainers were expected and normal, though even then there was an understanding that many clients could not afford retainers. A few spoke about the importance of retainers to running a financially solvent firm. But for some solos, retainers were something to be feared, not relied upon. Several solo practitioners simply do not take retainers, or do it only rarely. The solo practitioners who brought up concerns with retainers are all operating without support staff and they handle their own trust accounts. One attorney explained, "the less I can go through my trust account, I think the better off I am because it is a ton of paperwork." Another solo took a couple of retainers, but now "I am way too scared of accidentally messing up my trust fund to do it again." Yet another solo does not generally take retainers because "I don't want to get myself in implications with my trust account." There was also some worry about client perceptions in the smallest communities, but generally the concern with retainers was a fear of making mistakes with a trust account.

There are actually good reasons for solo practitioners to worry about legal ethics and their trust accounts. Solo and small firm lawyers are more likely to face discipline, and much of that discipline is because of mishandling of trust accounts.[268] Yet when these solo practitioners do not use a trust account, it puts them at financial risk. The true solos are already running on thin margins, and failing to collect retainers may mean they collect less of the money owed to them. This puts them at an economic disadvantage even compared to other rural, small firms. The time-intensive – and sometimes futile – practice of tracking down client payment was mentioned a lot, though no attorney articulated their clients' failure to pay as a material issue in judging their success in rural practice. The trouble of collecting money is not unique to South Dakota – a new solo practitioner in rural Wyoming similarly identified collecting payment as a challenging part of new rural practice.[269]

The business aspect of rural law practice hit the solo practitioners the hardest, though some lawyers who were originally hired by firms have taken over as managing partners or have become solos and are now facing the same business management concerns that solo practitioners faced right away. One way that rural practice programs could help rural practitioners, especially solos, is to provide more direct teaching about running the business side of a law firm. This type of training is built into incubator programs but existed more *ad hoc* in South Dakota. For example, one solo practitioner had interned in a large firm during law school and was able to sit down with the office manager for a few hours to learn bookkeeping, trust

---

[268] Leslie Levin, *The Ethical World of Solo and Small Law Firm Practitioners*, 41 HOUS. L. REV. 309, 311, 355 (2004).
[269] Tomisich, *supra* note 53, at 76.

accounting, and other business basics. Formalizing that training, or at least having a volunteer firm offer it to every new participant, could go a long way to helping new solo practitioners establish successful business practices.

LONG-TERM SUCCESS IN THE CONTEXT OF RURAL JOB LOSS

The information on rural economics and rural job loss is brutal. Rural communities can generally be "characterized by a trend toward rapid deindustrialization and catastrophic job loss."[270] This has hurt working-age men the hardest, and good jobs have been replaced with part-time, low-wage work, often in industries long thought of as feminine, such as hospitality and healthcare.[271] All rural places are not the same, and the rural Midwest is doing comparatively better than other parts of the country, yet that only means other rural areas are in even greater need of financial support for new lawyers.[272]

In Chapter 4, I wrote about how recruitment for law school should target working adults, not just students. In my interviews, the primary reason that rural working adults returned to school for a law degree was because they could not find a good job in their rural area. Before law school, they asked rural banks, ranches, implement dealers, and police departments for jobs, but were disappointed in availability, stability, or pay. One mid-career lawyer told me that while he wanted to ranch, his dad's "place wasn't big enough to sustain" them both. Instead, he sought out a career that would allow him to go back home. He acknowledged that pursuing a law degree in order to get back to a rural hometown is "probably backwards from how most people view law school" because of a perception that higher education, and law school in particular, is a ticket out of a small town. For him and many others, law school was actually a ticket back home, but in a well-compensated field. This relates deeply to what sociologists keep saying: It is hard to find a stable, well-paying job in rural America right now.

This context is key in how we judge the long-term viability of rural law practice. For smart rural residents who want to stay rural, career options are limited. The agriculture industry needs fewer workers; large manufacturing businesses have gone overseas. When rural residents cannot get good jobs, so go to law school then return as lawyers, they often create their own jobs and act, in many ways, as entrepreneurs. The traditional economic development strategy of recruiting established businesses has failed to create and sustain jobs, so rural communities have begun to focus more on supporting local entrepreneurs starting small businesses.[273] New lawyers fit this

---

[270] SHERMAN, WORK, *supra* note 159, at 29; *see also* WUTHNOW, *supra* note 31, at 86.
[271] Andrew Dumont, *Changes in the U.S. Economy and Rural-Urban Employment Disparities*, FED. RSRV. (Jan. 19, 2024), https://perma.cc/3DJY-V3K8.
[272] CURRID-HALKETT, *supra* note 72.
[273] Lori A. Dickes & Kenneth L. Robinson, *Rural Entrepreneurship*, *in* RURAL AMERICA IN A GLOBALIZING WORLD, *supra* note 58, at 595–96.

mold, not only because they represent other small businesses but because the lawyers themselves often create their own jobs.

When judging the financial situation of these lawyers, keep in mind that they have not entered rural practice because of the ability to earn a high salary. Some chose law school because it offered a higher standard of living than other rural professions, but there was a general understanding that they were sacrificing better paid urban jobs in order to reap the benefits of being rural. As Dylan Kirchmeier explained,

> We were always gonna live in a rural community somewhere. It was just setting ourselves up to the best way we could do that. But I don't know if a large majority of people that would look at it would see it that way. They might feel like they're sacrificing something to go to a small place.

Because the lawyers who have gone to rural America do so for quality of life, not earnings, I judge success based not just on comparisons to urban lawyers, but also in comparison to what they might earn in their rural communities without a law degree.

Comparisons to national data do provide some context. Studying Missouri rural lawyers in the 1980s, Donald Landon concluded that the primary difference between the earnings of rural and urban lawyers was that urban lawyers out-earned at the highest income levels. But, when looking at the middle-range salaries of lawyers, urban and rural lawyers were very similar.[274] National data on lawyer salaries today is similarly skewed by the biggest firms. Focusing more narrowly on small firms provides a better comparison. The national data for 2022 law school graduates working in small firms shows a median law firm salary of 70,000 dollars.[275] South Dakota's new rural lawyers made less fresh out of law school. Yet, as shown from Rachel Mairose's income growth from the first to the second year, the economic viability of rural practice cannot be judged on first-year salaries alone. In Missouri, Landon found that rural lawyers who had practiced for fifteen years were earning more than twice as much as lawyers practicing for less than five years.[276] In South Carolina, Chambliss found that longer-practicing lawyers specialized and increased their earnings.[277] In South Dakota, the rural lawyers have not been practicing that long. Yet even within that shorter time frame, lawyers consistently told me that as they became established in their rural communities, their finances improved.

Looking at national data is also skewed by the biggest cities with the highest costs of living. Many Americans in larger towns or cities think lower wages are justified in rural areas because of a low cost of living, yet that is not the experience of these lawyers. Housing is not as expensive in rural America as San Francisco or New York,

---

[274] LANDON, *supra* note 7, at 30.
[275] *Jobs & JDs, supra* note 42.
[276] LANDON, *supra* note 7, at 31.
[277] Chambliss, *supra* note 63.

but it is expensive and very often in short supply. Several participants commented on housing costs being just as expensive in their rural communities as what lawyers in South Dakota's largest communities pay, yet those city lawyers often earn a higher salary. Often, day-to-day needs are actually more expensive in rural areas. As one lawyer explained, "there's nothing I pay less for here. Actually, we pay more for everything." Take groceries, for example: With neither big grocery stores nor Walmarts, food costs more in rural America.[278] Plus, as that lawyer observed, "electric bills are more, water is more, Wi-Fi is more. Everything is more here."

Even with all of the costs of living in a rural area, for most of the South Dakota lawyers the growth in income by year five was enough to sustain rural practice. There were some lawyers who left rural practice partly due to low earnings, while others who have stayed remain unsatisfied with their incomes. And it is not simply what a lawyer earned. For two who departed, the financial issue was more related to the expense of paying their own health insurance. For one lawyer, it was a pure financial issue of having enough income to pay student loans without access to any loan forgiveness programs.

The overall financial stability of the participating lawyers was tied to their areas of practice, the size and location of their communities, and their mentorship. I need not rehash the variabilities of practice from earlier in the book, but suffice to say that if lawyers had a predictable salary from a firm or from the government, had good mentorship, and were in a community that brought them business, the lawyers felt more stable in their incomes and thus their ability to stay. Within private civil work, estate planning was particularly lucrative. Landon described estate work as "the land of milk and honey" for rural Missouri lawyers.[279] The same is true in rural Australia and in rural South Dakota, though estate planning is less important in South Carolina's poorest rural counties where lawyers are more likely to take personal injury work.[280] Two of the South Dakota lawyers with financial struggles landed in towns where established lawyers had cornered the estate planning business and there were no prosecutorial positions available. With those two options gone, there was no easy path for financial success.

Especially for the lawyers who grew up in lower socio-economic homes, the money is good. Several participants told me about their relative wealth compared to their blue-collar parents. One participant, who grew up ranching and would love to be a rancher, realizes he'll probably practice law forever because he's "making good money, and I very much enjoy the freedom that comes with making good money." It is all relative. A few participants view legal practice as only part of their income

---

[278] Keiko Tamaka, Patrick H. Mooney & Brett Wolff, *Food Insecurity and Obesity in Rural America: Paradoxes of the Modern Agrifood System*, in RURAL AMERICA IN A GLOBALIZING WORLD, *supra* note 58, at 650.
[279] LANDON, *supra* note 7, at 72.
[280] Mortensen, *supra* note 164, at 25; Chambliss, *supra* note 63.

streams, investing in real estate or ranching along with law practice. The older and more established attorneys who are now mentors often said the same thing: They diversified their work, often running businesses as well as a law office to ensure long-term financial stability.

While some lawyers bemoan lower rural salaries, other rural residents often see them as highly compensated. The perception that all lawyers make a lot of money was harmful to some participants. One participant was never able to get health insurance from the county, and his perception was the county commissioners were hesitant to pay the additional cost of health insurance for "young rich attorneys" who are already getting a stipend. Similarly, lawyers noted that clients think "it doesn't matter" if they fail to pay attorney bills because attorneys are "all rich." As one lawyer said, "people have a perception that attorneys make boo koo dollars, and that – especially for a rural attorney – that's just not the case."

For those who stayed, most anticipate that the stipend ending will not change their rural practice. For participants still active in their five-year commitment, no one is already planning to leave after the five years end. In fact, they are largely committed to permanency. Of course, some expect changes at the five-year mark. Several participants in private practice talked about their need to bill more to cover the eventual loss of the stipend. Participants with salaried positions want to see raises that reflect the amount of the stipend. One participant took a different view: He used the stipend to pay off his student loans, so he is not worried about a drop in income because he is debt free approaching the end of the five years.

Regardless of whether they left or stayed, the attorneys who have participated in this program agree that five years is the proper length of time. Two main themes emerged as lawyers told me why five years is appropriate. First, five years is seen as appropriate for getting integrated into a community in a way that forms long-term social bonds. Second, five years is appropriate for becoming a functional attorney. Functional in terms of knowledge and ability to competently practice law, perhaps also potentially adopting a niche practice area. And functional in terms of having clientele and work that creates financial stability for a lawyer. Zach Pahlke, who has finished his five years and stayed, explained that at the five-year mark "my career was stable enough" that though he "missed the stipend" it did not drop his standard of living and the five-year transition "was a controlled change."

None of this is to suggest that lawyers are in a perfect financial situation after five years. One participant who was just ending her five years explained that while she is "no longer living paycheck to paycheck" she is "still one emergency away from being financially ruined." Yet even the lawyers who did not feel financially comfortable generally acknowledged that there were more clients and cases they could take, but that doing more would be to the detriment of their personal lives. As one participant explained, a rural lawyer will be "as busy as you want to be" because "the work is there" in a rural community. There are two sides to this: On the one hand, rural lawyers should get to be picky about the amount and type of work they do. On the other hand, the more that lawyers reject work they do not want, the more that low-margin practice areas and low-income clients do not receive services.

Writing about Australia, one scholar explained: "Many regional and rural lawyers choose to sacrifice profit (and growth) in exchange for a 'better quality of life.'"[281] I heard the same thing from many South Dakota lawyers. A participating lawyer told me that the flexibility in work hours and being able to bring her baby to the office was worth the "trade-off" of more money in a bigger market. A mentoring attorney said something similar, that rural practice "is not all about a paycheck. It's about wanting to be part of that very intricately, closely knit community." A few participants have found themselves working too many hours at various points in their careers, but they have readjusted workload to make sure they can leave the office at a reasonable time. The flexibility and freedom offered by rural practice is important to these lawyers, even if it means a lower income.

LESSONS LEARNED

The rural practice of law does not offer the high incomes associated with the biggest firms in the biggest cities. But it can provide a solid career with long-term, stable, income. The data captured in the first ten years of this program shows the quick growth that lawyers have in income. The first year in rural practice will probably be hard, but the stipend payments helped most lawyers transition into a financially stable career. Lawyers in South Dakota are aided by a reasonable court-appointment rate and the existence of part-time prosecutor positions, decisions that other states may need to emulate. Most lawyers have created financially successful practices where they are part-time government employees and part-time private practitioners. Though even then they get left out of the best loan-forgiveness programs for government employees, which is just one more reason that direct support for rural attorneys is needed.

Ryan McKnight, who left the program after a year and now teaches at a university, tells his students "that you could make a good living" by going back to rural South Dakota to practice law, and that the average salary probably isn't much different than most lawyers in Sioux Falls. The difference, though, is that "you're doing it for yourself" and that "you're making a difference for that community, that town." Rachel Mairose embodies this: Her financial path shows a sparse first year, followed by financial security. She is now well-positioned in her community, serving as the local prosecutor, taking private clients, and doing volunteer work. The finances have worked for her, and they have worked for most lawyers in the program.

---

[281] Hart, *supra* note 255, at 121.

10

Community Impact

FIGURE 10.1 Rachelle Norberg

In 2019, a tornado swept through Burke, South Dakota, population 579. Rachelle Norberg was a new attorney in town – licensed for under a year. When the tornado hit, Norberg was on the Lower Brule Reservation drafting pro bono wills for tribal members. Norberg rushed home, putting her legal skills to work as Burke's city attorney, advising on property issues in the initial clean-up period. Later, Norberg volunteered for the tornado recovery, taking part in distributing donated funds.

Norberg volunteers a lot. Among the long list of her volunteer activities, she even keeps stats for her local high school football team. In addition, Norberg owns two businesses that employ local residents. She operates a busy legal practice, doing civil involuntary commitments, criminal defense, and general civil practice. She also owns and operates a title plant, ensuring that people in the county have good title when they purchase property.

Kelsea Kenzy Sutton, a local lawyer who was a county commissioner at the time of Norberg's contract, feels like her vote to approve Norberg's contract was a moment when she "made a difference" as a commissioner. Sutton sees Norberg as a major benefit to the community, noting that Norberg does a lot, in fact "maybe too much." Norberg cares deeply about the town of Burke, the place she grew up and where she is now firmly imbedded as an important community member.

For Norberg, the Rural Attorney Recruitment Program played a large role in bringing her back home and giving her financial support to begin her career. Accordingly, the Rural Attorney Recruitment Program played a large role in the community obtaining additional benefits through Norberg. The county commissioners split their vote three–two when approving Norberg and wanted proof that the expenditure was worthwhile. For five years, Norberg gave annual reports to the commission about what she financially contributed back into the county, ultimately proving to the commissioners that their investment was worthwhile.

Building on discussions about community acceptance (Chapter 5) and legal work (Chapter 7), this chapter looks broadly at what lawyers have brought to rural communities. It begins with discussions of volunteer work and pro bono legal work, then turns more directly to the communities themselves, addressing how local governments spend and save money on these lawyers, finally ending with a discussion of how these lawyers help to sustain rural communities.

VOLUNTEER WORK

Norberg is unique in facing a natural disaster that pushed her to assume an early leadership role in her community, but her hard work in legal practice and her dedication to public service is not unique. Austin Hoffman is a volunteer fire fighter; Derrick Johnson serves on the county's school board. Other lawyers serve on economic development boards or the Chamber of Commerce in their communities. There are also positions on a hospice board, a garden club, and a child protection team. One participant is a foster parent. Through various boards, they organize events: a bike rodeo, an ice fishing tournament, and an Easter egg hunt. They serve on county political boards and church boards.

For many lawyers, these community service activities are a core part of how they connect with the community and see themselves making a difference in the world. In rural communities, there is an expectation – even pressure – to volunteer. The pressure to volunteer can be difficult for those without time, but volunteering is good too. It helps "provide entrée to social networks," especially for those new to rural communities.[282] Volunteering provides benefits but can quickly become overwhelming. Author Kathleen Norris captures the culture of volunteering in rural towns. She says "[t]here are far fewer people than jobs to fill. Someone must be found to lead the church choir or youth group, to bowl with the league, to coach a softball team or little league, to run a Chamber of Commerce or club committee."[283] There is a danger here – with too few people and too many volunteer roles to fill, "capable people can find that they are doing too much."[284] The burden can fall especially hard on lawyers who can be "expected to be involved in a lot of community activities simply 'because I am the lawyer.'"[285]

As lawyers told me about their multiple volunteer roles, some acknowledged that volunteer obligations could overtake their family obligations and ability to achieve a work–life balance. The only lawyers without much community volunteer work are those who are busy with children. As one attorney said, "most of my career I've been either birthing a baby or nursing." Women who gave birth while in the program have found it difficult to do community service, especially for boards who meet in the evenings. Similarly, several attorneys with older children are cautious about how much their volunteer work takes them away from their kids. A few lawyers who were initially heavily involved in community service have stepped back because their children are in traveling sports or simply to capitalize on the time that their children are young.

Having children increases some types of volunteer work. Several lawyers with children coach their children's sports teams, including baseball, soccer, basketball, and volleyball. Two lawyers coach shooting sports through 4-H. Another participant referees youth basketball games. The focus on youth sports and local schools makes sense. Small rural communities often coalesce around schools.[286] Local public schools and their sports become a centerpiece of the community.[287] Ryan McKnight, a former Division I football player with NFL experience, was a volunteer coach in his rural community. Kirby Krogman doesn't volunteer with the team, though he is a self-described "avid White River Tigers basketball fan" and rarely misses a game. Krogman filled me in on a rivalry, the team's long history of making the state basketball tournament, and a particularly tough loss last season. Being present with youth sports – whether as a coach, referee, or fan – is a major way that community involvement happens in rural places.

Though not in all circumstances, the level of community involvement was often tied to feelings of acceptance and attachment. Jennifer English and her husband spent their first two years in Salem "trying to volunteer and get involved as much

---

[282] SHERMAN, PARADISE, *supra* note 70, at 79.
[283] NORRIS, *supra* note 198, at 80.
[284] *Id.* at 118.
[285] Tarr, *supra* note 209, at 50.
[286] BROWN & SCHAFFT, *supra* note 112, at 97–98.
[287] Schafft & Biddle, *supra* note 58, at 558–60; WUTHNOW, *supra* note 31, at 41.

as we could and at every turn we were snubbed and our ideas were never listened to." When the community did not accept English or the volunteer work she tried to provide, she withdrew from the community aspects of rural practice and has never developed the same attachment to place as most participants.

But for most lawyers, their communities were hungry for more volunteers and these lawyers were able to fill the types of jobs that must be done to make a community run. Volunteering normally led to community acceptance and community attachment, which in turn made lawyers happier with their choice to live and work in a small town. Rural sociologists have observed this same thing: That rural residents who engage in community-level work to improve the overall well-being of the community will be more attached to their rural communities.[288] And those more attached to their rural communities are more likely to stay, thus making community volunteer work important both for the communities and for keeping rural lawyers.[289]

PRO BONO

The Rural Attorney Recruitment Program contract now requires participants to take a pro bono case each year. Other than the full-time State's Attorneys who are prohibited by law from taking on outside cases, all participants do at least one pro bono case each year. For the participants who are members of the bar for the Rosebud Sioux Tribe, that bar membership requires they take a pro bono case in the Rosebud Sioux courts.

Beyond official pro bono cases, these lawyers are providing free or fee-reduced services in many ways. When I asked lawyers about pro bono, some said they did very little pro bono, but then went on to explain the legal work they do for free or reduced rate. It is not technically pro bono unless you start the lawyer–client relationship pro bono, but most of these lawyers are helping the economically vulnerable people in their communities by taking cases knowing they won't receive pay. The lawyers cut their hours or write off entire cases. These lawyers also take phone calls during which they give legal advice but rarely charge for that time.

While there is substantial wealth in these rural communities, especially for the ranchers and farmers with the biggest land holdings, there is also much poverty. Ryan McKnight, who worked in Haakon County for a year, explained that he and his wife Brittany Kjerstad McKnight took on pro bono cases because in his rural area it was hard for many of his clients to find employment, so clients could not "pay you for your services." Trying to charge might mean collecting "fifty bucks a month" for ten years, so instead the McKnights worked for free, or for a one-time payment of

---

[288] Brian M. Jennings & Richard S. Krannich, *A Multidimensional Exploration of the Foundations of Community Attachment among Seasonal and Year-Round Residents*, 78 RURAL SOCIO. 498, 501 (2013).

[289] Ulrich-Schad, Henly & Safford, *supra* note 182, at 389.

whatever the client had in hand that day, including being "paid in baked goods." Stephanie Trask, also in Haakon County, both cuts hours to reduce bills and if she has someone walk in who "really can't afford the representation" she will "let him know I can handle it." With lower-income clients, Trask charges based on the client's economic position. Many other lawyers said the same thing.

But there is a danger here. One lawyer wanted to do more pro bono, but "I also have to make a living." Another lawyer who enjoys helping "the downtrodden" worries about firm finances when she finds herself representing those clients or even providing them long, free consultations to help work through their problems. For many lawyers, consultations were free and a lot of legal advice was dispensed to walk-in clients or over the phone without charging. Cole Romey, who is starting to specialize in estate planning, says "it's like groundhog day" because he takes the same consultation phone calls all the time. He'll spend thirty minutes teaching them how the law works and never charges for those consultations, in part because "a lot of people can't afford it anyway, you can tell." Those limited interactions allowed legal advice to reach more people, but at the cost of lawyers not billing for their time.

Not a single South Dakota lawyer perceived their low bono or pro bono work as too burdensome, and for many it was a critical part of their identity as a small-town lawyer. When Chambliss interviewed lawyers in South Carolina, many of them had a similar positive view of pro bono work, but she also spoke with several lawyers who "expressed frustration at being expected to provide pro bono and discounted services and said that they rarely do so."[290] At least right now, in South Dakota there is a culture of providing pro bono services among the participating lawyers – perhaps because the Rural Attorney Recruitment Program requires it; perhaps because enough state bar leaders encourage it. In fact, several of these lawyers participate in the state bar's access to justice program which sends pro bono referrals. The stipend itself may also give lawyers increased financial freedom to take on more pro bono cases. This is how it worked for Dusty Ginsbach, who has done substantial pro bono work for people and organizations in his county. Ginsbach explains that "if I wouldn't have had the stipend, I probably wouldn't have taken on as many pro bono – *certainly* wouldn't have taken on all the pro bono cases I did."

Even though the participating lawyers do take pro bono cases, they are careful about protecting their time. Strategically, a lot of these lawyers do not announce up front that they are taking cases pro bono. Lawyers found it difficult to truly assess a client's situation up front, and lawyers prefer to start clients as fee paying, but switch to pro bono as the case progresses and the lawyer determines the client's real circumstances. Another reason for starting clients as fee paying is that, as one lawyer explained, the pro bono clients end up as "the worst cases" because the clients "realize they don't have to pay for anything" and treat the relationship differently. Some of the burden these lawyers feel from their pro bono clients might be based on legal

---

[290] Chambliss, *supra* note 63.

sophistication. Writing in 1976, a lawyer explained that new legal aid attorneys "who had practiced privately estimated that it takes almost five times as much time and effort to provide adequate representation to poor clients as it takes to provide similar representation in private practice" because the legal needs were more complex and the poor clients had generally not had prior interactions with lawyers, requiring that lawyers provide more education during the legal process.[291]

Beyond taking on pro bono clients, lawyers have found ways to provide legal assistance in their rural communities. Lawyers give presentations to groups in their communities about managing legal issues. Others have volunteered for traveling clinics hosted by the University of South Dakota Knudson School of Law. Rachelle Norberg had joined to help in a tribal wills clinic when the tornado swept through her hometown. Several attorneys frequently participate in legal clinics for veterans.

While the number of technical pro bono cases might be low for some of these lawyers, it is clear that free or reduced fee legal services are an important part of most participants' view of their role in the community. Clay Anderson, who "tr[ies] to always give back," will do several hours of pro bono work each week. Anderson says that "pro bono is something that I love doing, which is funny because I never thought I would." These participants are invested in helping the poor and strengthening their own local communities. While most do engage in community volunteer work, many participants see their pro bono or reduced fee work as the best way to give back to their community. Accordingly, rather than serve on community boards or volunteer at festivals, many would rather answer legal questions for free. In her South Carolina study, Chambliss found that longer-serving attorneys became less accessible over time, for instance by limiting walk-ins and free consultations.[292] Time will tell whether the South Dakota lawyers change, though Anderson is now the longest-serving Rural Attorney Recruitment Program participant and continues to do substantial pro bono work.

This pro bono work is important, but it will never be enough to serve the needs of the rural poor. Even decades ago when there were more rural lawyers, they were unable to take enough pro bono cases to meet those needs.[293] This brings me back to Jennifer English's view on rural practice, which is that there are insufficient paying clients available and states should invest in funding more legal aid attorneys in rural areas. Chapter 9, on economics, belies the conclusion that lawyers cannot make money in most rural communities, though English is correct that more free legal aid should be provided. One option would be to provide part-time employment with benefits to rural lawyers for certain types of legal aid work, leaving them with the rest of their time for private practice – much like what part-time prosecutors already do. When rural legal aid was first being envisioned, part-time lawyers were

---

[291] George, *supra* note 93, at 710.
[292] Chambliss, *supra* note 63.
[293] Kessler, *supra* note 50, at 274.

rejected in favor of full-time employees.[294] But in rural America, where it is hard to staff full-time legal aid jobs, perhaps part-time lawyers who are dedicated to their rural communities should be considered. The part-time legal aid attorney would provide services under a legal aid model while also benefiting from a stable income and benefits. Importantly, this could allow some of the poorest and most rural communities to sustain a part-time private practice lawyer.

Less appealing than part-time employment with benefits could be a judicare model, where private lawyers take poor clients and a legal aid organization pays for those services, much like doctors accept Medicare.[295] Legal aid advocates prefer salaried legal aid attorneys over direct provision by private rural lawyers, arguing that rural lawyers will have conflicts because of their other work, will not develop expertise in serving the needs of impoverished rural residents, and will worry about upsetting the local political and social structure.[296] They also argue that the aging lawyer population and the shortage of rural lawyers hampers the ability to use a judicare system.[297] Though I agree that it is important to have career legal aid attorneys serving rural areas, I think there is value to using private practitioners for some legal aid cases. Perhaps if we used the judicare model to ensure some steady income to rural lawyers (operating much like court appointments for criminal work), more rural lawyers could financially survive as private practitioners, thus allowing more lawyers to be available to take legal aid cases, and decreasing the conflicts advocates worry so much about.

GOVERNMENT EXPENSES AND SAVINGS

There are two ways in which these new rural lawyers take local government resources. First, local governments pay 35 percent of the annual stipend, less than 4,500 dollars a year for five years. Second, many of these attorneys are making their livings, at least in part, by working for government entities. Despite these two government outlays, governments are not wasting excess money to support these lawyers. In fact, the opposite is true – local governments may actually save money by supporting a new local lawyer.

When attorneys are local – whether they are prosecuting, defending, or providing another legal service – the government saves travel money. Counties know this, and it is part of the reason to participate in the program. This is also why a number of participating lawyers have felt an obligation to take court appointments. Counties also know that lawyers economically contribute in other ways. Program administrator Suzanne Starr would pitch participation to the counties in economic

---

[294] Barvick, *supra* note 51, at 547–48.
[295] Spain, *supra* note 100, at 377.
[296] *Id.* at 379; Barvick, *supra* note 51, at 550; Kessler, *supra* note 50; George, *supra* note 93, at 725–26.
[297] Barvick, *supra* note 51, at 550.

terms – that the participants would save tax dollars, add to the tax base, and help other local businesses.

Rachelle Norberg gave annual financial reports to the county commissioners about her financial contributions, detailed here. Over five years, the county paid 21,898.80 dollars in stipend payments. Norberg took criminal and abuse and neglect appointments, several of which she took on a pro bono basis without charging the county. Between the pro bono cases and the savings in mileage had the next closest attorney taken the appointments, she calculates between 3,750 dollars and 8,365 dollars in savings on court appointments. Then, in her role on the mental health board she offered a reduced hourly rate to the county, saving it 1,794.20 dollars. She gave six free training sessions related to the mental health board, calculated at 1,800 dollars in billable time. The direct savings to the county were somewhere between 7,344 dollars and 11,959 dollars. Plus, Norberg paid over 8,000 dollars in property taxes during her five years in the program and will continue to pay those long into the future.

The indirect benefits – those accruing to residents or other governmental entities – were even greater. Over the five years of the stipend payment, Norberg provided over 30,000 dollars worth of pro bono services to county residents, including preparing legal documents for eight new nonprofits in the county. Norberg paid over 32,000 dollars in state and city sales taxes on her business dealings during her time in the program. Add in that she bought two businesses plus an empty lot in town where she built a house, and it becomes very clear that the local community financially benefited from her arrival.

Norberg did not calculate how much local sales tax she paid on her own consumer purchases during the contract, but this is yet another way that local governments benefit. A different participating lawyer noted that though the county does pay her for taking court appointments, she always spends "that money back in the community." In her mind, counties hiring lawyers from out of town not only pay mileage, but then those lawyers are "taking that money and they're spending it in their community. It's not being reinvested here." That is true for both public and private dollars. When attorneys live locally, they pay taxes on their houses and offices, they collect local sales tax on their attorney services, they maintain a nice office which helps to keep property values up, and they pay sales taxes on their own consumer purchases.[298] They generally contribute to the financial well-being of the community.

Towns must have an economic base to survive, and lawyers are a part of that. Lawyers create jobs and pay taxes on their own businesses and provide legal work that allows local businesses to succeed. Rural communities generally lack the infrastructure needed to support new businesses. In bigger places there may be small business incubators, but not in these tiny towns.[299] A competent lawyer, though,

---

[298] South Dakota has imposed the sales tax on attorneys' services since 1988. *Matter of Discipline of Simpson*, 467 N.W.2d 921, 922 (S.D. 1991).
[299] Dickes & Robinson, *supra* note 273, at 594–95.

can provide services that fill in the missing knowledge and service gap. Eight of the participating lawyers regularly do business formation work in their legal practices.

COMMUNITY SUSTENANCE

In writing about declining communities in northwest South Dakota, Kathleen Norris observed: "When these people ask, 'Who will replace us?' the answer is, 'who knows, maybe no one,' and it's not easy to live with that truth."[300] That hard truth hit retired Chief Justice Gilbertson when he started to see lawyer offices close across rural South Dakota. That hard truth is hitting the aging lawyers in communities across the state. One mentoring attorney told me "I've had this discussion on what's going to happen in ten, fifteen years when we're done. When we fade out." For him, the reality is that "I don't know if anybody's gonna take my place." And it's not just the lawyers. He looks around at "the grocery store, the hardware store, or the dentist, or doctors, or lawyers." They are all at risk of disappearing and taking the community with them.

In many ways, the Rural Attorney Recruitment Program works because of localism. The lawyers and communities who have invested in this program do so because they believe they are making their communities stronger and are evidencing what Trevor Latimer acknowledges is one of the strongest arguments for localism, "that making the world a better place requires investment – not investment in the abstract, but investment in particular communities."[301] Someone with an opposition to localism (like Latimer) might accuse both the lawyers and the communities of being self-interested – they are each investing time and resources for something that helps their own local community for the selfish reason of wanting a strong local community that then further improves their own lives. A 1999 newspaper article from Sioux Falls essentially said this exact thing by accusing small counties of "parochialism" for wanting to keep local prosecutors.[302] The newspaper suggested that small towns not wanting to see "another job in town gone" was somehow narrow minded. But if a local community does not care about keeping local jobs, no one else will. Local investment to improve local communities is a good thing.

These rural lawyers are providing legal services that might not have otherwise been provided. In that way, the program lawyers are creating a new service and bringing legal representation to people who would not have had legal representation without the Rural Attorney Recruitment Program. Some of the services provided by these new rural lawyers will siphon off work from bigger communities: A local farmer might have considered driving to a bigger town to create an estate plan, but instead will decide to do it locally. In this instance, having a local lawyer does not increase overall economic output, but rather moves it from the bigger town to the

---

[300] NORRIS, *supra* note 198, at 173–74.
[301] TREVOR LATIMER, SMALL ISN'T BEAUTIFUL: THE CASE AGAINST LOCALISM 75 (2023).
[302] Young, *supra* note 262.

smaller. This is not bad for anyone. Lawyers in South Dakota's bigger communities are busy, oftentimes turning down work because they are too busy. Those lawyers are not being harmed by losing a small percentage of work to new rural lawyers. But the new rural lawyers – and the communities they serve – are substantially benefited by bringing the legal work back into the local area.

The rural lawyers who participated in the program were often driven by a desire to help their communities. One lawyer realized he was the only attorney signed up to take criminal defense appointments in a county and thought to himself, "What the heck? I guess I'm making a difference then." Private practice, even outside of pro bono work, can also achieve these goals. One lawyer told me "I hope I'm giving a service to the community." And he is. As just one example, he writes a lot of deeds, charging only 200 dollars to do so, which makes his firm no money. But it has "cleaned up so many property issues just doing simple deed work."

The program has attracted lawyers who want to make a difference. When I first interviewed Kristen Kochekian and Jennifer English in 2017, I was struck because both told me they moved to South Dakota because they viewed rural practice as public interest work. Kochekian explained that "I've always been public interest minded" and "I knew that if I was going to be in the [legal] field I'd be happiest when I was helping people." When I spoke with Kochekian's hiring lawyer, he explained that Kochekian excels at representing "the people who need help" in their rural community. Of course, none of these lawyers are full-time legal aid attorneys – they are, after all, earning their keep through paid clients. Yet they make a difference for individual clients and entire communities.

Rachelle Norberg explained, "My favorite part of my job" is being able to "look out the front office windows and look on either side of the street and say 'I directly got to help this person or this group or I got to do this project as part of being on a board.'" Norberg is happy in her practice because "I get to see it every day and I get to see it right away. I don't have to sit and wait" to see the impact. "I have literally generations of families that come to my office to have work done because this is where they've always come; this is where their parents had work done; this is where their grandparents had work done." Several lawyers mentioned the multigenerational aspect of serving clients as being a particularly satisfying part of rural practice.

When I asked mentoring lawyers about their views on the program, they were even more focused on benefits to the community. Greg Protsch said the program "was really beneficial to me, there's no question about that. And it was really beneficial to the residents of the county because if I would retire without Kristian [Ellendorf], there'd be no attorney in the entire county." That sentiment was repeated by other hiring attorneys. It also played into why established attorneys thought law students should consider rural practice. Emily Sovell sees it as a selling point that rural practice is all about "the small-town living; the camaraderie; and the things that you do for and with your community in these small towns."

It feels an overstatement to claim that a single lawyer moving to a rural community could change it. However, the small size of these communities means that even small shifts can be "highly influential on a community's economy, society, and environment."[303] Plus, it is difficult for the smallest communities to engage in meaningful economic development.[304] As sociologists David Brown and Kai Schafft argue about rural communities, "community development and economic development advance together. In fact, one might say that they are two sides of the same coin."[305] When rural lawyers help communities, they help sustain economic development. When communities invest their money to attract lawyers, they are providing a resource that will help their community members. As one rural lawyer in Wyoming explained, providing legal services in a small town means doing things "that are going to help the community be successful."[306]

Some of the small-scale community sustenance can be helped by having someone knowledgeable in town. One participating attorney told me that small-town attorneys are "problem solvers." She receives a large variety of questions: What do you do when your husband dies? What do you do when your neighbor's cows are out? How do you handle a foreclosure? What if a tenant leaves a cat in my apartment? How long should I keep my tax documents? Some of the questions are not legal, more "just general advice for pretty much any life questions." But there are few places in a small town where you can ask those questions, "except for your local attorney or maybe the sheriff's office." Landon said rural lawyers play a "helper" role in a rural community.[307] In Australia, the rural lawyer–client relationship has been described as having "a pastoral quality."[308]

There is reason to think that South Dakota communities are now understanding the value of the Rural Attorney Recruitment Program. Haakon County was skeptical of approving Ryan McKnight, but when the McKnights left, Haakon County was enthusiastic about participating again. In fact, a county commissioner called Stephanie Trask to recruit her. Fall River County rejected Willian Hustead, but later approved two lawyers hired into Hustead's firm. When Hustead ran into a commissioner who voted against him, Hustead mentioned wanting to hire another lawyer and inquired about whether the commission might approve what would become the county's second contract. Hustead figured "there's no way the commission would approve" a second contract, but the commissioner responded, "Oh, I think we would." Hustead "just about fell over" in surprise. Counties might have initially viewed the program as an unnecessary expense to support a well-compensated profession, but it seems that counties have figured out the investment is worthwhile.

---

[303] Ulrich-Schad, Henly & Safford, *supra* note 182, at 374.
[304] SHERMAN, PARADISE, *supra* note 70, at 5.
[305] BROWN & SCHAFFT, *supra* note 112, at 84.
[306] Tomisich, *supra* note 53, at 85.
[307] Landon, *supra* note 208, at 92.
[308] Mortensen, *supra* note 164, at 32.

LESSONS LEARNED

The vitality of rural communities is a struggle and, in all likelihood, will continue to be a struggle long into the future. Grassroot advocates, policymakers, and scholars strategize about how to strengthen America's rural communities, and why it is important to do so. Strengthening rural communities requires more than just placing a lawyer, yet lawyers can make a difference. The Rural Attorney Recruitment Program has made a quantifiable difference in bringing attorneys to rural communities in South Dakota over the last ten years. To the extent America wants strong rural communities (and, of course, I think America *should* want strong rural communities), programs that bring rural lawyers into rural communities are worth the investment. As Kathleen Norris observes, the small-town "paradise wasn't self-sufficient after all, and the attitude and belief that it ever was is part of the reason it's gone."[309] In order for small towns to be sustained, someone has to do the work.

Contributions to community is a major reason to reject remote provision of legal services as a silver bullet. A common refrain over the last few years has been that videoconference legal services can solve the rural justice crises. One mentoring attorney even posited that he sees viability in more remote representation of clients. Even though he is not convinced that attorney access must "necessarily be an in-person physical brick and mortar shop" he recognized in the next breath that it is still important for the communities to have a physical lawyer in town. A person who "adds to the tax base," and can "do other things" like "get on the school board."

An analysis of lawyers that starts and ends with the provision of legal services to clients misses one of the most essential reasons that rural lawyers matter. Rachelle Norberg is a classic example. Her list of community volunteer work is a mile long. She independently runs a law firm and a title company, providing critical services in a town with 579 people. She is continuously contributing to her community in big and small ways and has undoubtedly made her rural community a better place. When South Dakota developed its program, two main benefits dominated the discussions: access to justice and the economic viability of rural communities.[310] The program and its proponents have received criticism for focusing *too much* on rural economic viability instead of access to justice, but it seems to me that the two go hand-in-hand. As current South Dakota Supreme Court Chief Justice Steven Jensen says: "every one of those attorneys is a win for those local communities *and* the people that live there." We can celebrate both.

---

[309] NORRIS, *supra* note 198, at 47.
[310] Goetzinger & Morris, *supra* note 185, at 447.

11

Staying or Leaving

FIGURE 11.1 Amy Jo Janssen and family

Amy Jo Janssen grew up on a ranch in rural western Nebraska, starting her education in a one-room country schoolhouse. Janssen chose to come to the University of South Dakota for law school because it offered a much smaller community than the law schools in Nebraska. Following law school, Janssen wanted to establish a legal practice in a small, South Dakota town within a few hours' drive of her family. Fortuitously, she connected with Herb Sundall, a lawyer near retirement in Kennebec, South Dakota. Sundall was the only remaining lawyer in a firm with deep South Dakota roots – the Kennebec firm was originally started in the 1940s by a former South Dakota governor.

After law school, Janssen and her family moved to Kennebec, which, with a population of only 281, is the smallest community represented in South Dakota's Rural Attorney Recruitment Program. Janssen received county commission approval for the contract in 2014 when she began working with Sundall. But because Sundall was paying Janssen a stable salary, she strategically delayed her start in the program until Sundall retired in 2018 and Janssen took over the practice. Now, Janssen's stipend has ended, but she has no plans to leave. Janssen's family moved to Kennebec "with the intention to stay," and that is exactly what they plan to do. Janssen is now well-imbedded in the community. She has clients, she does public service work, and her children are in the school system. Those kids "like being here, they have friends, they like the community." Janssen is poised to stay in one of South Dakota's smallest towns permanently. A town of 281 residents (five of those being Janssen's family) has maintained a law practice against all odds.

In this case, the Rural Attorney Recruitment Program was an unqualified success: for Kennebec that kept a law office, for Sundall who was able to find a successor for his practice, and for Janssen who has a stable career in a welcoming community. In the course of my interviews, I teared up twice listening to lawyers tell their stories. Once was during my conversation with Sundall when he spoke about why he mentored Janssen. Sundall explained: "I think it's an obligation of mine to make sure that she's successful and that she gives the advice that I think my clients are entitled to." Sundall did not just feel an obligation to Janssen, he felt an obligation to his clients in his one-attorney town. Before finding Janssen, Sundall was "very concerned that I would maybe never get somebody to come in. And that bothered me because there's a lot of good people out there" that "deserve good representation." As he was nearing retirement, Sundall "almost felt like I was abandoning them if I just got up and closed the door and left. And, I couldn't do it." The Rural Attorney Recruitment Program helped Sundall, and the town of Kennebec, avoid that fate.

Overall, at the ten-year anniversary, twenty-four of thirty-two attorneys were still practicing law in their rural placements. That is a 75-percent retention rate for the first ten years of the program. This chapter includes information about why lawyers stayed and why lawyers left, though I begin with a more generalized discussion of choice. Basically, the idea that these lawyers are not stuck in rural communities; they choose to be there. Then I turn to the specifics of those who left the program, then those who stayed, always with a focus on how the policies of the Rural Attorney Recruitment Program played a role in the outcomes.

THE ROLE OF CHOICE

When I was in college, I signed up for an introductory Gender & Women Studies course. Agency became my new favorite word. I remember my dad, always game to hear about my academic interests, even started using it one Christmas break. I overused the word as a college kid, but the idea of individual agency – that people

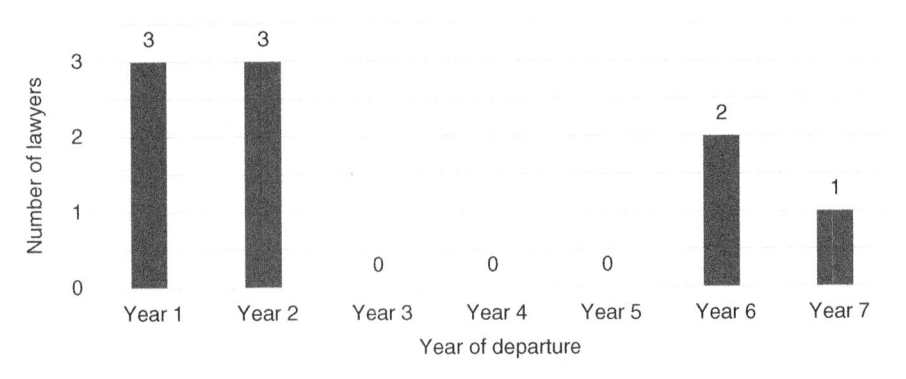

FIGURE 11.2 Year of participant departure

should be able to dictate their choices and, ideally, have the ability to control outcomes – still appeals to me. The Rural Attorney Recruitment Program is mostly in the business of increasing agency for rural lawyers. It offers an opportunity, but it cannot force participants to stay.

There is one way, however, that the program constrains individual choice. Because the contract requires that attorneys pay back the stipend if they leave in the middle of the program, the lawyers who have left either left quickly or after the stipend was finished. Eight participants left the rural practice of law. Five left during the five-year contract period and three left after the five-year contract period. One more attorney left a community during the contract period but immediately restarted the program in a neighboring county, so I do not consider her as a permanent departure from the rural practice of law. However, aspects of that lawyer's departure are relevant to understanding the program and are thus included in this discussion. Figure 11.2 shows the year of departure for the nine participants who ever left the program.

Of the nine departures, three left before receiving their first payment; three left before receiving their second payment; and three waited until after the five-year contract term was over and there would be no obligation to pay back any funds. The requirement of paying back the entire stipend amount constrained participants' ability to leave the program once they had accrued much payment.

There is a tension here. Several participants recommended either monthly payments or splitting payments so that new lawyers received a payment immediately. The problem with an earlier payment is that it would further constrain lawyers' ability to leave. As it is, several participants made the decision to leave immediately before they received payment because receiving a payment felt like an inflection point that required sticking it out for five years.

The data also suggests that there is a concern that lawyers will leave once the full five-year contract is completed and no repayment is necessary. That calculation is an inevitable part of a time-limited incentive program. When the incentive program expires, participants are no longer bound by any requirement to stay. Just as physicians sometimes leave rural areas after completing loan forgiveness programs, some rural lawyers will leave. But so far, it seems like the lawyers want to stay. Most of the lawyers who started lasted five years, and most of the lawyers who lasted five years plan to stay permanently. Some attrition, though, is not necessarily a bad thing. A lawyer unhappy with their work or personal life should not be stuck.

One participant who left the program very passionately told me that "in today's world, people move jobs really quickly." Job hopping may be a norm for today's generation of young workers, but that new cultural norm has not infiltrated the rural lawyers in this program.[311] Instead, these lawyers have been shockingly stable. Even for the eight participants who left rural practice, most have stayed in their first postprogram job. As Chapter 4 establishes, many of these lawyers had other jobs either before law school or after law school before entering rural practice. They are not afraid of changing jobs or careers when needed, but the rural practice of law has generally been satisfying enough to keep lawyers doing it.

In her book *The Heartland* historian Kristin L. Hoganson describes rural America as a place with lots of movement.[312] In this view, rural America is not isolated. Instead, people come and go, plus they generally engage with the broader world through travel, trade, and the sharing of ideas. Someone like Amy Jo Janssen who moved to Kennebec incapsulates what Hoganson argues: Even in the tiniest towns, where one might assume no one moves, people are entering and exiting. Even the lawyers who returned to their hometowns engaged in this coming and going. They left for college and law school then made the affirmative choice to return to rural America.

It may be, as Jennifer Sherman argues, that rural people "must be willing to forgo both economic and cultural capital, to live without movies and ballet lessons and fast food and many of the other amenities and opportunities available in most of the United States."[313] The digital age, especially that ushered in by COVID-19, has changed many of these sacrifices. It is easier than ever to access amenities through the internet. Perhaps ballet lessons are still missing and it can take an hour to get to the closest McDonald's, though some of these rural communities have a better drive-in movie theater than most cities. Lawyers talked about long drives to access shopping and restaurants, yet that was often balanced against shorter drives to access hunting, fishing, or agricultural land. The lawyers I spoke with were more than willing to forgo urban amenities to reap the benefits of living in a rural area.

Political scientists and sociologists write about "place attachment," a "bond people develop to a location where they would like to remain."[314] A number of factors influence place attachment, but overall rural residents have stronger place

---

[311] Eilene Zimmerman, *For Younger Workers, Job Hopping Has Lost Its Stigma. Should It?*, N.Y. TIMES (Aug. 9, 2023), https://perma.cc/J46H-27LU.

[312] KRISTIN L. HOGANSON, THE HEARTLAND: AN AMERICAN HISTORY (2019).

[313] SHERMAN, WORK, *supra* note 159, at 53.

[314] James G. Gimpel & Andrew Reeves, *The Urban-Rural Divide and Residential Contentment as Antecedents of Political Ideology*, 146 CITIES 104720 (2014).

attachment. This is important because place attachment "is a major component of life satisfaction."[315] This bolsters my findings that staying *is an affirmative choice* for these lawyers. Lawyers choose to stay in their rural communities because they want to. Of course, aspects of the community matter for this choice: When rural residents choose whether to stay or leave, they are more likely to stay in "areas where they have family and perceive there to be adequate recreational opportunities and high community trust and cohesion."[316] The longer a rural resident stays in their community, the stronger place attachment they feel.[317] The bet is that most attorneys who last five years will have built the community relationships to get them to stay for the remainder of their careers, and that has mostly been correct.

DEPARTURES DURING THE PROGRAM

Five attorneys left rural practice during their five-year contract, and one more attorney left a contract then restarted rural practice in another county. Of the five who permanently left the program during those five years, two entered teaching careers and three have remained lawyers. The five participants who left did so of their own volition, none were fired or faced repercussions at work that required a departure.

Elizabeth Steptoe had a great relationship with her mentor and hiring attorney but wanted more flexibility and less travel as she raised her young son. Plus, with her husband very busy on their farm, they found it "hard to mesh two big careers." A teaching job offered Steptoe the flexibility she wanted, and she remains open to returning to rural practice in the future. Of the participants who left during the five years, Steptoe was the only one who had returned close to home, living on the family farm and commuting to work in the neighboring county. She has not moved, simply changed careers. It is not surprising that some new lawyers would leave the field. Not everyone who gets a law degree wants to practice law, and not everyone who starts practicing law wants to keep practicing. The attrition rate from law firm jobs is pretty high.[318] And, on average, about 10 percent of new law school graduates never even enter the field, instead choosing JD Advantage Jobs, where law degrees are useful, but not required.[319] Some attrition from the legal field should be expected.

Kasen Lambeth was enjoying his full-time Deputy State's Attorney position in the rural practice program, but his friend and mentor was elected State's Attorney one county over, and Lambeth decided to take a job as her Deputy State's Attorney. When Lambeth moved, he was unable to continue in the program. Lambeth later

---

[315] *Id.*
[316] Ulrich-Schad, Henly & Safford, *supra* note 182, at 390.
[317] Jennings & Krannich, *supra* note 288, at 502.
[318] William Dougherty, *The Winners in Law's "Great Resignation" Will Be Firms That Focus on Innovation, Not Compensation*, ABA J. (Feb. 22, 2022), https://perma.cc/DPZ3-W6GW.
[319] *Jobs & JDs, supra* note 42.

became a solo practitioner, returning to rural practice by working in his original contract location of Elk Point, population 2,124. Lambeth ended up serving rural South Dakota for a number of years even outside of the program.

Evan Hoel's departure is more concerning from a programmatic perspective. Hoel was only in his rural community for three weeks before taking full-time employment as a public defender. Hoel was a solo practitioner and was primed for that departure by two fears – a fear of financial instability and a fear of inadequate mentorship to become a competent lawyer. The fears Hoel felt as a new solo practitioner were felt by others, including lawyers who suggested new solo practitioners needed more support. A more hands-on incubator program, or immediate funding for start-up costs, could prevent those types of concerns from leading to early program departures. Hoel had nothing bad to say about the program or his rural community. Simply put, he was not there long enough to really experience the rural practice of law.

The other two departures suggest a policy problem. Ryan McKnight and Amanda LaCroix both cite health insurance as the primary reason for their departures. LaCroix also had financial concerns with her practice, and the full-time attorney position she took with the state offered health insurance and a guaranteed income. McKnight similarly took full-time state employment, teaching at his alma mater. Before their departures, both McKnight and LaCroix tried, but failed, to obtain health insurance from their rural counties. Health insurance was hugely important for McKnight, whose wife was pregnant, and LaCroix, who had a very young child. Most of the lawyers working as even part-time prosecutors receive benefits through their employing county, though not all. The solo practitioners, unless they have health insurance because of military service, are the ones hit hardest with health insurance costs. McKnight and LaCroix fell into this category. Since their departures, the State Bar of South Dakota has made a health insurance plan available to its members. Ensuring health insurance is available to rural practitioners is a necessary part of a successful program to recruit and retain solo practitioners in rural areas.

Even for these lawyers who left after one or two years of practice, the program has been beneficial to them. For Ryan McKnight, the program "taught me a lot of resilience" and "compassion" that helps him navigate relationships with his college students. Elizabeth Steptoe developed a variety of skills. She increased her comfort level in dealing with people, found a renewed dedication to helping the downtrodden, and learned how to manage the growth of the family farm. For Amanda LaCroix, her time in the program has helped "tremendously" in her new job. She has practical experience which allows her to advise other state employees when they confront issues that LaCroix saw firsthand in practice.

While none of these lawyers completed the five-year commitment, and none are practicing law in rural areas today, it is not fair to say the program was a failure for them. Even where the program could have done more – like provide better mentorship or health insurance – there were still benefits from participating and spending even a short period of time in rural practice.

CHANGES AND DEPARTURES AFTER FIVE YEARS

As of summer 2023, fifteen participants had completed their five years in the program. Three of those fifteen participants left their communities entirely. Most of those participants made no changes following the end of their contract terms, but a few did. Two lawyers left their firms and became solo practitioners in their same communities, giving them more freedom to manage their own caseloads. Another participant joined a firm in a neighboring county following her contract and now splits her time between two counties. Dusty Ginsbach reduced his private clients to focus more on prosecutorial work and his second job working for an oil company.

Three attorneys left their rural communities after finishing their five-year obligation. Jake Fischer left after five years, returning to Minnesota where he attended law school and his wife grew up. Amanda Work left after five-and-a-half years. Though she was happy in her solo practice, her dream job as a federal public defender became available in Pierre. Casey Jo Deibert left in her seventh year for a full-time position in Pierre, where she now serves as the full-time State's Attorney.

Deibert was the only participant to leave for purely financial reasons. Deibert was "still drowning in school loans" after six years of rural practice and needed a higher-earning job. There are lessons to extrapolate from Deibert's experience. First, the county paying her to be a Deputy State's Attorney tried to be cheap with its prosecutor salary, making it hard for her to stay long term. Second, it helps when established attorneys (as they are able) share the wealth of valuable government contracts to make it financially possible for young attorneys to stay. Deibert would "go back in a heartbeat" to her contract county after her loans are paid or if a State's Attorney position became available. Her departure was not inevitable. Another lawyer who is considering moving away from her rural community thinks that getting more criminal appointments would have helped the finances of her practice and her feeling of community acceptance, increasing the odds that she would want to stay.

I asked each of these three departing lawyers if the program was a success for them, and they all said yes. Work noted how much she enjoyed her rural practice. Deibert noted that the program gave her purpose. Fischer noted the skills he developed. Work, who did criminal defense work in her rural community, now works as a full-time federal public defender. Deibert obtained experience in both prosecution and defense work, and now works as a full-time prosecutor. Fischer was more focused on civil work, and the skills have transferred to his new job. Overall rural practice "was a huge benefit" for Fischer and he learned to be "not afraid to try" something for a client.

THOSE WHO STAYED

Rural sociologists have studied what keeps rural residents in place and what makes them move. A focus on family and strong social ties in the community – including length of time living in that community – are aspects that keep rural residents in place.[320] The acceptance I discussed in Chapter 6 is critical here because "[t]he emotional aspect of sensing that a community is 'home' or that one belongs in a setting plays an important role in the formation of attachment to community."[321] But rural residents who are younger, unmarried, have higher education, and are newer to their rural communities are more likely to leave.[322] These lawyers are in the demographic most often pulled away by brain drain – they are highly educated and have the opportunity to move elsewhere. The lawyers are not stuck in rural communities, destined to practice law in one spot forever. Instead, lawyers choose to stay or choose to go.

Though eight participants have left the rural practice of law, twenty-four have stayed. Of those twenty-four, at the ten-year mark of the program, twelve were still in the five-year contract period, and another twelve had completed the contract. I asked each of those lawyers if they intended to stay in their community long term. Most said yes without any hesitation or qualification. A few are open to leaving if they meet someone and get married; one would consider leaving only for providing elder care for family members. Many lawyers are set on staying permanently. Austin Hoffman simply quipped, "if all else fails, I'll just buy cows and start farming again."

Two lawyers that have finished the five-year obligation think about leaving the rural practice of law. One participant plans to leave her rural community, though still thinks of the program as a success for her. While rural practice is "not even a little bit" like what she expected, she has enjoyed the "freedom" that has come with her rural practice, and she has learned "how to run a business." This participant, and one other, simply do not like practicing law. As one lawyer said, "I do not enjoy being a lawyer. It's really stressful. It takes a toll on your mental health." Legal work can be emotionally taxing, especially for lawyers who are empathetic by nature. Lawyers who do not like the actual practice of law can look for other work, though rural jobs are hard to find. One participant is actively working on a degree to become a licensed counselor rather than stay in the practice of law.

The rest of the participants generally enjoy being lawyers, though there are different degrees of this enjoyment. Most thoroughly enjoy doing legal work in their rural communities. They generally are fulfilled personally and professionally with their jobs, and many see themselves as public servants doing good for their communities. A few participants are more invested in ranch work than legal work, finding

---

[320] Ulrich-Schad, Henly & Safford, *supra* note 182, at 376, 385–86.
[321] Jennings & Krannich, *supra* note 288, at 500.
[322] Ulrich-Schad, Henly & Safford, *supra* note 182, at 385–86.

less satisfaction (but higher pay) in law, which is enough to keep them practicing law. For some, the intimate nature of these rural communities is not all good. As one participant said, "you live in a glass house" when you're a rural lawyer. Yet, that cost is worthwhile for the participants.

More than their legal practices keeps these lawyers in their rural communities. Anthropologist of law Michele Statz explains that "rural legal advocates experience professional *as well as* physical, material, and emotional obligations to a rural place."[323] Some stay because the hunting and fishing opportunities are good. More than that, though, many participants are just invested in the community itself. It is their childhood home or their adopted home, and they would not leave the community they have built. Sociologists have found that as an individual lives in a rural community longer, the natural amenities fade in importance as compared to the community.[324] Studies support that home and family keep people rural, and the same is true for these lawyers.[325]

For many of the participants with school-age children, the local school is a reason to stay. Multiple attorneys told me that they liked their school districts and saw them as a reason to move rural and a reason to stay. Not a single attorney told me they worried about their rural schools or saw bigger school districts as better, even though the bigger districts have more resources.

Children influence decision-making in other ways as well. One participant who got divorced after joining the program has stayed because a postdivorce move would implicate ability to successfully share custody. On the other hand, one law student who was signed up for the program changed her mind because of a divorce. Moving to a remote rural community was not a viable option postdivorce because it would have separated her children from their father. Realizing the best interests of her children were to be near to their father, she took a job in Sioux Falls in order to better share custody. Her personal preference was for rural practice; her family situation dictated against it.

Just as important as community, children, and recreation is financial stability. More than anything else, employment opportunities dictate where people want to live.[326] The finances and stability of practice are critical to keeping these lawyers in rural communities. Like many rural residents, these lawyers are willing to forgo higher salaries or fancier jobs to stay in a desirable place.[327] For the lawyers who have stayed, they express no desire for career "advancement" in any way other than becoming a better and more experienced attorney. Some hope that as

---

[323] Statz, *The Scandal of Particularity, supra* note 178, at 405.
[324] Joan M. Brehm, Brian W. Eisenhauer & Richard S. Krannich, *Dimensions of Community Attachment and Their Relationship to Well-Being in the Amenity-Rich Rural West*, 69 RURAL SOCIO. 405, 407 (2004).
[325] SHERMAN, WORK, *supra* note 159, at 126.
[326] Ulrich-Schad, Henly & Safford, *supra* note 182, at 387.
[327] SHERMAN, WORK, *supra* note 159, at 129.

their practices develop, they will have more time to enjoy other aspects of rural life, like ranching on the side. A few mentioned the possibility of judgeships in the future, but not as something they expected, rather as something they might eventually consider.

One way that the South Dakota program has allowed attorneys to stay is by being flexible in the coverage and administration of the program. Take for example the inclusion of maternity and military leave. Three participants are in the National Guard, requiring time off for training and deployments. The program is administered so those military commitments do not negatively impact participation in the program. For example, Austin Schaefer was deployed to Kuwait and Iraq in support of Operation Inherent Resolve. Schaefer's contract was paused from December 2022 until October 2023 when he returned to rural practice. Similarly, the program allows maternity leave for new mothers. Two participants delayed their entry into the program because of giving birth shortly after law school. Three more participants have had one or two children during their time in the program. That process has been easy – a simple email communication with the program administrator has been sufficient to schedule the maternity leave.

These types of accommodations are critical to keeping attorneys in the program. Without the ability to participate in military service or take time off after birth, any program might lose some participants. Across the legal profession, women have increased odds of leaving their jobs when they have children, facing a reality of insufficient leave, support, and flexibility. Balancing motherhood with a demanding career is part of what made Elizabeth Steptoe transition to teaching. Allowing a pause in work for new mothers allows more women to stay in the practice of law.

Programmatic flexibility also showed itself to be powerful in other ways. For the participant who had a bad start in one county then restarted in another county. For Amy Jo Janssen who was able to start the program only *after* her mentor retired, thereby ensuring support during her first few years in solo practice. For the participants where the local government agreed to pay their portion early, easing the earliest financial strain. And, perhaps most importantly, by giving a stipend that lawyers could spend however they wanted.

I asked every participant what the program could do better. One participant who left gave a list of proposed modifications, including replacing the general stipend with a transportation stipend, a childcare stipend, and a stipend specifically for the start-up costs for a new firm. Two lawyers suggested scrapping the stipend and implementing a loan-repayment program; another mentioned moving costs and down payment assistance. All of those are legitimate expenses for a new lawyer, and all could be covered with the South Dakota stipend. But what makes the South Dakota stipend so powerful – and so useful to rural practitioners – is its flexible nature. As Chapter 9 shows, these participants used their stipends in all sorts of important ways. It would be more expensive and more difficult to manage stipends targeted at specific costs, and no particular stipend could be tailored narrowly enough to meet the needs of all rural practitioners. Even loan forgiveness programs, so popular right now, are too narrowly targeted to incentivize the most lawyers.

The other way that the South Dakota program has been flexible is with regards to allowing any type of practice area and any type of firm situation. Jobs must be full time and must be in qualifying counties or municipalities, but otherwise lawyers can mostly create their own careers. After larger counties started using the program to subsidize full-time employee salaries, the option of being a full-time prosecutor was removed. A completely understandable choice, it still rankles some participants because one option for using the program is gone. Several attorneys wish that full-time government employees – whether prosecutors or tribal lawyers – could qualify for the program. Other states that have created rural lawyer incentive programs have often drawn them more narrowly. Administering a program that allows any type of employment in any practice area is presumably harder, but well worth the return on investment as lawyers find the career paths that work for them.

LESSONS LEARNED

There is no obvious metric to decide if South Dakota's Rural Attorney Recruitment Program has been successful. The lawyers behind implementing the program uniformly told me the program exceeded their expectations. The program has done more than any of the original planners thought. In that way, it is a success. It is also a success by being a first-in-the-nation policy response that has spurred national attention and emulation.

In my view, the numbers alone prove the efficacy of the program. Ten years after its implementation, 75 percent of the lawyers who set foot in a rural area under a program contract are still practicing law in their rural communities. Certainly, we could wish for 100 percent permanency in rural communities, but the fact that there are now twenty-four lawyers in rural South Dakota who have been helped by this program proves its success. Consider the improbability that Kennebec, a tiny town that most people see as nothing more than an interstate exit, could get a young attorney to serve the town for the next thirty years. Herb Sundall handing his firm to Amy Jo Janssen is a prime example of the good this program can accomplish.

Even among the participating attorneys, there is a difference in perspective on what success means. Perhaps it means practicing law permanently in a rural community; perhaps it means staying for five years. I asked the three attorneys who left after five years whether they thought of themselves as a success for the program. One said yes based on the services provided while in rural practice, and the other two not so much. They each said they feel "bad" about leaving because they view the point of the program as creating long-term rural lawyers. Several other participants talked about success being defined through longevity in rural legal practice, though others thought the point of the program, and thus its success, was to increase access to justice.

South Dakota's program has been, overall, a success. Not everyone is as thrilled as Austin Hoffman, who says: "The program is fantastic. I'm extremely happy our state did this; I hope our legislature continues this program." His praise is high, but few participants hold truly negative views about the program. Though not universal, even those who ultimately have disliked rural practice and want to change careers generally acknowledge the positive aspects of the program. It is not that these lawyers all think the program is perfect, but they recognize the program was able to help them get established in functional law practices in rural communities that have – for the most part – become their permanent homes. There is no question that the South Dakota program is good. The bigger questions are whether South Dakota stays committed to incentivizing rural lawyers by continuing to support and improve the program over time and whether other states will join.

South Dakota is a small state with strong connections between rural lawyers and those with policymaking capacity. Accessibility and intimacy of connections was critical to the creation of the Rural Attorney Recruitment Program in South Dakota. Other states, even states with substantially more resources than South Dakota, have generally failed to create similar programs. Yet states should take the success of South Dakota's program as evidence that it is worth funding rural lawyer recruitment in a meaningful way. Bus tours and networking events are not enough. Rural lawyers need real, concrete financial assistance to survive the first few years of practice, and it can be done at a reasonable price when it is crafted as a supplement, not a salary.

12

Conclusion

FIGURE 12.1 Dusty Ginsbach

Dusty Ginsbach practices law in Harding County, arguably the most rural county in South Dakota. Harding County has 1,178 residents spread over 2,671 square miles, for only 0.4 people per square mile. By the Census definition, 100 percent of the county is rural. The largest town, where Ginsbach practices, has a population of only 349. Ginsbach observes that "the biggest setback to rural practice in South Dakota is fear. People are afraid of what they don't know, and we're just not a brave bunch of lawyers."

Ginsbach observes that "people want a security blanket, and that security blanket looks like what everybody else has done and been fine with." He sees the "security blanket" for new lawyers as joining firms in the bigger South Dakota cities, oftentimes "getting worked to the bone" and "getting burnt out within the first two years." Yet, new lawyers are "comfortable with that because they have student loans to pay, and they have a reputation to uphold, and they are hungry. They want to gain experience, and they get taken advantage of." For Ginsbach, who chose rural practice from day one, "I would be more afraid of that than having the calm and quiet of a small community where you can still be as comfortable." A writer from rural Appalachia articulates the struggle of moving home to her rural community as an "ever-present struggle between the heart and the head."[328] The idea that one yearns to return home and live in a rural community, but the economics, the jobs, the internet access, and the housing weighs against the decision to move home.

Ginsbach does not see a solution to this fear. In his view "if people weren't afraid, then rural practice would be doing a lot better. So, I don't know what the answer is for the Rural Practice Committee to overcome that, or for the State of South Dakota to overcome that." I believe that overcoming this fear of rural practice is precisely why the Rural Attorney Recruitment Program was created. In fact, Chief Justice Gilbertson used the language of "fear" to describe why he was so focused on creating institutional support for rural lawyers.

For Chief Justice Gilbertson, the main reason for doing the financial incentive was to take away "the fear factor" of choosing small-town practice. In his view, financial assistance and good mentorship could combat the fear holding new lawyers back from choosing a career in a small town. This idea bears out in the way many of the participants view the program's influence on their decision to choose rural practice. The fear that Ginsbach and Gilbertson speak about is not the discomfiting, heart-racing fear of a dangerous situation. Rather, it is a combination of stress, risk-taking, and a fear of the unknown. Using such language, various participants explained the Rural Attorney Recruitment Program pushed them past the concerns of rural practice to give it a try. "It made it a little bit easier to come to terms with wanting to do rural practice because it gives you a little bit of that cushion to make it not as *scary*." "It certainly opened up some doors, because obviously being nontrad having family and kids to worry about, rural practice has a lot of *risks*, I would say." "That was a huge *risk*, coming back and opening my own practice fresh out of law school with absolutely no idea if I was going to be able to make enough money to put food on my table for my two kids and wife."

Participants not only saw the program as a way to push past the fear of rural practice, but they also saw it as an encouraging – and perhaps hopeful – start of their future. "It made it a lot more feasible to come home because I think it's kind of

---

[328] Kathleen M. Jacobs, *The Decision to Move Home*, DAILY YONDER (Oct. 12, 2023), https://perma.cc/NY2H-FZTS.

intimidating and hard to get a start in a rural community." "It helped – I'd probably say gave more of an option." "It probably would have either taken longer or I would have been a lot more hesitant about [rural practice]." "I can breathe a little bit, knowing that I'll be comfortable here, even [though] you could sign a lot higher-priced contract in a bigger city." "It was a thing that almost allowed me to come." "It would be something that would be helpful and make it so I could make it work."

The Rural Attorney Recruitment Program gave these lawyers hope for a career in rural practice. For many of them, it did what Chief Justice Gilbertson imagined. It turned the fear and risk into hope in the possibility of rural practice. It got lawyers over initial obstacles and committed to a career in rural South Dakota. Law professors Kathryn Abrams and Hila Keren have made the case that institutional interventions – including through law – can be used to cultivate hope.[329] Hope meaning "the ability to imagine new possibilities not encompassed by one's present condition; a sense of agency sufficient to consider oneself capable of pursuing, and attaining, distant objectives; and adequate imaginative, strategic, and material resources to develop, assess, and implement means for realizing such goals."[330] South Dakota's Rural Attorney Recruitment Program does just that. It gives hope to lawyers about the viability of rural practice.

More than that, the program also gives hope to rural attorneys wanting to retire but unable to find a new lawyer to take over the firm. The average age of rural attorneys continues to grow and there is consistent need for replacement attorneys to enter rural practice. The retiring attorneys I interviewed talked about their commitments to their rural communities and their fears of leaving a town with no lawyer. The recruitment assistance that came from the program gave hope to some of South Dakota's retiring lawyers and allowed them to find a successful transition for their rural firms in the communities they care so deeply about.

I leave the study of *clients* to future work. Someone else can – and should – study optimal ways for clients to access legal services in rural areas. There are a number of options that could be promoted. Logging onto the internet to see a remote lawyer? Walking into a local office to see a lawyer face-to-face? State-created forms to ease self-representation? Telephone hotlines for basic legal instruction? Drop-in hours at the local library? I cannot say what clients prefer or even the single best place for states to invest. What I can say is that though this book is not about the clients of rural lawyers, these lawyers generally see serving actual clients as an end-goal of the program. Rural America has been left behind in many ways, leading to despair, poverty, and discontent. It may be that the increased presence of lawyers in rural America creates hope for the clients of those lawyers. Abrams and Keren propose that legal representation can be used to foster hope in clients, and a study of clients in rural areas could flesh out how this operates.

---

[329] Kathryn Abrams & Hila Keren, *Law in the Cultivation of Hope*, 95 CALIF. L. REV. 319 (2007).
[330] *Id.* at 322.

Even bigger than the hope for individual lawyers and individual clients is an overarching hope I personally feel for rural America to survive and even thrive. While South Dakota's program stops at its border, the inspiration need not. Almost every state has a rural lawyer shortage, and almost every state needs an intervention. When rural communities are portrayed as toxic or unworthy, potential rural lawyers may avoid entering the profession despite all of the good parts of the profession.

It is my hope that the South Dakota program and its successes can give hope to other states. The fear of entering rural practice is not unique to South Dakota. An aging attorney in Oregon explained, "I think there are a lot of people who would be happy in a rural area, but they're afraid to come here."[331] There is room for Oregon, and the rest of the states, to adopt programs that cultivate hope in the face of this fear and allow rural lawyers to thrive.

Of course, no program is perfect, and even in South Dakota, which offers the most comprehensive support program for new rural attorneys, lawyers struggled. It is useful, in this context, to conclude with ideas for improvement by the people closest to the program. Throughout the book, I have interwoven ideas for improvement, though I collect them all here as a set of takeaways for consideration. I do not seek to overpromise on the universality of South Dakota's program to the rest of the country, yet I think it is fair to view middle America as a "vantage point" to consider the rest of the country.[332] Of course, there are limits to vantage points. Geography and local governments differ across the country. Take for just one example the idea of paying rural lawyers to provide open-office community hours: The best place to do this will vary. In a Walmart? At a tribal agency? At a courthouse? In the lawyers' office? At a library? Rural areas are different, and this is the trouble with proposing policy solutions too broadly: A proposal that seems out of touch with rural reality in one region may make sense in another.

Before discussing ideas for improvement, though, it is worth starting with the idea that not everyone agrees on what the "point" of this program is. It turns out that defining the "point" of the program is more controversial than I would have imagined. I thought it simple – to get lawyers into rural areas and hope they stay long-term. A few thought the point was about increasing access to justice, though most took a broader approach and thought about the program in relationship to rural livelihoods. A few participants thought the program should only be for lawyers joining firms, yet another thought the program "was intended to help solo practitioners," but *not* those joining firms. Another difference came to light with lawyer backgrounds – several participants thought the program should focus on participants with local ties, but another believes the program should only be for lawyers entering a rural community without preexisting ties.

---

[331] Collins, *supra* note 53, at 18.
[332] HOGANSON, *supra* note 312, at 256.

TABLE 12.1 *Suggestions for improvement*

Suggestion	Participating lawyers (32)	Potential participants (4)	Mentors (11)
Improve mentorship	11		
Support solos more	1		
Cover start-up costs	3		1
Increase dollar amount	3	1	2
Cover bar dues	1		
Pay at beginning of year or monthly	5		1
Extend years	1		
State fund, not locality			1
Cover tribal employees	1		
Change to targeting particular costs	3	1	
Health insurance	1	1	
Training for participants	4	1	
Better legal education	4		1
Supervised practice for solos until bar passage			1
Change time reporting	4		
Recruit new lawyers	6		8
Recruit firms to hire	4		1
Recruit communities	3		1

I view the goals and the point of this program as broad. It is for solo practitioners, and for those joining firms. It is for those moving to new communities, and those going home. South Dakota's legislation is broad enough to encompass a wide range of potential rural practitioners, bringing more lawyers into rural communities by casting a wide net of what qualifies.

With these varying perspectives in mind, I asked what should change in the South Dakota program. Table 12.1 reflects the suggestions and how often they were made.

By far the most common response from participants was a request for more mentorship. A few participants thought the Rural Attorney Recruitment Program itself should make mentorship more formal. One thinks it should be mandatory for participants to join an existing firm and more thought the program should encourage law firms to hire. Most provided suggestions for future lawyers: find mentors, take over an existing law practice, and find a firm that will pay a salary. Many of them realize the difficulty of finding a good mentor, and one attorney who had a particularly negative experience with her hiring lawyer suggested that an incentive be created to encourage aging attorneys to bring in and mentor new attorneys. A few mentoring lawyers also focused on convincing more firms to hire, with one suggesting a paid incentive for the retiring lawyer.

As one attorney said, the most difficult part of rural practice was "being able to make sure I'm knowledgeable enough" to handle cases. Mentorship helps, but so can training during and after law school. Several participants suggested law school classes that should be improved, especially on the nuts and bolts of running a law practice as a business. There were requests for more specific training, with a general recognition that such training was most useful once already in practice. Before COVID-19, there were meetings for Rural Attorney Recruitment Program participants, allowing both networking and continuing education. Many of the participants I interviewed did not even know about this past reality, but they suggested similar programming nonetheless. Attorneys who attended pre-COVID-19 trainings viewed those as important to their professional development and their ability to make referrals to other participating attorneys. Since I finished my interviews, those meetings have begun to return.

Community engagement was the next topic of suggestions. Several participants who were either rejected from a county or were accepted and later felt unwelcome suggested that the program itself should do more work before a county is approached with a particular participant. To some extent, the program did this by seeking out interested counties. In some places, it was a hiring attorney who did the legwork to make sure a community wanted a lawyer. But some participants and some hiring attorneys were still caught off guard with outright rejections from the county commission, or they later felt like locals did not want to bring them legal business. Mentors also spoke about this and how much work they did behind the scenes to get county commissioner approval; one suggested the program improve its "PR with the commissioners."

Finances were at the center of another set of proposals. The stipend amount has not risen with inflation, and there was a hope it would increase at least periodically with cost-of-living increases. Mentors who saw the stipend as a way to meet salary demands were likely to mention wanting to see an increase. And mentors absolutely did see the stipend as part of the compensation package for their new hires. For example, one participating attorney explained that the hiring attorney liked the idea of participating "because then he did not have to pay me as much."

More concerning than the total dollar amount for several participants was the timing of the payments. Two suggested monthly payments rather than annual payments, and several suggested that there be an initial payment at the beginning of rural practice to cover start-up costs. Certainly, a change to allow six payments spread over five years would allow an initial payment on day one, allowing basic expenses to be covered for solo practitioners. That, however, would create a lock-in effect for lawyers unable to pay back the stipend if they left the rural community, so unless the early money did not need to be repaid, such a structure could be problematic.

A good option would be to cover start-up costs for solo practitioners, but have those start-up costs come from another fund and not require repayment if a solo decides to leave. That additional stipend for an entirely new business is reasonable – as one solo practitioner explained, "there was nothing to walk into, and so I was building from the ground up and trying to get people to come back to the community for legal work." Another explained that even though she had prior practice experience, "starting from scratch is hard" for opening a new law firm, but having the stipend made her feel like, "I don't have to do this alone." An additional stipend for that situation might be warranted, as might coverage of bar dues for the solo practitioners in the first year or two. On the other hand, targeted stipends sometimes require more paperwork than they are worth. In Arkansas, incubator funding has required detailed accounting. That has been burdensome enough that the new program administrator is working to remove the detailed accounting requirements.

Solo practitioners are disadvantaged in other ways, and one lawyer who mentored a solo practitioner from afar proposed a special supervised practice rule to allow solo practitioners to somehow begin some supervised practice while waiting for bar results. New law school graduates joining firms can use supervised practice rules to begin working while waiting for bar results; solo practitioners cannot.

Several participants were happy overall with the program, offering no suggestions for change. But what these satisfied attorneys often offered was a suggestion for more and better recruiting from the high school level through law school. Many of these participants see more and more nearby lawyers retiring, with no new lawyers coming to replace them. They simply want more recruitment at every stage, as do the established attorneys. Three-quarters of the mentors I interviewed identified recruitment of the next generation of rural attorneys as a critical need in the program. Even with all the successes in recruiting, these lawyers look around and see aging colleagues across the state who need to hire the next generation.

Finally, there were a few comments about the administration of the program. The Unified Judicial System, which administers the program, requires that attorneys fill out time sheets to verify they have worked the minimum number of hours. No one had good things to say about this process. The participants complained, as did a program administrator. The same program administrator was skeptical of the state judicial branch even administering the program. There are other options. In Illinois, the state bar administers the program. In Arkansas, a faculty member at the law school administers the program, though that has created an issue in the past – when the faculty member left, the program went dormant for a few years. In South Dakota, because funding comes from the legislature, it is necessary to have the judicial branch of government administer the program. Plus, keeping the administration very institutionalized likely helps with sustaining the program over time.

In thinking about the program suggestions, very few suggestions offer major alterations. Instead, many of the lawyers suggested doing *more* of what the program already does. *More* mentorship. *More* funding. *More* support. *More* cohort building. There is room for growth in South Dakota, but the leaders who put the program together a decade ago should be proud of their creation and the successes it has engendered. Chief Justice Gilbertson is right: At some point, rural states just need to try *something* because "to do nothing is a guarantee of increased failure of the legal system in rural areas."[333] South Dakota's program might not be perfect, but it was a grand first attempt at crafting policy to solve the rural lawyer shortage.

Even with the hope that the program offers, difficulties will always remain. Rural lawyering is still hard work. Lawyers in small towns carry burdens – of doing community service; of managing conflicts; of helping the downtrodden and well-resourced alike. Austin Hoffman explained that as a rural lawyer, "you have a lot of very important things for a lot of people that you're dealing with all the time. I always tell people that 'I deal with the stuff that they don't want to.' That really is what it comes down to." As Amy Jo Janssen summarized, "life as a rural lawyer can be difficult, but it is very rewarding too" because rural lawyers have to be dedicated to supporting their clients in some of the most difficult moments in life. That dedication to clients as people; to improving people's lives; to sustaining communities, is what makes the career of a rural lawyer worthwhile.

---

[333] Gilbertson, *supra* note 2, at 443.

Postscript

I conducted my first interview for this book project on June 13, 2022. I met with the last Rural Attorney Recruitment Program participant on March 24, 2023, the day before the ten-year anniversary of the governor signing the legislation. Not much changed from then until July 1, 2023, the official ten-year anniversary of the legislation going into effect. But between July 1 of 2023 and when I finalized this book in November of 2024, a lot has happened. The Hustead Law Firm, which employs two participating lawyers, has opened a satellite office in the small town of Wall, bringing legal services to another underserved rural area. Following the 2024 election, three additional rural counties will have participating lawyers as State's Attorneys beginning in January 2025. Three 2024 graduates of the University of South Dakota Knudson School of Law entered the program. Several participants have finished their five-year contracts, and they have all elected to stay. One rural lawyer, who had previously completed her contract, has transitioned into a career in counseling. Furthermore, two lawyers who had left the program before the ten-year anniversary have now transitioned again, this time moving back to their home states. Kasen Lambeth moved to Las Vegas to be closer to his family. Evan Hoel moved to Minnesota. Those behind the scenes continue to promote and encourage the program. Project Rural Practice leaders began a new set of ambitious projects in October 2024. In short, South Dakota continues to push forward with successfully encouraging rural practice.

Appendix: Participating Attorneys

This appendix includes short biographies on all thirty-two participating attorneys from the first ten years of South Dakota's Rural Attorney Recruitment Program. The biographies include information on the status of participants at the ten-year anniversary in the summer of 2023, but also include updates if changes have occurred following that time.

Clay Anderson grew up in a military family but was deeply connected with his grandparents and their ranch outside of Miller in Hand County, South Dakota. Anderson completed his undergraduate studies at Regis University in 2009 then had a military career before graduating from the University of South Dakota School of Law in 2014. Anderson's Rural Attorney Recruitment Program contract was with Hand County and he offices in Miller. In addition to practicing law, Anderson is a businessman in his local community. Anderson started his career working with an established lawyer and now works as a solo practitioner in Miller.

Ashley Anson spent her early years in Idaho, then moved to the family ranch outside of Wessington Springs in Jerauld County, South Dakota. Anson received her undergraduate degree from Indiana University–Purdue University Indianapolis in 2010. She then worked for the *Saturday Evening Post* and served in the Army for a short period of time before graduating from the University of South Dakota School of Law in 2014. Anson simultaneously earned a Masters of Environmental Law and Policy from Vermont Law. Anson first signed a contract with Aurora County where she worked in White Lake, then signed a new contract with Jerauld County to work in Wessington Springs where she was a solo practitioner for over five years. At the ten-year anniversary, Anson remained in Wessington Springs but was associated with a firm out of Mitchell, South Dakota. Since then, she has begun working as a counselor.

Casey Jo Deibert grew up in Spearfish, South Dakota. Deibert completed her undergraduate studies at Chadron State College in Nebraska in 2007. After four years of work, she returned to school and graduated from the University of South Dakota School of Law in 2014. Deibert's Rural Attorney Recruitment

Program contract was with Perkins County where she worked out of Bison in a satellite office for an attorney. After six years in Perkins County, Deibert moved to Pierre, South Dakota, where she took a full-time prosecutor job that she continues to hold today.

Kristian Ellendorf grew up in Hurley, South Dakota. Ellendorf was in the National Guard and completed her undergraduate studies at South Dakota State University in 2010 then worked for several years, including as a law firm runner. Ellendorf then returned to school, receiving her law degree from the University School of Law in 2016. Ellendorf's Rural Attorney Recruitment Program contract is with Miner County where she works with an established law firm in Howard and is a part-time State's Attorney. In addition, she is a major in the South Dakota National Guard.

Jennifer English grew up in La Porte, Indiana. English completed her undergraduate education at Carroll College in Wisconsin in 2003. She then worked in a variety of jobs, including as a cruise ship karaoke host before returning to law school, graduating from the Ohio Northern University Pettit College of Law in 2017. English, who had never been to South Dakota, learned about the Rural Attorney Recruitment Program through national media coverage and signed a contract with McCook County. English opened a solo practice in Salem. In addition to continuing with a limited rural practice, English spends about 90 percent of her time doing drug and alcohol involuntary commitments in Minnehaha County.

Jake Fischer grew up on a farm outside of Parkston in Hutchinson County, South Dakota. Fischer completed his undergraduate (2005) and law (2009) degrees at the University of Minnesota. Following law school, Fischer worked in Minnesota for several years before returning to South Dakota and signing a Rural Attorney Recruitment Program contract with Douglas County. Fischer worked in Corsica in a law firm's satellite office for five years then returned to Minnesota following his contract.

Dusty Ginsbach grew up outside of Buffalo in Harding County, South Dakota. Ginsbach has served in the National Guard since 2002 and completed his undergraduate education at Chadron State College in Nebraska in 2009. Ginsbach worked for several years then returned to school and graduated from the University of South Dakota School of Law in 2013. Ginsbach moved home, signing his Rural Attorney Recruitment Program contract with Harding County and working in the town of Buffalo. Since completing his contract, Ginsbach has reduced his legal practice, now working part time with a limited private practice and as the State's Attorney for Harding County. Ginsbach also works for Continental Resources and serves in the South Dakota Army National Guard.

Evan Hoel grew up in St. Paul, Minnesota. Hoel completed his undergraduate education at the University of Minnesota in 2013. Hoel then graduated from the University of South Dakota School of Law in 2018. Hoel signed his Rural Attorney Recruitment Program contract with Dewey County, starting a solo practice in Timber Lake. Hoel worked as a licensed attorney in Timber Lake for only three weeks before deciding to leave rural practice. Hoel worked as a public defender in Rapid City, South Dakota, for five years and moved to Rochester, Minnesota, in 2024 to work for Southern Minnesota Regional Legal Services.

Austin Hoffman grew up on a ranch outside of Eureka in McPherson County, South Dakota. Hoffman obtained his undergraduate degree from South Dakota State University in 2010 then worked for five years as a news reporter in Sioux Falls, South Dakota. Hoffman returned to school, graduating from the University of South Dakota School of Law in 2016. Hoffman's Rural Attorney Recruitment Program Contract was with McPherson County and Hoffman set up a solo practice in Eureka, where he remains today.

Amy Jo Janssen grew up on a ranch outside of Gordon, Nebraska. Janssen received her undergraduate education at Chadron State College in Nebraska in 2011 and her law degree from the University of South Dakota School of Law in 2014. Janssen signed her Rural Attorney Recruitment Program contract with Lyman County and joined a one-attorney firm in Kennebec. Now that her hiring attorney has retired, Janssen is a solo practitioner in Kennebec.

Derrick Johnson grew up in Tyndall in Bon Homme County, South Dakota. Johnson received his undergraduate (2013) and law (2017) degrees from the University of South Dakota. Johnson signed his Rural Attorney Recruitment Program contract with Bon Homme County and spent his first few years working in Scotland with a firm. In 2023, Johnson transitioned to solo practice in Springfield, a different town also located in Bon Homme County. Johnson's five-year contract is still active as of 2024.

Mason Juracek grew up in Gregory in Gregory County, South Dakota. Juracek received his undergraduate degree from Dakota Wesleyan University in 2019 then graduated from the University of South Dakota Knudson School of Law in 2022. Juracek signed his Rural Attorney Recruitment Program contract with Tripp County, the third lawyer to do so. Juracek is working in Winner as a Deputy State's Attorney and in private practice. Juracek's five-year contract is still active as of 2024.

Dylan Kirchmeier grew up in Webster in Day County, South Dakota. Kirchmeier received his undergraduate (2017) and law (2020) degrees from the University of South Dakota. Kirchmeier signed his Rural Attorney Recruitment Program contract with Sisseton, a city in Roberts County. Kirchmeier works as the full-time State's Attorney for Roberts County and his five-year contract is still active as of 2024.

Kristen Kochekian grew up in High Point, North Carolina. Kochekian received her undergraduate degree from East Carolina University in 2001 then graduated from the Oklahoma City University School of Law in 2005. After several years of legal work in North Carolina, Kochekian decided to join the Rural Attorney Recruitment Program after learning about it through the national media. Kochekian signed her contract with Spink County and has practiced in Redfield with a law firm since 2015.

Kirby Krogman grew up on a ranch outside of White River in Mellette County, South Dakota. Krogman received his undergraduate degree from Chadron State College in Nebraska in 2014 and graduated from the University of South Dakota School of Law in 2018. Krogman signed his Rural Attorney Recruitment Program contract with Mellette County and has always been a solo practitioner in White River. Krogman operates a private law firm and serves as State's Attorney in Mellette and Jones Counties. Krogman was an active program participant at the ten-year anniversary, though his contract has since concluded.

Amanda LaCroix grew up in Rapid City in Pennington County, South Dakota. LaCroix completed her undergraduate studies at the University of Utah in 2014 and graduated from the University of South Dakota School of Law in 2017. LaCroix signed her Rural Attorney Recruitment Program contract with Bennett County and opened a solo practice in Martin. In her second year of the program, LaCroix left the program and moved to Pierre to work for the South Dakota Department of Education, where she continues today.

Kasen Lambeth spent his earliest years in Cedar City, Utah, then moved to Las Vegas, Nevada, as a child. Lambeth completed his undergraduate studies at Southern Utah University in 2011. Lambeth relocated to South Dakota for law school, graduating from the University of South Dakota School of Law in 2017. Lambeth began his career working in Vermillion, South Dakota, in a small firm then was hired as a full-time Deputy State's Attorney in Union County. Lambeth entered into a Rural Attorney Recruitment Program contract with the city of Elk Point to cover his work as a Deputy State's Attorney. In his second year of the program, Lambeth left Union County to take a Deputy State's Attorney position in Clay County then later transitioned into solo practice serving the towns of Vermillion and Elk Point, which was his job at the ten-year anniversary. Since then, Lambeth has returned to Las Vegas, Nevada, to be closer to family.

Rachel Mairose grew up on a farm outside of Kimball in Brule County, South Dakota. Mairose obtained her undergraduate degree from Briar Cliff University in 2015 then graduated from the University of South Dakota School of Law in 2018. Following law school, Mairose clerked for a state trial court in South Dakota then signed her Rural Attorney Recruitment Program contract with Aurora County and joined a law firm in Plankinton. Mairose continues to practice in Plankinton and is now the State's Attorney of Aurora County.

Ryan McKnight grew up in Sioux Falls in Minnehaha County, South Dakota. McKnight earned his undergraduate degree from South Dakota State University in 2011. Following a year as an offensive lineman with the Cincinnati Bengals, McKnight received his law degree and an MBA from the University of South Dakota in 2015. McKnight signed his Rural Attorney Recruitment Program contract with Haakon County and opened up a practice in Philip with his wife Brittany Kjerstad McKnight. The McKnights practiced in Philip less than a year before McKnight joined the faculty of the South Dakota State University Ness School of Management and Economics, a job he continues to hold today.

Cody Miller grew up outside of Spink in Union County, South Dakota. Miller worked in law enforcement during and after college, ultimately receiving his undergraduate (2013) and law (2020) degrees from the University of South Dakota. Miller signed his Rural Attorney Recruitment Program contract with Wentworth in Lake County and joined a law firm in Madison. Miller remains with that firm, now as a partner.

Abigail Monger grew up in Sargeant Bluff, Iowa. Monger received her undergraduate (2018) and law (2020) degrees from the University of South Dakota. Monger signed her Rural Attorney Recruitment Program contract with Bon Homme County and joined a law firm in Tyndall. At the ten-year anniversary, Monger was an associate attorney with the firm and a Deputy State's Attorney. Since then, Monger has been elevated into firm partnership and has become the State's Attorney for Bon Homme County. Monger's five-year contract is still active as of 2024.

Rachelle Norberg grew up on a farm outside of Burke in Gregory County, South Dakota. Norberg received her undergraduate (2015) and law (2018) degrees from the University of South Dakota. Norberg signed her Rural Attorney Recruitment Program contract with Gregory County and took over a firm and title company in Burke where she remains today. Norberg was an active program participant at the ten-year anniversary, though her contract has since concluded.

Zachary Pahlke grew up in Winner in Tripp County, South Dakota. Pahlke received his undergraduate (2010) and law (2014) degrees from the University of Nebraska–Lincoln with a year between working for Dell. Pahlke moved home, signing his Rural Attorney Recruitment Program contract with Tripp County and joining his parents in private practice in Winner. Pahlke previously served as the State's Attorney in Mellette County and now serves as the State's Attorney in Tripp County as well as having a limited private practice.

Victor Rapkoch grew up in Shelby, Montana. Rapkoch received his undergraduate degree from Ave Maria University in 2011 then worked for a few years, including operating a shark-hunting business in Florida. Rapkoch learned about the Rural Attorney Recruitment Program while he was choosing a law school, which led him to choose the University of South Dakota School of Law where he graduated in 2016. Rapkoch signed his contract with Marshall County and joined a law firm in Britton. In his fifth year of practice, Rapkoch opened a solo practice in Britton which he continues to run today along with his position as the Marshall County State's Attorney.

Cole Romey grew up on a ranch outside of Oelrichs in Fall River County, South Dakota. Romey received his undergraduate degree from Chadron State College in 2013. Romey worked in banking for several years then returned to school and graduated from the University of South Dakota School of Law in 2020. Romey then clerked for a justice of the Supreme Court of South Dakota for one year in Rapid City before joining the program. Romey's Rural Attorney Recruitment Program contract is with Fall River County and Romey joined a law firm in Hot Springs. Romey's five-year contract is still active as of 2024.

Austin Schaefer grew up working on farms and ranch operations outside of Leola in McPherson County, South Dakota. Schaefer received his undergraduate degree from South Dakota State University in 2013. Schaefer worked for four years at Daktronics before returning to school, graduating from the University of South Dakota School of Law in 2020. Following law school Schaefer clerked for a trial level court in South Dakota and obtained a tax LLM from the University of Denver Sturm College of Law in 2022. Schaefer signed his Rural Attorney Recruitment Program contract with Fall River County and joined a firm in Hot Springs. Schaefer is active in the Judge Advocate General ("JAG") Corps of the South Dakota Army National Guard. Schaefer's five-year contract is still active as of 2024.

Jackson Schwandt grew up on a dairy farm outside of Milbank in Grant County, South Dakota. Schwandt received his undergraduate (2010) and law (2015) degrees from the University of South Dakota with a break between when he worked at the local cheese factory and tried selling tractors. Schwandt signed his Rural Attorney Recruitment Program contract with Grant County, joining a firm in Milbank. Schwandt continues to work in that private firm and serves as the Grant County State's Attorney.

Elizabeth Steptoe grew up in St. Lawrence in Hand County, South Dakota. Steptoe received her undergraduate (2019) and law (2020) degrees through a 3+3 program from the University of South Dakota. Steptoe is the only participant to have multiple local governments sign her contract. Hyde and Sully Counties as well as the cities of Onida and Highmore agreed to contribute to her contract. Steptoe lived in Hand County during her time in the program and left the program in her first year to become a teacher. Steptoe did not move away from rural Hand County when she left the program, the only participant to stay local after leaving rural practice.

Stephanie Trask grew up on a ranch outside of Elm Springs in Meade County, South Dakota. Trask received her undergraduate degree from Chadron State College in 2005 then worked for Dakota Rural Action for five years before returning to school and graduating from the University of South Dakota School of Law in 2014. Trask worked at a law firm in Rapid City, South Dakota, before

Haakon County reached out and asked Trask to move to Haakon County and take over as State's Attorney. Trask then moved to Philip and Haakon County signed her Rural Attorney Recruitment Program contract. Trask opened a solo practice, which she continues today, though she has stepped down from the State's Attorney role.

Cassie Wendt grew up on a ranch in rural Jackson County, South Dakota, with the nearest town being Philip, located in Haakon County. Wendt received an Associate's Degree in Paralegal Studies in 2005 from Western Dakota Technical Institute then worked as a paralegal while completing her undergraduate degree at Colorado Technical University in 2008. Wendt graduated from the University of South Dakota School of Law in 2012 and began her legal career as a prosecutor in Butte County, South Dakota. After a decade in that role, Wendt moved home in 2022. Jackson County, where Wendt lives, signed her Rural Attorney Recruitment Program contract, though Wendt runs her solo law firm out of Philip, in Haakon County. Wendt became State's Attorney for Jackson and Haakon Counties in January 2025. Wendt's five-year contract is still active as of 2024.

Amanda Work grew up in Spencer, West Virginia. Work obtained her undergraduate degree (2006) and master's in teaching (2008) from West Virginia University and taught school for three years before returning to school. Work graduated from the University of South Dakota School of Law in 2014. Tripp County signed Work's Rural Attorney Recruitment Program contract and she worked in Winner as a satellite office for a law firm. After her contract ended, Work transitioned to her own solo practice then left Winner to become an assistant federal public defender in Pierre, South Dakota.

Kathy Zenner grew up in Lake Hiawatha, New Jersey. Zenner earned her undergraduate degree from the University of South Florida in 1995 then graduated from Stetson University's College of Law in 1998. Zenner gained legal experience in Colorado in a public defender's office and a law firm before stepping away from law to raise children. Zenner reentered law with a full-time Deputy State's Attorney position for Union County. Zenner became State's Attorney for Union County in January 2025. Zenner's contract was signed by the city of Elk Point and is still active as of 2024.

Index

abuse and neglect cases, 2, 100, 103, 149
access to justice, 19, 24–25, 29, 107, 153, 164, 169
agriculture
    as alternative to legal practice, 161
    background in relevant to practice, 105
    communities, 65–66
    farmers/ranchers as clients, 88
    financial difficulties of, 49, 137
    influencing lawyer career decisions, 52, 59, 157
    jobs, 5, 48, 137
    lawyers background in, 44, 49, 125, 139, 154
    and off-farm employment, 49, 53, 158
    relative wealth, 145
    as supplements to legal practice, 129
    subsidies for, 71, 133
American Bar Association, 2, 16, 25, 31, 35, 58, 77
Anderson, Clay, 38–39, 59, 147, 175
Anson, Ashley, 39, 97, 113–14, 175
Arkansas
    Dale Bumpers (senator), 17, 22, 87
    incubator, 35–36, 74, 128, 171–72
    interviews with residents, 41
    study of, 15, 43, 74
Ashton, South Dakota, 66
Ashwood, Loka, 19
Association of American Law Schools ("AALS"), 45
Aurora County, South Dakota, 113–14, 125–26, 175, 178

bar exam, 38, 57, 78, 118, 127, 172
Barnett, Tom, 30–31
bedroom communities, 27, 65
Belle Fourche, South Dakota, 90
Bennett County, South Dakota, 83, 178
Berkeley Law, 5, 37
Bison, South Dakota, 176
Bon Homme County, South Dakota, 177, 179
brain drain. *See* out-migration from rural America
Britton, South Dakota, 80, 179–80
Brown, David, 29–30, 102, 152

Buffalo, South Dakota, 166, 176
Bumpers, Dale (senator), 17, 22, 87
Burke, South Dakota, 3, 73, 142–43, 153, 179
business development, 103
Butte County, South Dakota, 90, 129, 181

California, 5, 36, 52
Chambliss, Elizabeth, 17, 41, 87, 105–6, 134, 138, 146–47
Cheyenne River Sioux Tribe, 83
childbirth, 144, 163
city attorneys, 101–2, 142
Clerk of Courts
    as mentors, 112, 119
    providing referrals, 87, 128
clerkship, 56–57, 64, 118, 125–26, 130
clients
    as deserving representation, 155
    fee-paying, 26
    inability to pay, 23–25, 27, 36, 96, 107–8, 131, 145
    multigenerational, 151
    of legal aid organizations, 23
    and sexism, 87–88
    travel, 2, 21, 23, 27
    willingness to use rural lawyers, 86–88
clinics providing legal services
    justice bus programs, 36
    tribal wills clinic, 142, 147
    veterans, 147
communities in rural America
    acceptance of lawyers, 79–84
    as accepting of outsiders, 80
    as attractive to lawyers, 161–64
    differences among, 65, 169
    involvement with helping acceptance, 82
    lawyers helping sustain, 150–52, 155
    resilient, 29
    as skeptical of outsiders, 17, 78–79, 82
commuting, lawyers to work, 74

conflicts
  as city attorney, 101
  faced by rural lawyers, 91, 104, 108
  part-time prosecutors, 93–94, 104
  prosecuting and defending, 98–100
  with family law cases, 104
consultations, 134, 146
coronavirus. *See* COVID-19 pandemic
Corsica, South Dakota, 176
Corson County, South Dakota, 26
country lawyers. *See* lawyers, rural
county seats, 66–67
court appointments
  for criminal defense, 91, 95–98
  importance to finances, 128, 130
  pay rates, 130
COVID-19 pandemic, 7, 29, 157, 171
criminal defense
  court-appointed, 91, 95–98
  as financial stability, 131
  as main income, 96
  mentorship for, 111–12
  of private clients, 96
  by program participants, 95–98, 143
  by prosecutors, 98–100
  shortage in rural areas, 97
  in tribal court, 96
culture in rural America, 6, 80–82

Dakota Plains Legal Services, 27
Daugaard, Dennis (governor), 32, 38, 67
definition of rural
  from the Census Bureau, 5
  for South Dakota's program, 32, 65
  varying across studies, 17, 65
Deibert, Casey Jo, 38, 46, 97, 104, 113–15, 131, 160, 175–76
Dewey County, South Dakota, 177
divorce. *See* family law
Douglas County, South Dakota, 113

economic decline
  job loss in rural America, 137–41
  lawyers combating, 3, 26
economic development, 137, 151–52
economies in rural communities, 25, 66, 96, 137–41
education in rural America, 17
Elk Point, South Dakota, 42, 80, 93, 159, 178, 181
Ellendorf, Kristian, 39, 58, 80, 116, 121, 151, 176
employment in rural America, 50, 137–41
English, Jennifer, 23–24, 27, 39, 48, 58, 61, 75, 77–81, 83, 87–88, 97, 101, 144–45, 147, 151, 176
estate planning, 26, 91, 97–98, 102–4, 107, 112, 133, 139, 146
Eureka, South Dakota, 58, 72, 128, 177

Fall River County, South Dakota, 63–64, 152, 180
family law, 91, 103–5, 108, 133
finances of rural practice
  after stipend ends, 140
  agriculture as supplement, 129
  in context of economic decline, 137–41
  court-appointed work, 131
  government pay, 128, 130–34
  high-paying practice areas, 26, 139
  historical, 13, 18
  importance of stipend, 58, 127–28, 130
  importance to lawyers staying, 162–63
  lawyers with second jobs, 129–30
  mentorship costs, 116
  pay structures, 116, 126–27
  pro bono as a burden, 146–47
  prosecutor pay, 131–33
  sparse in beginning, 126–30
Finch, Atticus (fictional character), 14, 18–19
Fischer, Jake, 38, 58, 74, 113–15, 160, 176
Fort Pierre, South Dakota, 1

GI Bill, 15
gender of rural lawyers, 40, 52–55, 163
Georgia, 86
Geu, Tom (dean), 31
Gilbertson, David (justice), 1–2, 9, 11, 29–32, 34, 52–53, 67, 96, 150, 167–68, 172
Ginsbach, Dusty, 39, 62, 119, 129–30, 146, 160, 166–67, 176
Goetzinger, Pat, 9, 30–31
government, local
  as antilawyer, 64
  cost-sharing in South Dakota program, 32, 67–68, 70–71, 75, 78, 93
  importance of, 68
  lawyers working for, 100–2, 142
  limited budgets, 71, 75, 93
  recruiting lawyers, 70, 152
  signing contracts for stipend, 63–64, 68–72, 78, 80, 143, 155
  spending on lawyers, 2, 20, 69, 97, 130–34, 140, 148, 152, 160
Governor's House Program, 73
Grant County, South Dakota, 54, 180
grants
  writing, 3
  matching, 68, 71, 75–76
Gregory County, South Dakota, 177, 179

Haakon County, South Dakota, 54, 70, 74, 90–91, 99, 145–46, 152, 179, 181
Hand County, South Dakota, 175, 180

Harding County, South Dakota, 129, 166, 176
health insurance, 39, 62, 129–30, 132–33, 139–40, 159–60
high school
   career counselors, 46
   internships, 47, 122
   job shadowing, 47
   teachers encouraging law school, 46–47
higher education. *See* law school
Highmore, South Dakota, 54, 180
Hoel, Evan, 38, 83, 95, 159, 174, 176–77
Hoffman, Austin, 39, 46, 52, 58, 72, 102, 104, 128, 143, 161, 165, 173, 177
hometown
   acceptance in, 79, 82
   investment in, 162
   predictor of staying, 60
   prosecuting in, 95
   working in, 13–14, 43, 45, 52, 58–59, 79, 113
Hot Springs, South Dakota, 63–66, 180
hourly rates, 23, 88, 131, 135
housing in rural America
   cost, 72, 139
   difficulties obtaining, 72–74, 139
   mobile homes, 72
Howard, South Dakota, 80, 116, 176
Hughes County, South Dakota, 81
Huron, South Dakota, 7
Hustead, William, 63–65, 152, 174
Hyde County, South Dakota, 180

Illinois, 7, 13, 34–35, 41, 128, 172
immigration
   European immigrant celebrations, 6
   immigrants in rural America, 6–7
   lawyer, 50
incubator programs
   in Arkansas, 35–36, 74, 128, 171–72
   in California, 36
   to encourage rural practice, 35
   in Montana, 35
Indian Country
   Cheyenne River Sioux Tribe, 83
   definition, 26
   difficulty of rural practice, 26
   estate planning, 26, 107
   Lake Traverse Reservation, 28
   lawyer shortage, 26–27, 113
   lawyers practicing in, 26–27, 83, 101
   legal aid provision, 27
   Lower Brule Reservation, 142
   Oglala Sioux Tribe, 83, 91
   Pine Ridge Reservation, 83, 91
   poverty, 26
   program participation in, 26, 92
   recruitment in, 48
   Rosebud Sioux Tribe, 26, 101, 106, 145
   as rural, 6
   Sisseton Wahpeton Oyate, 28, 83, 93
   Standing Rock Reservation, 115
   taxation, 75, 93
   traditions and culture, 6
   tribal courts, 96, 106–7, 145
   Yankton Sioux Tribe, 6
indigent clients. *See* rural poor
internet access in rural America, 25
internships
   for college students, 122
   for high school students, 47, 122
   for law students, 59, 110–11, 118, 122
   stipends for, 37, 43, 122
Iowa, 41, 43, 72, 106, 125, 179

Jackley, Marty (attorney general), 94, 112
Jackson County, South Dakota, 26, 74, 90–91, 99, 101, 181
Janssen, Amy Jo, 39, 46, 49, 58, 61, 104, 116, 154–55, 157, 163–64, 173, 177
Jensen, Steven (justice), 34, 153
Jerauld County, South Dakota, 175
Johnson, Derrick, 39, 62, 96, 102, 116, 131, 143, 177
judges
   career for rural lawyers, 22, 163
   and court appointments, 96–97
   historical, 20
   influence on rural lawyers, 44, 77, 108, 118–19
   as mentors, 57, 119
   opinion on rural lawyers, 29, 106
   part-time, 21
   and pro se litigants, 21
   rural need for, 2, 15
   traveling, 21, 99
   in tribal courts, 20
   tribal judges, 26
   without law training, 20–21
judicare, 23, 148
Juracek, Mason, 39, 46, 82, 110, 122, 177
Justice Buses, 36

Kansas, 21–22, 29, 35, 84, 103, 105
Kennebec, South Dakota, 116, 154–55, 157, 164, 177
Kentucky
   Leslie County, 12–14, 18
   nonlawyer judges, 21
   southeastern, 4, 12–14
   University of Kentucky, 18, 47
Kern, Janine M. (justice), 57
Kirchmeier, Dylan, 28, 39, 51, 56, 74, 83, 92–93, 138, 177

Kjerstad McKnight, Brittany. *See* McKnight, Brittany Kjerstad
Knudson School of Law. *See* University of South Dakota Knudson School of Law
Kochekian, Kristen, 58, 61, 80, 102, 117, 119, 131, 151, 177–78
Krogman, Kirby, 39, 42–43, 49, 51, 62, 96, 109–10, 112–13, 144, 178

LaCroix, Amanda, 39, 47, 58, 73, 83, 111, 159, 178
Lake County, South Dakota, 179
Lake Traverse Reservation, 28
Lambeth, Kasen, 39, 42–43, 80, 158–59, 174, 178
Landon, Donald, 3, 17–18, 45, 84, 103, 138–39, 152
Las Vegas, Nevada, 42, 44, 174, 178
law firms
   mentorship in, 116–17
   working in, 102–6
law school
   choosing to attend, 45–50
   cost, 16, 18
   elite education, 55–56
   historical, 13, 16
   in larger communities, 16, 18
   online degree, 16
   and preparation for practice, 118
   promoting rural practice, 37
   time commitment, 16
lawyers
   career options, 14
   clothing choices, 80–81
   economic backgrounds, 15
   public perception of, 15
lawyers, rural
   affordability for clients, 21, 107–8, 146
   aging, 7, 9, 15, 30, 155, 168, 172
   as the children of lawyers, 45
   and communities, 2–3, 31, 102, 121, 143, 146–47, 150–52, 161–64
   as entrepreneurs, 134, 137
   finances. *See* finances of rural practice
   gender, 40, 52–55
   as generalists, 14, 91
   historical, 13–14, 20
   as increasing access to justice, 24–25, 49, 77, 88, 107, 145–48
   as legal aid attorneys, 22–23
   mentorship. *See* mentorship
   missing from scholarship, 19–20
   not a fallback career, 18, 56, 58, 62, 138, 157–58, 161–64
   as parents, 45, 52, 55, 58, 62, 74, 80, 82, 84, 95, 144, 159, 163
   part-time work, 50, 129–30
   as politicians, 22, 31
   in private practice, 22, 102–6
   as problem solvers, 3, 152
   as protectionist, 68, 85, 88
   size of hometowns, 43
   as societal equalizers, 19
   as specialists, 98, 105–6, 108, 138, 140
   traits of, 14
   work–life balance, 54, 140–41, 144, 162–63
lawyers, urban
   job availability impacts rural practice, 9, 29
   as mentors to rural lawyers, 111
   serving rural clients, 7, 20, 22, 25, 36, 101
   as specialists, 14–15, 37, 101
   working against rural interests, 19
legal aid
   as career for rural lawyers, 22
   constraints in serving clients, 23
   disproportionate funding to urban areas, 22–23
   funding, 21–22
   hiring private attorneys, 23
   historical, 22–23
   in Indian Country, 27
   need for more lawyers, 24, 27
   need in rural America, 23–25, 107, 147
   preference for full-time attorneys, 23
   as providing access to justice, 24
   in rural areas, 22–23, 36
Legal Services Corporation ("LSC"), 23, 25, 27
legislature of South Dakota, 28, 30–34, 40, 51, 131
Lemmon, South Dakota, 78
Leola, South Dakota, 180
Leslie County, Kentucky. *See* Kentucky
licensure
   alternative pathways, 37
   bar exam, 38, 57, 78, 118, 127, 172
Lincoln, Abraham, 13–14, 16, 18, 22
loan forgiveness
   to encourage rural practice, 30
   for full-time government employees, 93
Loan Repayment Assistance Programs ("LRAPs"), 37
local government. *See* government, local
localism, 150
low bono
   instead of pro bono, 145
   provided by rural lawyers, 91, 134, 145–48
Lower Brule Sioux Tribe, 142
Lust, David (legislator), 31–32
Lyman County, South Dakota, 177

Madison, South Dakota, 179
Mairose, Rachel, 39, 51, 61, 82, 118, 125–26, 130, 138, 178
Marshall County, South Dakota, 179–80
Martin, South Dakota, 30, 58, 73, 83, 111, 178

maternity leave, 163
McCook County, South Dakota, 77–78, 97, 176
McKnight, Brittany Kjerstad, 38–39, 52, 70, 99, 111–12, 119, 128, 145, 152, 159, 179
McKnight, Ryan, 38–39, 45, 51–52, 70, 73–74, 103–4, 110–12, 119, 123, 128, 141, 144–45, 152, 159, 178–79
McPherson County, South Dakota, 46, 177, 180
Mellette County, South Dakota, 26, 109–10, 178–79
mentorship
  by Clerk of Courts, 112, 119
  for criminal defense, 111–12
  by judges, 57, 119
  in law firms, 116–17
  by paralegals, 111, 119
  as program requirement, 34, 123
  for prosecutors, 110, 112, 117, 132
  of rural lawyers, 84, 109–24
  sacrifices by established lawyers, 116, 120–22, 132
  in satellite offices, 113–16
  of solo practitioners, 109, 111–13, 119
  by state bar members, 119, 123
  as succession planning, 36
  by urban lawyers, 111
Metzger, Pamela, 96
Milbank, South Dakota, 180
Miller, Cody, 39, 45, 58, 102, 179
Miller, South Dakota, 59, 175
Miner County, South Dakota, 176
Miniard, John B., 12–16, 18
Minnesota, 21, 36, 38, 43, 55, 160, 174, 176
Missouri, 17, 20, 43, 45, 84, 103, 127, 138–39
Mitchell, South Dakota, 175
Monger, Abigail, 39, 58, 82, 95, 179
Montana, 16, 35, 43, 50–51, 129, 179
Morris, Bob, 9, 30–31

National Guard, 129, 163, 176, 180
Native Americans. *See* Indian Country
Nebraska
  Chadron State College, 175–78, 180
  dual licensure in, 105
  law schools, 16, 55, 154
  lawyers from, 31, 43, 154
  Rural Law Opportunities Program, 37
networking, 16
Nevada, 37, 42–43, 178
Norberg, Rachelle, 39, 73, 101, 103, 119, 142–43, 147, 149, 151, 153, 179
Norris, Kathleen, 78–79, 81–82, 84, 86, 144, 150, 153
North Dakota
  Indian Country, 59, 115
  law school affordability, 16
  rural attorney stipend, 7, 29, 34–35
  rural lawyer shortage, 129

Office of Economic Opportunity, 22–23
office-share agreement, 116
office space, 72, 74–75, 111, 113, 115, 122, 126, 129
Oglala Lakota County, South Dakota, 26
Oglala Sioux Tribe, 83, 91
Onida, South Dakota, 180
Oregon, 35, 169
out-migration from rural America, 18, 29, 50–51, 62, 161
overhead for law firms, 24, 116, 126–27, 129

Pahlke, Zach, 39, 45, 58, 100, 106, 109–10, 112, 119, 122–23, 140, 179
paralegals, 111, 119
part-time legal work, 129–30
pathway programs
  to recruit rural lawyers, 37, 123
  Rural Law Opportunities Program, 37
Penfield, Shane, 31, 114–15
Perkins County, South Dakota, 114, 129, 176
Philip, South Dakota, 52, 54, 59, 73–74, 91, 101, 108, 111, 119, 128, 179, 181
Pierre, South Dakota, 8, 38–39, 160, 176, 178, 181
Pine Ridge Reservation, 83, 91
pipeline programs. *See* pathway programs
place attachment, 157–58
Plankinton, South Dakota, 82, 125–26, 178
poverty
  of clients, 145–46
  historical, 18
  in Indian Country, 26
  persistent poverty, 27, 75
  rural poverty rate, 25–26, 49, 168
  War on Poverty, 22
practice areas
  abuse and neglect, 2, 103, 149
  abuse and neglect cases, 100
  business, 91, 103, 149–50
  civil litigation, 91, 102–6, 143
  criminal defense, 95–98, 143
  estate planning, 26, 91, 97–98, 102–4, 107, 112, 133, 139, 146
  family law, 91, 103–5, 108, 133
  free or reduced services, 92
  generalists, 91
  government, 100–2
  involuntary commitments, 101, 143
  municipal law, 101–2, 142
  probate, 26, 102–3, 135
  property, 103
  prosecution, 92–95
  prosecution and defense, 98–100
  real estate, 102–3, 135, 143, 151, 153
  tax, 103

Index

Presho, South Dakota, 20
press coverage of the Rural Attorney Recruitment Program, 40, 82
pro bono
  as a burden, 146–47
  as identity of rural lawyers, 146
  in Indian Country, 142, 145, 147
  more needed, 107
  as a program requirement, 34, 145–46
  provided by rural lawyers, 91, 142, 145–48
pro se litigants, 21
probate, 26, 102–3, 135
prosecution
  by defense lawyers, 98–100
  election of prosecutors, 13, 22, 54, 91–92
  finances of, 131–33
  full-time prosecutors in program, 39, 59, 92–93
  full-time prosecutors not eligible for stipend, 34, 92–93
  importance of local prosecutors, 94
  mentorship for, 110, 112, 117
  part-time prosecutors, 39, 93–94, 134
  rural lawyers as prosecutors, 13, 26, 28, 54, 92–95
  threat of consolidation, 132, 150
Protsch, Greg, 116, 121, 151
Pruitt, Lisa, 7–8, 15, 35, 43

racial diversity, 6–7, 83
racism, 88
Rapid City, South Dakota, 8, 30, 38, 44, 58, 63, 83, 112, 177–78, 180
Rapkoch, Victor, 39, 46, 48, 51, 80, 106, 117, 119, 179
Raymond, Margaret, 98
reading the law, 13, 16
real estate, 102–3, 135, 143, 151, 153
Recruitment Assistant Pilot Program, 32
Redfield, South Dakota, 66, 178
remote legal services
  challenges with, 36
  for legal aid, 25
  by rural lawyers, 59
  by urban lawyers, 7, 105, 153
reservations. See Indian Country
retainers, 136
retirement benefits, 129–30, 132
riding circuit. See travel
Roberts County, South Dakota, 28, 54, 92–93, 177
Romey, Cole, 39, 49, 56–58, 63–65, 97, 146, 180
Rosebud Sioux Tribe
  involuntary commitments, 101
  lawyer shortage, 26
  poverty, 26
  Sicangu Oyate Bar Association, 106, 145
  tribal courts, 106, 145

Rural Attorney Recruitment Program (SD)
  importance of flexibility, 34, 74, 163
  press coverage, 40, 82
  requirements, 34, 71
  stipend. See stipend in South Dakota
  success of, 155
  suggestions for improvement, 170–73
rural communities. See communities in rural America
rural education. See education in rural America
rural lawyers. See lawyers, rural
rural poor
  difficulties in serving, 146–47
  meeting legal needs of, 15, 23, 25, 134, 145, 147

Salem, South Dakota, 27, 77–81, 144, 176
Sandel, Michael, 55–57
satellite offices, 113–16
Schaefer, Austin, 39, 46, 63–65, 163, 180
Schafft, Kai, 29–30, 102, 152
schools, local
  benefit to rural lawyers, 155, 162
  as building community connections, 80
  as important to community, 144
  lawyers on school board, 22, 143, 153
  lawyers representing, 102
Schwandt, Jackson, 39, 52, 58, 102, 180
Scotland, South Dakota, 116, 177
self-representation. See pro se litigants
sexism, 87–88, 104
Sherman, Jennifer, 19, 52–53, 157
Sicangu Oyate Bar Association. See Rosebud Sioux Tribe
Sioux Falls, South Dakota, 8, 44–45, 51, 61, 126, 136, 141, 162, 177–78
Sisseton Wahpeton Oyate, 28, 83, 93
Sisseton, South Dakota, 28, 30, 83, 92, 177
solo practitioners
  after working in a firm, 117, 160
  argument for additional support, 128, 159
  finances, 127, 136
  mentorship of, 109, 111–13, 119
  not taking retainers, 136
  overhead costs, 129, 159
  program departures, 159
  success rate in program, 111
South Carolina, 17, 41, 87, 105–6, 127, 134, 138, 146–47
South Dakota Supreme Court, 37, 56, 115
Spink County, South Dakota, 66, 178
sports
  important to community, 144
  lawyers coaching, 80, 144
  as volunteer work, 143–44
Springfield, South Dakota, 102, 177
Standing Rock Reservation, 115

Starr, Suzanne, 58, 64, 69–70, 77, 148
State Bar of South Dakota
    mentorship program, 123
    role in establishing Rural Attorney Recruitment Program, 30–31
    as welcoming, 119
State's Attorney. *See* prosecution
Statz, Michele, 3, 25, 62, 162
Steele, John, 125–26
Steptoe, Elizabeth, 38, 58, 74, 117, 123, 158–59, 163, 180
stipend in South Dakota
    flexibility, 155, 163–64, 170
    full-time prosecutors excluded, 34, 92–93
    importance to lawyers, 126–28, 130
    justifying reduction in pay, 133
    keeping lawyers rural, 128
    law creating, 32
    length of time, 32, 140
    paid for by others, 71
    refusal to pay, 70–71
    requirement to pay back, 156
    residency requirement, 74
    set amount without inflationary increases, 32, 171
    use by lawyers, 129
stipend programs for lawyers
    failed attempts, 35
    Illinois, 7, 34–35, 128, 172
    North Dakota, 7, 29, 34
stipends for medical professionals, 31–32
Strain, Mick, 113
student loans
    constraining career choices, 16–17, 30, 139, 160, 167
    forgiveness programs, 16–17, 30, 35, 37, 139, 141
    stipend used to pay, 129
succession planning
    as mentorship, 36, 121
    programs to facilitate, 36
Sully County, South Dakota, 180
Sundall, Herb, 116, 154–55, 164
supervised practice, 37, 118
Supreme Court of the United States, 20–21
Sutton, Kelsea Kenzy, 3, 143

taxes
    keeping sales tax local, 3, 149
    tax base, 3, 64, 75, 93, 149, 153
Thorne, Sarah, 29–30
Timber Lake, South Dakota, 83, 177
title company. *See* real estate
Todd County, South Dakota, 26, 101
Tomisich, Ashli, 17, 41, 118
Trask, Stephanie, 39, 75, 89, 99, 101–2, 111, 118–19, 146, 152, 180–81

travel
    clients to court, 21
    clients to lawyers, 2, 23, 27, 105
    judges to court, 21, 99
    lawyers to clients, 7, 36
    lawyers to court, 2, 13, 20, 69, 97, 100, 110
    lawyers wanting to limit, 100
    students to law school, 16, 18
tribal courts, 106–7, 145
Tripp County, South Dakota, 72, 109–10, 113, 177, 179, 181
trust account management, 113, 115, 137
    finances, 136
trusts. *See* estate planning
two-career households, 17, 39, 59, 83, 110, 125, 127, 129
Tyndall, South Dakota, 82, 177, 179
tyranny of merit, 55–57

Unified Judicial System, 30, 32, 93, 97, 172
Union County, South Dakota, 93, 178–79, 181
University of South Dakota Knudson School of Law
    affordability, 16
    career services, 58, 61
    Dean Tom Geu, 31
    encouraging rural practice, 29, 59
    involvement with Project Rural Practice, 31
    pro bono clinics, 142, 147
    stipend tied to tuition, 32
    students at, 29, 45, 51, 55, 80, 125, 154, 174–81
urban lawyers. *See* lawyers, urban
urban view of rural, 4–5

Vehle, Mike (legislator), 30–32, 67, 75
Vermillion, South Dakota, 39, 178
volunteer work, 79–80, 143–45

Wall, South Dakota, 63, 174
Wendt, Cassie, 39, 49, 59, 73–75, 90–91, 95–96, 108, 111, 181
Wentworth, South Dakota, 179
Wessington Springs, South Dakota, 175
White Lake, South Dakota, 175
White River, South Dakota, 42, 113, 144, 178
wills. *See* estate planning
Winner, South Dakota, 45, 82, 102, 109–10, 177, 179, 181
Work, Amanda, 38, 82, 89, 96, 102, 113–15, 160, 181
work–life balance, 54, 140–41, 144, 162–63
Wyoming, 17, 41, 85, 118, 136, 152

Yankton Sioux Tribe, 6
Yankton, South Dakota, 4

Zenner, Kathy, 39, 52, 181
Ziebach County, South Dakota, 27

Made in the USA
Las Vegas, NV
12 March 2025